Parliaments and Legislatures Series

Samuel C. Patterson, General Advisory Editor

Parliaments and Legislatures Series

General Advisory Editor
Samuel C. Patterson, Ohio State University, USA

The aims of this series are to enhance knowledge about the well-established legislative assemblies of North America and western Europe and to publish studies of parliamentary assemblies worldwide—from Russia and the former Soviet bloc nations to Asia, Africa, and Latin America. The series is open to a wide variety of theoretical applications, historical dimensions, data collections, and methodologies.

POLITICAL CONSULTANTS

❧ IN ❧

U.S. CONGRESSIONAL ELECTIONS

Stephen K. Medvic

THE OHIO STATE UNIVERSITY PRESS
Columbus

Library of Congress Cataloging-in-Publication Data

Medvic, Stephen K.
  Political consultants in U.S. congressional elections / Stephen K.
Medvic.
    p. cm. — (Parliaments and legislatures series)
  Includes bibliographical references and index.
    ISBN 0-8142-0873-8 (alk. paper)
      1. Campaign management—United States. 2. Political campaigns—
United States. 3. Political consultants—United States. 4. Elections—
United States. 5. United States. Congress—Elections. I. Title. II. Series.
JK2281.M384 2001
324.7'0973—dc21

                                                        00-012773

Text and jacket design by Gary Gore.
Type set in Trump Mediaeval by Sans Serif.
Printed by Thomson-Shore, Inc.

The paper used in this publication meets the minimum requirements of the American
National Standard for Information Sciences—Permanence of Paper for Printed Library
Materials. ANSI Z39.48-1992.

9 8 7 6 5 4 3 2 1

Contents

Foreword

The modern world of congressional campaigning and electioneering in the United States has come to be heavily populated by political consultants, those experts and specialists who become integral parts of the congressional campaign staff. There was a time when professional consultants thrived only in the bailiwick of the presidential campaign, but this is no longer true. Today, many congressional campaigns employ political consultants, and they are now important objects of political analysis. What roles do political consultants play in congressional campaigns? How has the use of political consultants changed in recent years? How much influence do political consultants exert in congressional campaigns? How should political consulting be shaped in the future? These are the central questions addressed in Stephen Medvic's seminal study.

In the *Dorsey Dictionary of American Government and Politics*, political consultants are defined as "advertising specialists who are for hire to sell political candidates." But as Medvic amply demonstrates, today's political consultants work far beyond the domain of advertising—to include campaign management, speech writing, public opinion polling, computer applications, public relations, fund-raising, personal and political advice, and legal assistance. Scholars have noted the growing involvement and influence of consultants in presidential campaigns, but their role in contests for the U.S. Congress has not been investigated very systematically. Medvic initiates a line of theorizing about the consultants' role, tying his empirical work to conceptions of the act of voting in elections and the part played by voters' *schemas*—patterns of information and judgments making up their cognition about political candidates. Political consultants are now deeply involved in the processes of communication between candidates and voters in congressional elections. They are the practitioners of *deliberate priming*, "brought into a campaign to determine which issues their client should emphasize and how those issues should be framed."

The grounding for Medvic's analysis of consultant influence is provided by a collection of data for consultant activities during the 1990 and 1992 elections of members of the U.S. House of Representatives. Consultants were identified as those who worked in two or more campaigns, were relatively highly paid, or were members of the American Association of Political Consultants. Based on these parameters, Medvic establishes the incidence and growth of congressional campaign consultancies; 45 percent of the 1990 congressional candidates hired one or more consultants, and this proportion had grown to 63 percent in 1992. Undoubtedly, by the 1990s political consultants had become a significant element in American contests for congressional seats.

These political consultancies paid off for many congressional candidates. Most notable, Medvic finds, is the vote gain attributable to a "political consultant effect" for congressional challengers. In brief, Medvic's statistical analysis supports his claim that "hiring a political consultant significantly helps challengers run more competitive races," whether they are Republicans or Democrats. The general professionalization of congressional campaign politics and the pervasive role of electronic and other media in congressional contests has produced the realities in which political consultants may shape election outcomes.

Political consultancy in parliamentary elections is not confined to contests for seats in the U.S. Congress. Professional consultants are now involved worldwide in aggressive, competitive campaigning for seats in parliament. And, for that matter, a good many American political consultants take their skills abroad to manage parliamentary campaigns. The political consultant has become an international figure, nearly as much at home in Hungary or Russia, Germany or Britain, South Africa or Venezuela, as in the United States. Indeed, Medvic's analysis should provide an impetus not only for replication in other legislative elections in the United States but also for comparative studies focusing on parliamentary elections in many democratic countries.

Has the rise of political consultants in House elections made congressional campaigns better or worse? Some commentators and pundits think the injection of professional consultants in campaigns makes them overly Machiavellian, too deceptive, excessively negative, overly poll-driven. The author concludes his analysis by addressing some of the salient normative issues raised by the growing role of political consultants in congressional campaign politics. Medvic is fairly agnostic in appraising the growing role of political consultants. He acknowledges the major criticisms of the influence of political consultants, but he decries the many unsupported and excessive claims offered by critics. The author's thoughtful book provides invaluable preliminary analyses and insightful appraisal that enhances our understanding of professional consulting in elections to Congress.

SAMUEL C. PATTERSON

Preface

Political scientists are just now turning their attention to the activities of professional political consultants. Although Stanley Kelley explored the activities of "professional public relations men" over forty years ago and Larry Sabato detailed their role in elections in the early 1980s, follow-up research failed to materialize. This is particularly true for systematic empirical research but also for theoretical work. As a result, numerous questions remain unanswered (and some have yet to be clearly articulated) with respect to what consultants do, the effects of their activity, and the normative consequences of those effects.

This book attempts to find answers to some of those questions, both theoretically and empirically. First, I develop a theory that explains what consultants do for congressional candidates and their campaigns. Next, I examine a number of fundamental questions about consultant influence in congressional elections. While the empirical analysis is only an indirect test of the theory, I wanted to address what I see as the most glaring gaps in the literature; that is, the lack of theoretical perspective on consultant activity and the lack of quantitative analysis of their influence. I hope the fit between the two parts will be clear to the reader.

If I am at all successful in filling in those gaps, it is due in large part to the assistance of numerous individuals and institutions. The project began as a dissertation at Purdue University and, as such, benefited from the collective wisdom of my committee. They were James McCann, who provided much needed optimism as well as methods advice; Mark Gibney, who graciously agreed to be added in the eleventh hour and who could be counted on to ask the "big picture" questions; William Shaffer, who offered valuable comments on every word of this and many other projects; and, finally, Silvo Lenart, to whom I will always be indebted for the personal sacrifices he made for his graduate students. Without his guidance, this book and my career would never have left the starting gate. Keith Shimko served as something of an ex officio member of my committee and deserves a great deal of thanks for his wonderful advice and for allowing me to try his patience with my worrying. He is a dear friend and mentor.

Three institutions gave me support along the way. Generous funding for this project came from the Purdue Research Foundation in the form of a dissertation grant. I also benefited greatly from a Goldsmith Research Award from the Joan Shorenstein Center on the Press, Politics, and Public Policy at the Kennedy School of Government, Harvard University. I wish also to thank Old Dominion University and all of my colleagues there; they provide a marvelous environment for teaching and scholarship.

I must mention a group of scholars with whom I have been fortunate to serve on panels and at conferences. They are truly at the forefront of studying political consultants, and I have been influenced by them in countless ways. They are, in no particular order, James Thurber, Paul Herrnson, David Farrell, Robin Kolodny, Kelly Patterson, Candice Nelson, David Magleby, David Dulio, and Dave McCuan. Their insights and suggestions were of great benefit to me in writing this book.

The final product was much improved with the assistance of Charlotte Dihoff, Beth Ina, and Malcolm Litchfield of Ohio State University Press and Samuel Patterson, the series editor for Parliaments and Legislatures. Three anonymous reviewers gave their time and also contributed a great deal to improving the final manuscript.

The book was completed in memory of Barbara Hinckley, who saw it off the ground but passed away before it landed in print. I will never again learn so much from one person so quickly.

My family has been extraordinarily devoted. Words cannot express how much I owe to my parents, Nancy and Steve, for their support and guidance throughout the years; my sister Allison is simply an inspiration; and my in-laws, Bobbi and Jim Fisher, have helped in so many ways. Without the love and patience of my wife, Emily, I could not have completed this book. She was quick to forgive the late nights (and weekends) I spent at the office and slow to complain when I put the book before other commitments. Her strength is remarkable—and infectious—and I cherish our friendship. Finally, the book is dedicated to our son, Colin. While I was completing this book, he was learning to walk and talk. Coming home to his smiling face and playfulness makes the frustrations of teaching and writing magically disappear.

. I .

Introduction

It has been said that politicians campaign in poetry and govern in prose. If that is so, and if we wish to continue the analogy, then political consultants are the poets, crafting verses that candidates recite in the public readings that are our elections.

However, consultants are not only artisans. They also possess technical skills that have been applied to rapidly advancing technological innovations. This book will examine those skills from a number of perspectives. My purpose is to understand consultant activity in congressional elections. As such, I discuss what it is consultants do for congressional candidates and develop a theory of consultant activity and influence. The primary goal of the study, however, is to examine the effectiveness of consultants in helping their candidate-clients gain votes. Consultants have risen to prominence in part because of the perception that they can, in fact, deliver votes—a perception that has yet to be shown empirically. I will explain the plan of the book in more detail below. But first, a brief introduction to the political consulting phenomenon is in order.

The Ascension of Professional Political Consultants

For decades, American political campaigns have been undergoing a process of increasing sophistication and technological transformation that has altered the traditional concept of elections and representative democracy. This process, which began, according to most accounts, in the 1930s, reached an apogee by the early 1990s that can best be described as the "professionalization" of American campaigning. Whether or not they were the catalyst for this alteration, professional political consultants were certainly the beneficiaries of the change.

The fruits of campaign professionalization have accrued to political consultants in terms of both money and fame. On the first score, 45 percent of all congressional campaign spending in 1990 and 46 percent in 1992, or $118 million and $248 million, respectively, passed through the hands of political consultants (Fritz and Morris 1992, 45; Morris and Gamache 1994, 83). While much of that money represents the cost to firms of providing services (conducting polls, producing advertisements, etc.) or of subcontracting, we can rest assured that a large amount went to pay the salaries of the consultants.[1]

In addition to the exorbitant amounts of money they command, some consultants have even become celebrities. James Carville and Mary Matalin, who worked on opposite sides of the fence in the 1992 presidential campaign, became media stars when their romance-on-the-hustings became public knowledge. After the election, the couple coauthored a best-selling book (for which they were paid a $900,000 advance) and commenced with a lecture tour while Carville "starred" in *The War Room* (a documentary about the Clinton campaign) and Matalin began hosting *Equal Time*, a CNBC talk show. (She would later become co-host of CNN's *Crossfire*.) A profile in *People* magazine solidified the couple's entry into "the cult of celebrity," leading Carville to acknowledge that he had "become more of a character than a consultant" (Bowman 1994).

Other consultants have similarly risen to celebrity status. By the time he reached his midthirties, Frank Luntz, who helped construct (and sell) congressional Republicans' 1994 "Contract with America" on the basis of his polling and focus group research, had been profiled in numerous national magazines including the *New York Times Magazine*, which called him "Washington's latest Wunderkind" (Kolbert 1995, 46). At a time when few politicians command the attention of biographers, Lee Atwater, the late Republican consultant, recently had his life story documented (Brady 1997). Even little known regional consultants often find themselves in "the cult of the consultant" (Strahinich 1995, 28).

If campaign technique and strategy are newsworthy (as they are increasingly deemed to be by the media), then certainly the technicians and strategists themselves deserve coverage. But there is a more self-interested reason for the media's role in the cult of consultant celebrity. "A symbiotic relationship has developed between the press and political consultants, which has helped both groups enormously," according to Larry Sabato (1981, 310). CNN's Bill Schneider explains that "reporters and consultants feed off each other. . . . Reporters make consultants celebrities, and consultants give reporters great copy and the inside dope on what's really happening" (in Strahinich 1995, 28; see also Sabato 1981, 310–11). Yet Sabato contends that the "full-fledged" celebrity status of consultants is "totally out of hand. Their egos—and the media's willingness to feed them—now overshadow issues and candidates and parties" (in Fineman 1993).

Additionally, Dan Nimmo and James Combs (1992) point out that consultants have increasingly been used by the media as pundits (100–106). This may be a logical outcome of reporters' emphasis on campaign strategy as opposed to policy discussions. When strategy becomes central to a news story, consultants, as experts in the field, will naturally be called upon to interpret the strategic context of campaigns, the decisions made and tactics employed, and the corresponding results. In this environment, every utterance from a candidate, every public action, becomes a calculated attempt to persuade voters of something, and since consultants are behind it all, only consultants can make sense of it for the public.

Finally, because consultants often thrive on being in the national spotlight, even seemingly damaging news can be advantageous to campaign handlers. The 1993 race for governor of New Jersey gained national attention, at least in part, because it showcased "two campaign titans" against one another: Republican consultant Edward Rollins and his archrival, James Carville (Berke 1993a, A1). Just days after helping Christine Todd Whitman win the governorship, Rollins suggested that he had allocated $500,000 to African American precincts with the express intent of suppressing the vote in those areas (see Connolly et al. 1993 and Berke 1993b). Although he later withdrew his charge (claiming that the story had been fabricated to show up Carville), Rollins became a media magnet overnight (Fineman 1993). Undoubtedly, to the extent that people could recognize his name, it was the result of the scandal and not his professional skill. Although he had a difficult time finding work for a short time after the incident, Rollins would eventually work for Bob Dole's presidential campaign in 1995. (He resigned after allegedly making anti-Semitic remarks at a political roast.)

The recent widely publicized scandal involving consultant Dick Morris had more to do with Morris's own personal behavior than with electoral tampering. Nevertheless, the coverage of, first, his presence in the Clinton campaign (see the cover story of the September 2, 1996, issue of *Time*) and, second, his "meltdown" (see *Time* and *Newsweek* for September 9, 1996) indicate just how central even rogue consultants have become in the new "political-media complex" (Swanson 1992). Indeed, Morris is certainly the only political operative to appear on the cover of a national news magazine in two consecutive weeks. And, undoubtedly as a result of his infamy, he has already landed three books deals— including one in which Morris (1999) fancies himself a contemporary Machiavelli—as well as a political commentator's post on Fox News and a Web site that surely attracts attention because of its creator and not its content.

Despite the attention being lavished upon consultants by the media, political scientists have, until recently, largely ignored their rise to prominence. Serious consideration of what it is that consultants actually do has been offered by only a handful of scholars. In those cases where consulting has been examined, it has been done in a rather anecdotal manner, focusing on techniques and supplying abundant examples of their implementation. While detailed descriptions of the mechanics of consulting are invaluable to our understanding of the profession, we have reached the point at which more rigorous analysis is required to get a complete picture of the professionalization of American campaigning. Missing from political science journals are both quantitative and qualitative analyses of political consulting (or, for that matter, any reference to consulting at all). Furthermore, even the few books that have been written on the subject lack a theoretical foundation with which to explain the role of political consultants in American campaigns generally or congressional elections specifically.

Having said all this, I should note that the tide may be turning. One increasingly sees papers on political consultants at academic conferences. A recent issue (June 1998) of *PS: Political Science and Politics* devoted a symposium to the topic, and a generous grant from the Pew Charitable Trusts has recently been made to examine the topic. The study resulting from that grant, *Improving Campaign Conduct,* has been undertaken by American University's Center for Congressional and Presidential Studies under the leadership of James A. Thurber. That project has already begun to focus attention on political consultants among academics and the media. It has also produced an edited volume specifically on the role of consultants in elections (Thurber and Nelson 2000) and one on campaign advertising (Thurber, Nelson, and Dulio 2000). If that sort of attention continues, we will surely have answers to many of the questions that are just now being asked.

Congressional Elections Research and the Consultant as a Campaign Resource

Too often when consultants have been the focus of scholarly interest, it has been in the context of presidential election research. The vast majority of consultants, however, will never work in a presidential campaign. Far more will handle congressional campaigns, making those elections central to understanding consultant activity. To this point, however, congressional elections scholars have been concerned with voters and voting behavior or key campaign resources like money but not with campaign elites. With regard to voting behavior studies, Darrell West (1993) notes that while "the focus has yielded rich dividends, the preoccupation with American voters has distracted researchers from candidates and other political elites. Campaigners are crucial in elections. They set the choices available to voters. They influence the rate of political change. They establish the perimeters of the electoral arena. Nevertheless, research on leaders has virtually disappeared from library shelves" (148). One could argue that consultants are among the campaign elite too often ignored by election scholars. This book, then, seeks to shed light on the activity of this group of political elites as well as on the congressional candidates that hire them.

Notwithstanding the scant attention paid to political elites, the study of congressional elections has produced a number of interesting and important findings. It has been evident for some time, for example, that voters in House races lack basic knowledge of the candidates. During a campaign, fewer than half of all voters can recall the name of the incumbent in a given race, and less than 20 percent can do so for the challenger. The level of recall for open seat candidates' names falls between that of incumbents and challengers at roughly 34 percent (Jacobson 1992, 118). Of course, recall of candidate names requires more from voters than does simple name recognition. The former asks voters to remember the names of candidates, while the latter provides a list of names from which the voters can choose. Recognition of incumbents, challengers, and open seat candidates is over 90 percent, 50 percent, and nearly 80 percent, respectively (118). Nonetheless, if voters cannot even remember the names of the candidates, they cannot be expected to possess more complex information such as candidate issue positions.

In such a low information environment, citizens rely on "cognitive shortcuts" to make voting decisions. Early research suggested that the most important such shortcut was partisanship (A. Campbell et al. 1960). This was clearly true for the 1950s and 1960s. According to Gary Jacobson (1992), party-line voters made up three-quarters of the electorate as late as the early 1970s (111). By the late 1970s, however, incumbency was becoming a crucial factor in the outcome of elections. Roughly half of all partisan voters defect from their party's candidates to vote for an incumbent, and less than 10 percent switch to a challenger (Jacobson 1992, 115). Given the fact that incumbents are better known than challengers, this makes perfect sense. But incumbents are also evaluated more positively than challengers, "and these positive perceptions . . . are more important in explaining the vote than mere recognition" (Hinckley 1981, 25).

Incumbents enjoy other advantages over their opponents as well. Most of these relate to the resources that incumbents have at their disposal such as name identification, the franking privilege, the ability to perform constituency service, and (though its impact is controversial) superior fund-raising capabilities. Ultimately, then, congressional election research is concerned with the study of campaign resources, at least when it is not examining voters. In this book, I am interested in exploring the impact of a resource that, strangely enough, is rarely discussed as such. Political consultants, however, are as much a resource as money, and once data are collected on their presence in campaigns, their impact can be measured just as easily (see Medvic 1998 and 2000).[2]

Consultants themselves may take umbrage with this classification (as might scholars; see Johnson 2000, 42). After all, they are unique individuals whose abilities and experiences make them more or less valuable to the candidate/clients who hire them. But there is plenty of theoretical reason to believe that the variation in consultant ability is minimal. Marjorie Randon Hershey (1984) uses "social learning theory" to explain how campaigners "learn" to run effective campaigns. As she notes, "In social learning terms, [a] campaigner's 'memory' consists of the situations he or she has faced (or learned about) in the past, the individual's responses to those situations, their results, and the expectations derived from them" (60–61). This means that consultants will generalize from past experiences and develop "models" that can be applied to future campaign situations.[3] Given their vast experience, professional consultants are likely to learn campaign lessons more completely than amateur campaigners. Add to this the fact that most candidate campaigns face similar contexts (e.g., only two major party candidates, "gotcha" journalism, voters with roughly similar levels of knowledge and interest, etc.), and it is only a slight exaggeration to suggest that consultants, as campaign resources, are interchangeable.

When conceptualized in this way, rather than as individual talents who vary greatly in terms of what they can accomplish in a campaign, consultants can be systematically analyzed. Indeed, this book treats professional campaign handlers like any other resource in attempting to measure the impact of consultants on congressional elections.

The Present Study

Although political consultants are much more prominent now than when Larry Sabato studied them twenty years ago, the "relative dearth of published materials on consultants" that he found remains in place today (Sabato 1981, xiv). With this study, I am attempting to fill some rather large gaps in our understanding of consultants. In so doing, I hope to build on the aforementioned interest that is emerging among political scientists in political consultants and their influence on American, and specifically congressional, elections.

A scholar can approach subject matter from four perspectives. One can *describe* the topic under examination; provide a *historical* account of the phenomenon; offer *theoretical* insights, both empirical and normative, into the operation and/or consequences of the phenomenon; and examine the subject *empirically*, using quantitative and/or qualitative methods.

We have ample descriptive and historical accounts, both scholarly and popular, of consultants and their activities. Thus, the gaps I am attempting to fill in the study of consultants refer to the other two approaches to research. First I develop a theory of consultant influence in chapter 3 (after providing an introduction to previous work on consultants and the "proto-theory of consultant influence" in chapter 2). Although normative accounts of the impact of consultants are legion, I hope to explain that impact in empirical terms. Without a theory to guide us, our study of political consultants, or any phenomenon, proceeds in the dark. "Theories," as Alan Isaak (1985) suggests, "explain and organize existing knowledge." But they are also used "to suggest and to generate hypotheses" (169). Needless to say, political science is currently without a theory that explains consultants' behavior or predicts their influence in elections (see Thurber 1998).

In developing a theory of consultant influence, I am seeking to cast as wide a net over the subject as possible. To my mind, a theory of political consulting should explain most, if not all, of what consultants do. It should, of course, address consultant activity. But it should also deal with voters and the campaign strategies and messages that are produced by consultants. It should explain whether and how professional consultants differ from amateur campaigners and how consultants influence elections (which, after all, is why they are hired in the first place). One book cannot possibly test all of the hypotheses embedded in such a theory, and this book examines just one aspect of the theory. Nevertheless, I thought it necessary to start an investigation into the topic in this manner. I hope the theory proves fruitful and can provide a basis for further exploration into consultant activity. I must acknowledge, however, that to some extent the theory can stand alone and that its implications will be tested herein only in part. My hope, therefore, is that readers will see the benefit of beginning an empirical analysis with theory and will not regard the result as disjointed.

In fact, although the theory addresses many aspects of consultant activity that are not further investigated in the book, theoretical development is crucial to the empirical analysis I do conduct. I have chosen to examine the influence of consultants on elections because this seems to be the most fundamental empirical question raised about consultants. If they do not have an influence on election outcomes, further study of their activity may be pointless (although normative questions would be raised by the channeling of vast sums of money to "professionals" who cannot deliver what they claim). Yet without some theoretical guidance, such an analysis seems to me foolhardy.

Thus, based on part of the theory developed in chapter 3, I fill some gaps in empirical research on political consultants in chapters 4 through 7. Not only do we not know the extent to which consultants influence elections, we are not even clear about the extent to which they are used by congressional candidates.

I will conclude the study with a chapter on the implications of the use of consultants in American elections. This is not a new endeavor. Virtually all prior work on consultants has contained the obligatory chapter on the impact of consultants on democracy. Nevertheless, armed with evidence of consultants' electoral influence (or lack thereof), I hope to provide some original thoughts on this question.

The findings herein should be of some relevance to those interested in elite behavior, whether in terms of consultants-as-elites or in terms of congressional candidates' behavior (e.g., in hiring consultants). It serves as political communication research because, as we will see, consultants are most often described as communications experts. However, the project is principally concerned with congressional elections and broadly addresses issues of representative democracy. Thus, I hope scholars of various fields will find something relevant in these pages.

The need for such a study, I assume, is clear. When nearly half of all campaign spending is filtered through an industry, that industry ought to be examined by political scientists. That it has not been says more, perhaps, about the difficulty in approaching the topic than about the study of politics as an academic discipline. Although this project aims to cover much ground, its modest goal is to lay a foundation for further exploration into the effect of consultants on congressional elections.

. 2 .

Foundation for a Theory of
Consultant Influence

This chapter examines the foundations for an empirical theory of political consultant influence. While political scientists have some understanding of the history of campaign handling, we lack a theory explaining what it is consultants do. In other words, whether we think political professionals matter in elections or not, we have no reason to believe either possibility and no explanation for the findings of potential studies. This chapter explores a number of issues related to the study of consultants: barriers to such study, definitional concerns, and the role and functions of campaigns generally. In addition, I briefly discuss the present lack of theory in this field and review what could be considered a proto-theory of consultant activity. These matters set up the theoretical development that follows in the next chapter.

Barriers to the Study of Political Consultants

That there exists a paucity of work on what is clearly a significant phenomenon in American politics can be explained in a number of ways. Mark Petracca (1989, 11) argues that the lack of easily accessible data sources, confusion over what it means to "consult," and scholarly interest in voting behavior as opposed to political institutions (where, presumably, consultants are most active) all contribute to political scientists' neglect of professional campaign consultants. Additionally, many political scientists believe it is virtually impossible to find significant effects for any congressional campaign variable other than money or incumbency status. Thus, even if consultant data could be collected, quantitative analysis of consultants seems futile. This project deals with each of these barriers to inquiry and, I hope, overcomes the futility of a systematic study of consultants.

I begin by addressing the last of the aforementioned difficulties and then turn to Petracca's explanations. Because it is a definitional problem, and therefore uniquely important for understanding this project, I will confront Petracca's second point in a separate section.

While campaign expenditures and the incumbency advantage seem to be the final explanatory word on congressional elections, I maintain that, at least in the case of campaign expenditures, the picture is not as clear as it might appear. Money in and of itself does not attract votes.[1] Expenditures must be allocated in at least a minimally efficient way in order to have an impact. Spending 95 percent of a $500,000 campaign budget on snacks for volunteers would not help a candidate win. Of course, few campaigns spend so unwisely. Nevertheless, the point should be obvious: Campaign expenditures do not buy votes directly. Instead, they make it possible to purchase those things (polling, advertising time, expert advice, etc.) which are necessary to obtain victory.[2] As Gary Jacobson (1980) notes, money is "the basic and most flexible resource for acquiring means to reach voters" (24). One of those means, I suggest, is the advice of political consultants.

As for the incumbency advantage, it is true that officeholders seeking reelection rarely lose. The explanations for this are manifold. Richard Fenno's (1978) "home styles," David Mayhew's (1974a, 1974b) "advertising," "credit claiming," and "position taking," and Morris Fiorina's (1977a, 1977b) "constituency service" arguments are examples of such explanations. Perhaps most important, voters recognize congressional incumbents but are unacquainted with their challengers (at least in the House). Ultimately, as Barbara Hinckley (1981) noted, "For a large number of House voters, essentially no choice is provided: one candidate is known and the opponent is not" (51). Thus, other campaign-specific variables may not prove significant influences on an incumbent's share of the vote. For nonincumbents (challengers and open seat candidates), however, many factors have been found to be electorally significant. Thus, consultants may not help incumbents because the latter benefit so greatly from simply holding office, but political professionals may very well affect the nonincumbent's campaign.

Petracca's (1989) first point, that the lack of data on consultants hampers efforts to study them, while true in the past, is less of a problem today. Since 1986, *Campaigns and Elections* magazine (hereafter *C&E*) has compiled a "Campaign Scorecard" for each election cycle. This scorecard lists the nation's top political consulting firms, the type of consulting they do, and the clients who hired them. Beginning in 1990, *C&E* employed a methodology that provided a reliable and, I would argue, valid measure of professional consultant activity. Unlike the previous two scorecards, which relied on surveys of consultants, 1990's was compiled from Federal Election Commission disbursement/disclosure forms as well as follow-up calls to campaign staffs and local reporters when necessary (Beiler 1991, 27). From FEC reports, the *C&E* staff could determine which candidates hired which consultants if, indeed, they hired handlers at all. This enabled *C&E* to list virtually all the clients for whom a consultant worked, including those who lost (which is difficult to do when relying on consultants to reveal their clients).[3] The 1992 scorecard followed a similar methodology, which will be described in detail below (Mundy 1993, 20).

In addition to the *Campaigns and Elections* data, extensive studies of campaign spending in the 1990 and 1992 congressional elections have been published (Fritz and Morris 1992; Morris and Gamache 1994). The *Handbook of Campaign Spending* for both years itemizes each campaign's finances according to eight spending categories and provides substantive information about every House and Senate race per election cycle. Included in such information are the names of consultants hired by the candidates. All the data presented in the *Handbook*, like that in *C&E*, were culled from FEC reports.

Petracca's (1989) third potential barrier to systematic analysis of consultants is the disciplinary bias of political scientists in favor of behavioral as opposed to institutional approaches to research questions. The result is a move "away from the analysis of electoral institutions in which consultants now play such a commanding role" (11). While such a bias surely exists, it should not be overstated. To begin with, there are studies that have examined the campaign functions of institutions (Mayhew 1974a, 1974b) as well as the institutional context of campaigns (e.g., on congressional campaigns in the media, see Clarke and Evans 1983 and Vermeer 1987). The behavioral bias did not hinder these studies, and there is little reason to believe that it would prevent an institutional examination of consultants, should someone wish to undertake it. Furthermore, the implicit assumption that campaigns and consultants can *best* be studied in institutional (or, for that matter, behavioral) terms is dubious. Multiple perspectives on any given subject are necessary given the inherent advantages and disadvantages of any single approach. Finally, even in an institutional study of elections, the actors within campaigns (i.e., consultants) could be studied behaviorally just as members of Congress routinely are.

Professional Political Consulting Defined

There are reasonable grounds for believing that variables other than money and incumbency are influential in congressional elections and, given the *C&E* lists and *Handbook* information, researchers now have access to data on political consultants. In addition, the behavioral bias of political science does not present much of a problem for the study of consultants. Nevertheless, confusion over what it means to "consult" (Petracca's second obstacle to the study of campaign handlers) still exists.

Although practitioners respect the difference, political scientists have often conflated "consulting" and "managing." In the present project, political consultants will be broadly defined as people who are hired by a campaign to provide advice and/or services based on their expertise in a given area of campaign activity (see Sabato 1981, 8).[4] The *Political Resource Directory* includes thirty-four campaign services that are offered by thousands of professional organizations, most of which are political (as opposed to commercial) consulting firms.[5] Consultants specialize in the delivery of these often highly technical services.

One such service is campaign management. Whereas many candidates use "advisers" (whether or not they are actually consultants), all campaigns have managers. A campaign manager is simply someone who handles all of the day-to-day activities of a campaign (Joyner 1969, 152; Nimmo 1970, 39) and is responsible for implementing the overall campaign strategy (Shadegg 1972, 32–4; Luntz 1988, 62–66; Goldenberg and Traugott 1984, 21). The campaign manager, then, is primarily an administrator (Schwartzman 1989, 9). Among other things, a manager must order yard signs and bumper stickers as well as office supplies, organize volunteers, schedule the candidate's appearances, and set up press conferences (Salmore and Salmore 1989, 76; Steinberg 1976, 48–58). In larger campaigns, most of these activities will be delegated to various coordinators, whether paid staffers or volunteers, and it is the campaign manager's responsibility to do the delegating. Furthermore, given his/her role in the campaign, the manager is present (often at campaign headquarters) on a daily basis. It is only in extraordinary cases, like a presidential campaign, that a consultant will serve as the day-to-day campaign manager (Newman 1994, 123). Nevertheless, there are consulting firms that specialize in campaign management. They advise clients on how best to organize their campaigns but usually do not oversee the daily operation (although they may supervise the initial organization).

The "professional" aspect of consulting remains to be addressed. Because members of the consulting industry are not licensed, a consultant in the broadest sense of the term is anyone who hangs a "Political Consultant" shingle outside his/her office. However, consultants can be considered professional when they engage in consulting on a more or less full-time basis and handle more than one campaign per election cycle.[6] As noted above, many campaigns have individuals on whom they rely for strategic advice. Often, however, these people are longtime party activists or the candidate's trusted friends who do not assist other campaigns simultaneously. Even if paid, therefore, they would not fit the present conception of a professional political consultant.

The extent to which political consulting qualifies as a profession is an open question. For some, the consultant's lack of "theoretical underpinnings" renders his/her occupation a craft rather than a profession (Nimmo 1970, 66). Others, like Rosenbloom (1973), disagree, arguing that the operational theory of consultants "may not be well stated, or even completely accurate, but it does exist" (106). Boiney and Paletz (1991) concur with Rosenbloom, noting that consultants "possess, at least implicitly, models of the voters' decision-making processes" (3). In fact, Boiney and Paletz construct a practitioner's model of voting behavior based on a study of political advertising in 1984 (1991, 13–19). They find that the political advertising model contains all the elements that political science models of voting behavior use and more (21). In other words, political consultants are guided by a theoretical framework even if they are not fully aware of it.

Yet, as Rosenbloom (1973) realizes, an occupation requires more than simply an operating theory to qualify as a profession (105). In her classic work on the subject, *The Rise of Professionalism*, Magali Sarfatti Larson (1977) suggests that the characteristics of a profession include a "professional association, cognitive base, institutionalized training, licensing, work autonomy, colleague 'control,' [and a] code of ethics" (208). "These characteristics," she maintains, "appear in various combinations in all the modern professions" (208).

If we believe Rosenbloom and Boiney and Paletz, political consulting does, indeed, have a cognitive base. It also has a professional association with a code of ethics.[7] Furthermore, consultants enjoy work autonomy, which Larson (1977) claims exists when a profession is "allowed to define the very standards by which its superior competence is judged" (xiii). The remaining three characteristics, however, are lacking in the political consulting industry.[8]

Does meeting four out of seven characteristics make an occupation a profession? Larson emphasizes the fact that "the professional phenomenon does not have clear boundaries" (1977, xi). For my purposes, the question of the political consulting industry's professional status will remain unanswered. Nevertheless, I will refer to certain consultants as "professionals." Specifically, I consider a professional political consultant anyone whose income is derived, at least in part, from providing service to multiple political clients per election cycle including, but not exclusively, a political party. This conceptualization puts consultants somewhere between "member of a profession" and "a person paid for a service" and has a number of operational advantages. For example, it allows us to distinguish between party operatives and political consultants.

The former are employed solely by a political party while the latter may have a party as one among a number of clients but will also work for individual candidates (Medvic 1997). Most significantly, my conceptualization enables a distinction to be drawn between the amateur campaigner who works for one campaign and the professional who works for many.

For measurement purposes, I operationalize "political consultants" to include members of campaign firms who worked on at least two congressional and/or statewide races in one election cycle, were among the highest grossing consultants in their fields (according to the *Handbook of Campaign Spending* for 1990 and 1992), or were members of the American Association of Political Consultants.[9] Again, this definition is sufficiently narrow to exclude part-time or nonprofessional campaign handlers while being broad enough to include all those operatives who make a serious attempt at consulting for a living. In the end, well over three hundred professional consulting firms per election cycle qualified for this data set.

One other point of clarification about consultants is necessary. Traditionally, consultants are categorized according to two types—generalists and specialists (Sabato 1981, 9, 13–14; Luntz 1988; Salmore and Salmore 1989, 217). Generalists are presumably responsible for coordinating various aspects of a campaign and establishing a "campaign plan" or overall strategy (Sabato 1981, 9, 13). Specialists, as the name implies, focus on the provision of specific, usually technical, campaign services including polling, direct mail, fund-raising, computer assistance, and advertising (9, 14). Given the theory I will develop below, I maintain that the distinction between these two types of consultants is no longer valid. Specifically, I argue that generalists are themselves specialists of a certain kind and any other conceptualization of them misses an important point about their role in congressional campaigns. I continue to use the title "generalist," however, because that is the industry's accepted name for these consultants.

Having addressed the problems that have hindered the study of political consultants in the past, I turn now to the context in which consultants operate. In order to explain the role of consultants in campaigns, it is first necessary to understand the place of campaigns in elections. Therefore, a brief discussion of the functions of campaigns is in order.

The Functions of Campaigns

Political campaigns are primarily understood as candidates' efforts to win elections for party nominations or to public office.[10] Conventionally, election campaigns have four goals: informing the electorate of the issue positions of oneself and/or one's opponent; persuading them to vote for you and/or against your opponent; activating the partisan predispositions of those who should be one's supporters while not activating those of your opponent's potential supporters; and mobilizing your supporters and/or demobilizing the opposition.[11]

Campaigns also serve other functions in the American electoral system. In particular, they play a symbolic role in our political culture and a republican role in our representative democracy. These tasks are not, of course, mutually exclusive, nor are they equally beneficial for democracy. Nevertheless, I address each of them because they are all tied to the activities of political consultants.

Symbolic

On one level, campaigns are symbolic events (Edelman 1985, 3, 18; Gronbeck 1978; Nimmo and Combs 1980, 107–16). As such, they are an essential part of the "ritual dramas" (Nimmo and Combs 1983, 49) that create the "symbolic expression of popular will" which, in turn, legitimizes future government action (Nimmo 1970, 7; see also Edelman 1988, 97).[12] At a minimum, campaigns legitimize the electoral *process* by perpetuating two "primal American myths": acquiescence, a "'fail-safe' rationale for choosing leaders," and quiescence, a reassertion of "the values associated with campaigning and its outcomes (free-and-open decision-making, public accountability, . . . the two-party system) in order to remind a citizenry that it is 'happy' and 'content' with its electoral system" (Gronbeck 1978, 273; see also Trent and Friedenberg 1995, 4, 50). According to this view, campaigns and elections maintain at least an illusion of democracy, whether or not one can say it actually exists in any meaningful sense.

A more radical variant of this view holds that the "democratic facade" serves propertied or wealthy interests (Hellinger and Judd 1994, 123–218; Parenti 1995, 179–202). It is the role of the campaign, then, to create the appearance of elites at odds and in competition "without any serious attention being paid to the wishes of the general public" (Hamilton 1972, 4).

Republican

Gore and Peabody (1958) suggest that, in addition to being the site of symbolic politics, campaigns are "the institutional device through which the principle of representation [is] not only elaborated but implemented" (55). By forging consensus on major issues, campaigns ensure the broadest possible representation (68). This assumes, of course, that the consensus emerging from a campaign reflects majority opinion in the electorate.

That position is difficult to maintain if one takes a multidimensional view of policy preferences rather than a unidimensional (or left-right) perspective. It is also difficult to separate the role of campaigns in a republican system of government from that of elections themselves. Nevertheless, any discussion of the functions of campaigns must acknowledge their importance in such a system.

Informative

The original concept of the "informing function" of campaigns posited for them an educational role (Kelley 1960, 8–9; see also DeVries and Tarrance 1972, 73; Meadow 1989; Salmore and Salmore 1989, 10). In this view, campaigns provide voters with enough (factual) information to enable them to make a rational choice at election time (Kelley 1960, 8–10). Early work on voting behavior assumed that information (namely, issue positions) was necessary for rationality in voting. In that these studies found voters' information levels to be low (Campbell et al. 1960, 171–76, 186; Converse 1962), their authors had to conclude that voters were not acting rationally at the polling place, at least according to classical democratic theory (Berelson, Lazarsfeld, and McPhee 1954, 308).

But as Anthony Downs (1957) pointed out, "Paradoxically, it seems to be rational for parties to encourage irrationality in voters" (160). In other words, candidates may not selflessly provide information to voters when that information would be damaging to their electoral hopes. Since any piece of detailed information is going to be viewed negatively by some of the voters, the parties (or candidates in a candidate-centered system such as ours) are likely to offer only vague bits of information (135–37). Thus, vague information about policy positions can be seen by each voter "in a light which brings it as close as possible to his own position" (136). As Downs notes, "Ambiguity thus increases the number of voters to whom a party may appeal" (136; see also Shepsle 1972; Page and Brody 1972; Page 1976).

In the years since the early voting behavior studies, political scientists have come to evaluate Downs's paradox in more complex terms and have reconciled the voters' low level of information with rational action on their part (see Feldman and Conover 1983; Lau 1986; Miller, Wattenberg, and Malanchuk 1986; Zaller 1992, 216–64; Lodge, Steenbergen, and Brau 1995). Samuel Popkin (1994), for example, suggests that voters engage in "low-information rationality" when thinking about politics (7, 9–17). This means they use information shortcuts to make judgments about, and evaluations of, policies and candidates (13–15).[13] Because the information-processing heuristics that are used in political thinking are similar to those used in everyday situations, their application to politics is now seen as rational and unproblematic (Feldman and Conover 1983; Kinder and Fiske 1986; Sullivan et al. 1990; Popkin 1994, 65).

This revised approach to voter rationality has, to a great extent, changed the role of the campaign. Campaigns are no longer seen as vehicles for voter education. It is now understood that the rational campaigner will disseminate only partial (and often ambiguous) information. And "reasoning voters" maintain rationality even when they use only part of the incomplete information they are given. Under these circumstances, the role of the campaign organization is to determine which pieces of information can be used to the candidate's advantage and to disseminate only that material (Salmore and Salmore 1989, 10). In addition, campaigns attempt to provide voters with information about their opponents that will disadvantage them before the latter can "define" themselves. At the same time, the opponent is following an identical strategy. Thus, we no longer expect candidates to supply voters with all the relevant information about themselves and their issue positions. Campaigns, after all, are designed to win elections. Besides, candidates have never acted as objective issue informants.

Persuasive

Implicit in the idea of campaigns as information disseminators, though often treated as a separate function, is the idea that campaigns attempt to "persuade" voters to vote for their candidates.[14] While this seems intuitive, its realization depends, to a large extent, on how we define persuasion. I will not attempt to offer a final definition of persuasion (see Nimmo 1978, 99–100, for a nice summary of the differing views on the subject). Instead, I will simply say that if by persuasion one means a change in a prior attitude, then contemporary campaigns do not, and indeed could not, persuade voters to choose one candidate over another. If, on the other hand, one understands persuasion to be the activation of already held attitudes, then campaigns do, in fact, persuade voters (Lazarsfeld, Berelson, and Gaudet [1944] 1968, 74). A few words about this distinction are in order.

Nimmo (1978) suggests that in political campaigns "there is an effort to evoke the natural loyalties of one's party followers and get them to vote accordingly" as well as an attempt "directed at the opposition, not designed to convert partisan beliefs and values but to convince people that in this campaign they would be better off voting for the candidate of a different party" (162). Nimmo's explanation of the functions of a campaign follows from the early work of Lazarsfeld, Berelson, and Gaudet ([1944] 1968). They argued that "campaigns are important because they *activate* latent predispositions" (74; emphasis in original). Thus, between two-thirds and three-fourths of the voters who in May did not know how they would vote eventually "crystallized" their votes for the party corresponding to their political predispositions (74).

Campaigns also "reinforce" voters' predispositions by keeping them "in line" and reducing their "defections from the ranks" (Lazarsfeld, Berelson, and Gaudet [1944] 1968, 87). Fully 15 percent of all voters in Lazarsfeld, Berelson, and Gaudet's study were "waverers" who initially intended to vote one way, moved away from that intention (to either "Don't Know" or to the other party), and returned to their original preference in November (65).

Finally, very few voters are "converted" to cast their ballot for the party other than their originally stated preference. Indeed, Lazarsfeld, Berelson, and Gaudet concluded that of all the potential campaign effects, conversion was clearly the least likely to occur (104). Whereas half of all voters never deviated from their original party preference, only 8 percent converted (66). The absence of conversion effects was due to the fact that "the people most open to conversion—the ones the campaign managers most wanted to reach—read and listened [to the campaign] the least" (95).

These findings were crucial for allaying the fears of researchers working after World War II. The concern at the time was that audiences were "highly vulnerable to the direct media influences of propaganda campaigns" (Lenart 1994, 11; Katz 1963, 80).[15] Before the minimal or "limited effects" school of thought (Klapper 1960), the notion held sway that media effects worked one way (from communicator to audience) and that attitudes were delivered as if injected with a "hypodermic needle" (Trent and Friedenberg 1995, 96–98; Ansolabehere, Iyengar, and Simon 1995, 15–17). But the "social influences model" (Trent and Friedenberg 1995, 98–103) suggested that democracy was safe from the manipulative possibilities that seemed to have been actualized in Nazi Germany.[16]

Later work would confirm the finding that the campaign's ability to convert voters was virtually nonexistent (Berelson, Lazarsfeld, and McPhee 1954). Party identification was soon found to be the most significant determinant of the vote, and this, of course, was out of the campaign's control (Campbell et al. 1960). Eventually, political scientists suggested that candidate evaluations were also important in a person's voting decision (Stokes 1966). While candidates can often shape their images for the electorate, there is still some limitation on a candidate's ability to control evaluations of him/herself. As for issues, they continued into the 1970s to be seen as having little relevance for the vote.

Following the turbulent 1960s, however, that view began to change. Although V. O. Key Jr. (1966) had made the "perverse and unorthodox argument . . . that voters are not fools" (by which he meant they can and do vote on issues) half a decade earlier, he found little support among his contemporaries (7). Soon, however, political scientists began painting a more subtle picture of the American voter. Issues were found to play a significant role, at least occasionally, in voters' decision-making calculus (RePass 1971; Pomper 1972; Nie, Verba, and Petrocik 1976; Carmines and Stimson 1980, 1989). And today, according to Niemi and Weisberg (1993), voting behavior scholars are "concerned not with whether issues matter but with which issues matter and how they matter" (138). Evidence of issue voting has profound implications for the belief that campaigns matter. If people, at least occasionally, vote based on issues, then "[c]hanging issues changes the campaign, if not the outcome" (Popkin 1994, 58).

One research tradition in particular has been very successful in revealing how campaigns can affect voting behavior.[17] This body of work, known as "schema theory," argues that people construct "mental models" (Johnson-Laird 1983) when they receive communication of any kind. These models, known as "schemata" (Rumelhart 1980, 1983) or "schema" (Bartlett 1932), are cognitive structures that organize information. Within each schema are pieces of information, called nodes, that are linked in as yet undiscovered ways. When a person receives stimuli from the outside world, different parts of a given schema are activated. This activation process determines the person's reaction to the stimuli. Schemas may serve to integrate new information or to retrieve bits that have previously been stored (Milburn 1991, 73).

Additional research, which has grown out of the schema tradition (see Lodge and McGraw 1991), uses an "on-line model of information processing" (Hastie and Pennington 1989) to reveal how voters can make judgments about candidates without recalling specific information about those candidates (McGraw, Lodge, and Stroh 1990; Lodge, Steenbergen, and Brau 1995). Under such a model, voters receive campaign messages, add them to a "running tally" (or "on-line tally") of past messages, and evaluate the candidates at a later date, based on their tally. Thus, campaign information is used to make judgments, and those judgments last over time, but the specific information is quickly forgotten. That citizens' memories are short, then, presents no substantive or normative problems for scholars working in this voting behavior tradition (see Lodge, Steenbergen, and Brau 1995, 321–22).

I have briefly discussed schema theory in order to note that it has implications for campaigning. While my theory of consultant influence relies on schema theory, for now the most relevant point of schema theory is the fact that one's schema activation is triggered by her/his environment, parts of which are at least sometimes under the control of communicators (Higgins, Rholes, and Jones 1977; Sharp and Lodge 1985; Lodge and Hamill 1986; and Milburn 1987). By presenting cues, or using specific "signs," a communicator brings to the foreground certain nodes within a schema rather than others (Biocca 1991a, 47). Once those nodes are elicited, they are used for on-line processing. The information sent by a campaign will be added to the mental tally sheet of the voter in different ways, depending upon which part of the schema was tapped. Thus, communicators, or information providers, have some influence over the cognitive processes that people engage in as they receive information, store it, and use it in future evaluations.[18]

It should be noted that texts (e.g., campaign messages and ads) have multiple meanings and that interpretations depend on a number of things including context, the shared experiences of the audience, and the perspectives of individual audience members. Thus, while campaign messages will resonate in similar ways with many voters because of their commonality, the same messages will be viewed from hundreds of perspectives based on the individual characteristics of the voters. Given the potential for multiple interpretations, it should be clear that schema activation is a dynamic process and, as such, is quite difficult to control or manipulate. As Biocca (1991a) notes, "Communication always fails to some degree" (39). This condition is of utmost importance for the theory of consultant influence to be developed below.

All of this is to say that political scientists have traveled a long road to reach the conclusion that campaigns can impact voters. "Like the manic-depressive whose mood swings from one extreme to another," notes Denise Baer (1995), "political science has alternated from treating campaigns as propaganda with vast power to alter voter preferences, to deeming them irrelevant, to again viewing campaigns and campaign strategies as quite potent and effective in determining elections" (48). The persuasive function of campaigns, then, is just beginning to be understood with the subtlety it deserves. Even some who defend the "minimal effects" model, like Steven Finkel (1993), suggest that "the *potential* does exist for campaigns to move individuals away from their vote dispositions" (18, emphasis in original).

Activation

I have already briefly discussed the campaign's activation function. To be precise, Lazarsfeld, Berelson, and Gaudet ([1944] 1968) differentiated between activation and reinforcement. The former occurs when campaigns draw out voters' political predispositions. In fact, Lazarsfeld, Berelson, and Gaudet created an "index of political predisposition" that included just three factors: socioeconomic status (the higher, the more Republican), religion (Protestants were Republican, Catholics Democratic), and place of residence (Republicans were rural dwellers and Democrats were urbanites) (25–26). As the authors concluded, "Social characteristics determine political preference" (27). For those voters who declared themselves undecided in May of the election year, the campaign's role "was not to form new opinions but raise old opinions over the thresholds of awareness and decision" (74). This activation process takes place in four steps: campaign communications stimulate interest; this interest increases exposure to campaign information; that exposure is selective; and, as a result, one's vote crystallizes according to predispositions (75–76).

A somewhat different process is that of reinforcement. Here, the job of the campaign is "to secure and stabilize and solidify [the partisan's] vote intention and finally to translate it into an actual vote" (Lazarsfeld, Berelson, and Gaudet [1944] 1968, 88). Partisans are people who know in May how they will vote in November. Thus, the electoral object is simply to keep them "in line" during the campaign (88). In 1940, 53 percent of the voters knew six months in advance how they would vote in November (103). Such numbers have declined somewhat in recent years, but at least one-third continue to know how they will vote in the general election before the party conventions and nearly 60 percent make up their minds by the end of the conventions (Flanigan and Zingale 1991, 162).

In practical terms, campaigns rarely differentiate between activation and reinforcement. Consultants usually break down the electorate into three groups: those who are for their candidate, those who are against him/her, and those who are undecided (Johnson-Parker and Parker 1994, 38; Bradshaw 1995, 31–32). Too often, however, the undecideds are treated as an undifferentiated mass of people who, given their predilection for "split ticket" or "switch" voting, are really independents and, therefore, equally persuadable by either campaign (Beaudry and Schaeffer 1986, 30–32; see also Johnson-Parker and Parker 1994, 38). When consultants lump all undecideds together, they overlook the fact that such voters have differing partisan predispositions. In fact, as Keith et al. (1992) have convincingly argued, most of the voters who call themselves independents behave as though they were party identifiers. Campaigns run the risk, therefore, of creating and disseminating messages that not only are unsuccessful at activating their own partisans but may crystallize those predisposed to the other party.

Even Bradshaw (1995), whose blueprint for strategy design recognizes that the "undecideds" will split between the two parties, eventually combines "supporters" and "targeted undecideds" into "our voters" and treats that group as a unified, undifferentiated whole (32). Perhaps the best explanation for why consultants neglect to distinguish between activatees and reinforcees is what I will call "single theme-ism." A candidate's theme, or message, is his/her answer to the question "Why am I running for this office, at this time, and why should I be elected?" (42–43; Faucheux 1994, 47). It is, in other words, the rationale for why a candidate should be elected and his/her opponent defeated (Shea 1996, 148; Bradshaw 1995, 42; see also Salmore and Salmore 1989, 112).[19] According to many consultants, candidates must have "message discipline" to be successful. This means picking one, and only one, theme and sticking to it (or "staying on message") in all circumstances.[20] "'Theme' is not a word that should ever have an 's' on the end; there is only one theme" (Bradshaw 1995, 42). Similarly, political operative Mary Matalin has written, "The absolute rule of message dissemination and message penetration is consistency and repetition. The principle is the same for political campaigns or companies: Everyone says the same thing, *over* and *over*" (Matalin and Carville 1994, 80; emphasis in original; see also Shea 1996, 154).

Covington et al. (1993) have examined "single theme-ism" empirically using the Issue of the Day (IOD) strategy adopted by the Reagan 1980 campaign. There are three parts to an IOD approach, all of which are meant to manage the media coverage of a campaign. The first two involve the candidate's actual relationship with the media: the candidate's *accessibility* to the press is to be infrequent and the *formality* of the interactions is to take the form of highly structured press conferences rather than off-the-cuff conversations. Of interest here is the third aspect of the IOD, *homogeneity* of the message (785). Covington et al. (1993) define this feature as "the degree to which the messages delivered to the press over some period of time are unified in content, creating a single, easily identified, and consistent theme" (785). Such a theme, claim the authors, "is most likely to influence the public's image of a candidate," whereas "a variety of messages may deter any single message from being retained, combining to create a confused and less persuasive image" (785). The study reveals that the IOD strategy is effective at influencing, but not entirely determining, the way the press covers a campaign. In the last week of the 1980 election, for example, the Reagan campaign was able to inject its message into two-thirds of the print and television news stories. Overall, television reporting was considerably more influenced by IOD than was print, the latter having more time to make the news and, therefore, needing to rely less on the campaigns for information (791–92). We might expect, of course, that congressional campaigns would be less effective in shaping the news, but the aforementioned study shows that the media are not immune from the image-shaping efforts of campaigns.

Given this proclivity for campaigns to disseminate consistent, simple messages, it is difficult for them to differentiate among voters to any great extent. To do so would complicate matters and thereby seriously threaten the candidate's ability to maintain message discipline. It is the case that campaigns discuss different issues with different groups of voters. Note, however, that each issue will fit with the overall theme of the campaign.[21] Nevertheless, the use of multiple issues doesn't mean campaigns target voters based on whether they need activation or reinforcement. Instead, voters are "segmented" into demographic groups, and these groups, in turn, are fed issues based on their collective characteristics (Newman 1994, 67–85). This process, known as "targeting" (or "narrowcasting" when it is done through media), enables the campaign to tailor its message to disparate groups. There is a limit, however, to such tailoring. Union members, for instance, may be given a candidate's position on labor issues, but the campaign will not craft separate messages for union members who are definite supporters and those who are potential supporters.

This is not to say that campaigns, especially well-financed ones like presidential or some senatorial campaigns, do not make relatively fine distinctions among voters. Targeting (via direct mail, telephone, or television/radio advertising) in such races is complex and utilizes specific, and often subtle, demographic characteristics to segment the electorate (Newman 1994, 67–85). Furthermore, the rapid advance of technology is increasingly making such tactics available to congressional and lower-level campaigns.[22]

The point here, which has perhaps been made in too much detail, is not to criticize consultants for neglecting to recognize the difference between activation and reinforcement. It is simply to suggest that they do not, in practice, distinguish between the two.

Mobilization

Mobilization is a party's/campaign's effort to increase participation among its supporters (Rosenstone and Hansen 1993, 25–26). In effect, campaigns mobilize as they activate and vice versa. In other words, campaigns' efforts to increase turnout among their friends also help solidify their partisans' support just as attempts to trigger partisan predispositions simultaneously encourage supporters to vote. Activation and mobilization, then, are two sides of the same coin.

On the other hand, some mobilization activities (e.g., get-out-the-vote drives, or GOTV) are specifically designed to increase turnout, not influence preferences. To the extent that mobilization is targeted toward those who are likely to yield benefits without inordinate cost (Rosenstone and Hansen 1993, 30–33), a campaign's efforts are directed toward those who are a good bet to vote for the candidate sponsoring the drive, including both the aforementioned activatees and reinforcees (Beaudry and Schaeffer 1986, 103–6). Recall that in Lazarsfeld, Berelson, and Gaudet's study ([1944] 1968), two-thirds and three-fourths of those with Republican and Democratic predispositions, respectively, voted accordingly (74). Thus, simply increasing turnout among those likely to be predisposed toward one's campaign could reap enormous rewards.

Campaigns can increase participation among supporters through direct or indirect means (Rosenstone and Hansen 1993, 26–30; Huckfeldt and Sprague 1992). Direct mobilization occurs when the campaign contacts the voter him/herself. This type of mobilization can take the form of literature distribution, door-to-door canvassing, or telephone contact. Early studies of mobilization found that party efforts to increase turnout are successful (Gosnell 1927; Eldersveld and Dodge 1954; Eldersveld 1956). Kramer (1970–71) specifically found that door-to-door canvassing significantly increased turnout in presidential elections, and Lupfer and Price (1972) concurred, arguing that only face-to-face (i.e., door-to-door) contact, as opposed to that by telephone or through literature, increased participation at the polls. This was later amended by Adams and Smith (1980), who found that telephone canvassing/GOTV calls also increased turnout.

On the other hand, Huckfeldt and Sprague (1992) found that party contact did not significantly increase turnout among those who did not vote in the primaries (80). Since nearly all primary voters turn out in the general election, voter contact appears to have little ability to mobilize. Nonetheless, Price and Lupfer (1973) have suggested that mobilization will best occur in areas where predispositions favor the canvasser but turnout is traditionally low. And Jackson (1996a) has argued that campaign factors matter for turning out voters once they have registered to vote, an act which itself is determined by an individual's sociodemographic characteristics.

Elsewhere, Dawson and Zinser (1976), Cox and Munger (1989), and Jackson (1996b) have shown that a campaign's overall mobilization effort, as measured by campaign expenditures, has a positive impact on turnout in congressional elections. As opposed to sociodemographic factors, Jackson (1996b) contends that "elite activity, as measured by campaign spending, appears to be the primary agent of political mobilization" (432). These findings are not substantiated by Caldeira, Patterson, and Markko (1985), who show that mobilization occurs when the race is contested, there is a high level of party competition, and there is a senatorial race being run simultaneously.[23] The significant variables in the latter study are ones that are out of the hands of any given campaign. Those results, therefore, would cast doubt on a campaign's ability to mobilize its supporters.[24]

Indirect mobilization takes place when those individuals contacted through direct means themselves contact others (Rosenstone and Hansen 1993, 27–30). This process takes place through social networks like families, churches, workplaces, and bowling leagues. When a person who has been contacted by a campaign urges friends or colleagues to vote (and to do so for a particular candidate), they have helped their party indirectly mobilize other members of the electorate. According to Huckfeldt and Sprague (1992), "The initial contact has cascading consequences in the collective deliberations of democracy" (70). Thus, mobilization, like most campaign communication, takes place in two steps: campaigns contact active members of the electorate and they, in turn, contact less active citizens (Katz and Lazarsfeld 1955; Katz 1957).[25] "Direct mobilization reverberates through indirect mobilization" (Rosenstone and Hansen 1993, 28).

Campaigns may also attempt to demobilize the opposition's supporters. Reports of the use of "street money" in the New Jersey gubernatorial campaign of 1993 added fuel to the fire of those who have argued for years that political consultants regularly attempt to suppress the vote, by using either accepted, legal practices or (accepted) illegal ones.[26] More common than street money, however, is the use of negative advertising, which some researchers have found keeps turnout down. Ansolabehere and Iyengar (1995) used experiments to determine that the use of negative ads reduces intentions to vote by 4.6 percent, a statistically significant decrease (104; see also Ansolabehere et al. 1994). The authors conclude by suggesting that "the practice of attack advertising, which has become the dominant message of modern political campaigns, alienates people, especially nonpartisans, from politics and actually depresses intentions to participate in the electoral process" (101).

Those results contradict an earlier study by Garramone et al. (1990) in which the researchers found no significant difference in the intention to vote between those who saw negative advertisements and those who saw positive advertisements. Ansolabehere et al. (1994) were critical of that study, however, because the authors used fictitious ads and an artificial setting for their experiment, thereby casting doubt on the results (829).

Ansolabehere and Iyengar (1995) are not sanguine with regard to the motivations of political consultants in the face of their findings. Indeed, "Consultants brag about using negative advertising to depress turnout, when higher turnout may hurt their candidate" (102). Such cynicism, however, is somewhat excessive. If consultants use negative ads when low turnout benefits their candidates, then presumably their opponents in all those races are using nothing but positive spots in hopes of increasing turnout.[27]

In reality, both candidates in a race use negative ads, primarily because it works to create negative impressions of the target candidate. If consultants take the demobilizing effect of negative ads into account, it is only as a secondary consideration. Of course, consultants whose candidates could benefit from low turnout may realize that using negative ads will prompt their opponent to respond with attacks, thereby decreasing turnout as a result of the overall negative tone of the campaign. But if all consultants recognized this formula, they would not take the bait and respond with attack ads when they needed higher turnout. Critics cannot have it both ways. Either consultants use negative advertising to lower turnout, in which case the critics cannot explain the fact that negative advertising is virtually always used by both candidates in a race, or consultants use attack spots to create negative impressions about one's opponent, in which case turnout considerations are minimal or nonexistent. All of this is to say that the charge that consultants use attack ads to lower turnout for strategic advantage is rather simplistic. Demobilization is not always to one's advantage, and when it is, it is not as easily achieved as is often thought.

These, then, are the primary functions of the campaign. If I have spent an inordinate amount of time describing them, it is only to establish the context within which political consultants operate. For now, note that all of the aforementioned functions involve communication, in one form or another. As renowned political consultant Joseph Napolitan (1972) has suggested, "So far as I am concerned, there are only three steps to winning any election, here or abroad: First, define the message the candidate is to *communicate* to the voters. Second, select the vehicles of *communication*. Third, implement the *communication* process" (2; my emphasis). Obviously, communication will prove important in theorizing about the influence of consultants in election campaigns. Having outlined the campaign functions, I now turn to the development of a theory of consultant influence.

Toward a Theory of Consultant Influence

In its most basic form, the hypothesis of this study is that political consultants have an impact on congressional elections. In order to specify what that impact is and to establish more detailed working hypotheses, it will be necessary to develop a theory of consultant influence. First, however, the paucity of theoretical work on consultants should be addressed. In doing so, I set up the development of my theory of consultant influence, which can be found in the next chapter, by tracing the evolution of what I call the proto-theory of consultant behavior.

The Present Lack of Theory

The existing work on political consultants is amazingly atheoretical (Thurber 1998). This is due, in large measure, to the fact that most of it has been written by journalists and practitioners.[28] While these contributions are often insightful descriptions of the work consultants do in specific campaigns, they are not written in accord with accepted rules of scientific inference, one essential element of which is a theory about the phenomenon under examination (King, Keohane, and Verba 1994). Of course, that is not the purpose of such accounts and I do not mean to suggest that it ought to be. Nevertheless, because it is not grounded in theory, nor does it produce results that can be incorporated into one (since, where they exist, the findings are not generalizable to all campaigns), journalistic/practical writing about consultants remains entertaining but largely fruitless for rigorous analysis of political operatives. Unfortunately, the academic literature is not much more theoretical than the popular writing and, until recently, has remained largely descriptive and/or anecdotal.

Proto-Theory

Given this state of theoretical affairs, our understanding of the role, behavior, and impact of political consultants in American elections is primitive at best and limits the ability of political scientists to examine consultant influence. Nevertheless, some of the previous work on consultants hints at a theory, resulting in a framework that is proto-theoretical. To set the stage for the development of a comprehensive theory, a review of that work will be useful.

Stanley Kelley Jr.'s (1956) early book on public relations professionals in American politics was the first to shed light on the activities of political consultants from an academic perspective. Using case studies, he showed how political professionals apply the techniques of mass media communications to enhance their candidates' ability to disseminate their messages. According to Kelley (1956), the professionals are members of a "skill group" that has mastered the technical aspects of public relations (4). Essentially, the technical problem facing any candidate is "the selection of the media of communication in such a way as to achieve a maximum effect on the consumer within given budgetary limits" (54).[29] Kelley's argument is that only experts in mass persuasion can effectively shape the campaign environment to gain "wide circulation for a point of view" (202; 201–6). Public relations professionals are, in other words, "propaganda specialists" (3). Having taken the place of the party boss,

these professionals would continue to rise in influence as mass persuasion became more important to the aims of candidates (210).

Kelley also noted that campaign professionals situate themselves
"between those who seek power and those who bestow authority" (3).
Traditionally, political operatives worked "behind the scenes" (*Behind
the Scenes in Politics*, 1924; Cunningham 1956). The new campaign handlers, however, were repositioned, at least conceptually. Kelley (1956) did
not explain in detail how the new role as mediator operated, but he
clearly recognized an important element of the professionally run campaign. Consultants, as political communication experts, help candidates
disseminate messages to audiences who are likely to support the candidate but who need to be activated (53); they make offensive (as opposed
to defensive) campaigns possible and enable candidates to attack, or "to
press on the public issues that are to one's own advantage" and "not just
to give one's own side of the question but to *define* the political situation" (48; emphasis in original); and, finally, they shape "verbal environ-
ments" in which voters will react positively to the themes they create
(201).

Many of Kelley's conclusions about professional campaigners (like
their supposed interest in always increasing turnout—as opposed to the
party boss who always wanted to decrease it—as well as the professionals' alleged emphasis on issues) may no longer hold and may not even
have held when Kelley wrote his book. Nevertheless, his descriptions of
the role of public relations people in politics necessarily influence our
understanding of consultants today.

Robert Pitchell (1958) followed Kelley's work with an examination of
the activities of a handful of public relations firms in California. He
notes that in the absence of party organization, candidates are forced to
turn to professional campaign managers who "place emphasis upon mass
communications as the quickest and least expensive (per voter reached)
campaign technique" (279). Of course, these managers are experts in
mass media manipulation (282).[30] Still, Pitchell concluded that professional operatives may not be as successful as is usually thought because
there is no "push-button technique for electing the candidate" who hires
them (300).

Pitchell also mentioned one of the "cardinal rules" of Whitaker and
Baxter, the most successful campaign firm of the first half of this century, if not of all time. That rule, which virtually everyone who writes
about them dutifully notes (see Kelley 1956, 46–47; Perry 1968, 13;
Nimmo 1970, 61; and Mitchell 1992, 83–86), is that "there must be
strong control from the top" if a campaign is to be successful (Pitchell
1958, 289). That means that every aspect of the campaign, especially the
finances, must be handled by the campaign's manager. Karl Lamb and

Paul Smith (1968) call this view the "comprehensive model" of campaign decision making. As they describe the model in its ideal form, it "calls for a hierarchical structure" including "functional specialization, unbroken lines of authority, and complete internal communication" (21). All decisions in a campaign of this sort are made "at the pinnacle of a pyramid-like campaign organization" (21). The model originated in the 1934 California lieutenant governor's race (Mitchell 1992, 83–86) and has been articulated by many campaigners since then (see Shadegg 1972, 36–37; Van Riper 1967, 137–38).

The comprehensive model has been shown to be unrealistic and virtually nonexistent (Hershey 1974; Levin 1962, 307–9) as well as counterproductive (Corsino 1985). According to Lamb and Smith (1968, 26–29), a number of defects in the model keep it from being fully realized, although some campaigns have attempted to put it in place. In reality, as Xandra Kayden (1978) maintains, "If there is any single rule that dominates political decision making it is this: *decisions are made by whoever happens to be in the room at the time*" (11; emphasis in original). This is particularly true of "professionalized" (as opposed to "personalized") campaigns that are defined, in part, by diffused responsibility and decision making (9–10).

While no campaign runs according to the ideal, some organizations are more comprehensive than others, such as the Goldwater presidential campaign of 1964 (Lamb and Smith 1968, chs. 3–8; Kessel 1968). Lamb and Smith have argued that the comprehensive approach is less successful than the alternative, which they call the "incremental model" (29). "Decisions are coordinated through mutual adjustment, an endless process of bargaining and compromise" (32). Authority is dispersed and fragmented (33), and there is no differentiation between means and ends, as there is in the comprehensive model (32). Thus, many more people are responsible for campaign decisions, and a diversity of ideas are considered. When the campaign staff consists of numerous professionals, the incremental model is better able to take advantage of their knowledge and talents. Indeed, Lamb and Smith (212–15) find that the incremental model is a more successful approach in terms of staff morale, intraparty cohesion, and voter persuasion/activation/mobilization because it is best suited for the uncertainty of the campaign environment.[31]

The relevance of campaign decision-making models for a theory of consultant influence should be clear. Today, no consultant would insist on omnipotence in a campaign. As consulting becomes more specialized, campaign operatives know that they must rely not only on the skill of various other handlers (as is allowed for in the comprehensive model) but on the knowledge, insight, and advice of numerous members of the campaign team (as is required by the incremental model). Without necessarily realizing it, those scholars researching campaign decision making showed how the contemporary professionalized campaign, characterized as it is by extreme specialization and fragmentation of duties, is likely to be more effective than an old-style, centralized effort.[32]

Building on Kelley, and to a lesser extent Pitchell, other scholars examined consultant behavior by offering updated descriptions of professional campaigning at approximately ten-year intervals (see Nimmo 1970; Sabato 1981; and Luntz 1988). Unlike the other two books of its kind, Dan Nimmo's book *The Political Persuaders* attempts to build a theory for the phenomenon under study. Of interest to him are "the techniques of modern election campaigns," and he includes the obligatory chapters on pollsters and media specialists as well as one on professional managers. Although he argues that "students of politics . . . must not only describe the detailed activities of campaign professionals, but must begin examining the broader impact of the new technology of political persuasion," Nimmo himself focuses primarily on the former (1970, 68).

Like Kelley, Nimmo sees political professionals as experts in mass communication (1970, 6).[33] The communications sciences, suggests Nimmo, "have made the persuasive efforts in political campaigns into a highly specialized activity requiring the expertise of specialists in management, research, and media" (33; see also 112–14). Indeed, it was the need to utilize the latest in mass communication techniques that led to professional campaign handlers in the first place (37).

Nimmo offers a twist, however, to Kelley's argument that campaign professionals are technical wizards. Whereas Kelley had argued that the consultant's skill was essential for the selection of the proper media of communication (1956, 54), Nimmo adds that consultants are also experts in resource allocation (1970, 38). "Their major contribution to a campaign is rationality in allocating scarce resources—time, money, and talent" (41; see also Sweeney 1995, 15, 24–26). Political parties used to be the "basic planning agency" for a campaign, and candidates could rely on them not only to obtain important resources (i.e., money) but also to help with the efficient use of those resources. Since the decline of party organization in electoral campaigns, office seekers have had to get independent help to use the candidate-centered technology that now dominates elections (Agranoff 1972b, 10).[34] That technology is increasingly put to use gathering and using resources. The arrival of the computer in campaigns, for example, means that specialists are required to operate them and to pick software to handle a variety of campaign tasks.[35] Thus, for Nimmo, consultants remain important for their technical know-how, but their skills are now put to use for resource allocation as much as for voter contact.

In other areas, such as Nimmo's conceptualization of where consultants are situated in the campaign, Kelley's influence is direct. Nimmo holds that "the modern political campaign is a mediated one" (1970, 133), by which he means not only that campaigns are waged on television, radio, and in the print media but also that professional operatives now serve as political middlemen. "Instead of direct, spontaneous, personal contact between candidates and voters," he notes, "we find professional management firms, pollsters, and communications specialists mediating between political leaders and followers" (163). Nimmo's implication is that "professionally mediated campaigns," or those using political consultants, will be different than nonprofessionally mediated ones (see his chapter 5). Indeed, it is not even clear that candidates without consultants are waging a "mediated" campaign at all.

With that in mind, Nimmo begins to build his theory of consultant influence. He bases it broadly on a theory of persuasion which assumes that society is "a differentiated mass" and that individuals within groups "absorb the bulk of their information directly from communications media rather than from one another" (31).[36] These individuals simultaneously share tendencies with other members of society while reacting "in different ways at different times to different stimuli." As a result, appeals to voters "must be diversified accordingly" (31). From here, Nimmo establishes a "field theory of campaign effects." He recognizes that previous studies uncovered few if any effects of campaigns on voting behavior. But that is due, he contends, to adherence to a theory of attitudinal effects rather than one of perceptual effects (179). Because "modern campaign technology is aimed not at attitude change but at perceptual shifts," the early voting behavior literature overlooked an important goal of the contemporary campaign (168). Granting that the campaign will not change the minds of those voters most interested in the race, Nimmo suggests that uninvolved (or uninterested) voters are the target of consultants. Even then, however, the goal is not to convert opponents but to "activate sympathetic perceptions" (192–93).

Because interested and involved voters are committed to their present attitudes, campaigns have little hope of changing their minds. But those who are less interested and less involved are consequently less committed to their attitudes. Nimmo argues that in such cases, "the intent of persuasion is not to change attitudes directly, but rather to break through the weak perceptual barriers and convince the individual of alternative ways of acting, each of which conforms to his basic predispositions instead of being contrary to them" (180). To do this, the campaign must create ambiguous messages so that each voter can project onto them what he/she wishes them to say. As Nimmo recognizes, the authors of *The People's Choice* suggested just such a strategy: "A campaign argument will be particularly successful if a variety of meanings can be read into it" (Lazarsfeld, Berelson, and Gaudet, cited in Nimmo 1970, 181). The contemporary criticism that campaigns are devoid of specifics has precisely this strategy in mind, regardless of how baseless this criticism may be.

Ultimately, Nimmo's (1970) theory rests on the uses-and-gratifications approach to communication (180; see McLeod and Becker 1981). From this perspective, voters, particularly but not exclusively disinterested ones, look to (or use) campaign communications for entertainment (or gratification), not information. They read news about the campaign or watch political advertising for pleasure.[37] Thus, receiving campaign communication is not work but recreation, or "play" (Nimmo 1970, 185; see also Stephenson 1967). As a result, uninterested voters are spectators and, therefore, relatively inactive in the communication process. Campaigns, in turn, "must teach [the voter] a temporary political role." It becomes the job of the consultant "to see that his candidate's role successfully converges with those played by voters, a task in which he has had marked success in contemporary America" (Nimmo 1970, 193).

In many ways Nimmo's theoretical work is groundbreaking for those who wish to understand consultant influence. There are, however, a number of problems with the field theory of campaign effects that need to be addressed before offering an alternative theory. To begin with, it draws a distinction between only two types of voters—those who are interested/involved and those uninterested/uninvolved. As Nimmo realized, voters respond in myriad ways to campaign appeals. Even the most sophisticated voter segmentation model could never capture the extent to which voters are actually unique; a twofold conceptualization certainly cannot. At the same time, such models often ignore those things which all voters have in common. Although Nimmo acknowledges this (31), his theory makes no allowance for the fact. For example, among uninterested voters, some may be more likely to respond to issue appeals, whereas others would be moved by images (although the issue/image distinction is something of a false dichotomy). And among those with even the slightest issue concerns, some may react to the abortion issue just as others can be reached on taxes, the budget, defense, or crime, to name a fraction of the possibilities. Thus, *a theory of consultant influence must take into account the voters' simultaneous commonality and distinctiveness.*

Second, Nimmo never really says how consultants "teach" voters a "role" for themselves. Most of the book is dedicated to how consultants do what they do, but it is not clear from his theory how the technical operations affect the voters' perceptions. This is a particularly difficult problem to overcome. Any theory explaining consultant influence must account for what consultants do, the voters' attitudinal/perceptual structures, and how consultant behavior actually taps those structures. Nimmo's theory, unfortunately, overlooks the last of these.

Finally, although the uses-and-gratifications approach posits a role for the user, Nimmo continues to view the voter as basically passive or "quiescent" (192). As discussed briefly above, recent work in schema theory suggests that voters have a more psychologically active role in the campaign than had been previously thought. As a result, a theory of consultant influence should recognize the voters' cognitive activity while enabling the campaign to have some impact on those voters. I hope to overcome these problems with the theory I develop below. Nevertheless, my theoretical work on this subject owes a great deal to Nimmo. He is the only scholar to have attempted a theory about consultants, and future work on the topic is indebted to him because of it.

Following Kelley and Nimmo, many other contributors to the "proto-theory" of consultant influence stressed the technical skill of the campaign operative. A relatively large number of them take the campaign management and organization approach that Smith (1982) says "trad[es] on 'practical' expertise" (50). Although most of the "how-to" books by practitioners fit into this category, some academic work does as well. Most notably Agranoff (1972a and 1976) and Rosenbloom (1973) take this approach, which holds that consultants (or "campaign professionals") are successful because they are experts in mass communications or public relations (see also Bloom 1973; Denton and Woodward 1985, chapter 3). This is also the assumption, though often unstated, of those writers concerned with campaign technologies (Meadow 1984, 1985; Selnow 1994), of those who take a management or marketing approach to campaigns (Steinberg 1976; Mauser 1983; O'Shaughnessy 1990b; Newman 1994), and of the authors of the best descriptive books on consultants, namely, Blumenthal (1982), Sabato (1981), and Luntz (1988). The latter summarizes the consultant-as-expert thesis when he writes, "The fact is, modern campaign technology has so complicated the process of running for public office that it has passed the stage where a statewide candidate can independently and completely manage his own campaigns. Most candidates recognize the need for expert advice. . . . The minimum tools required to compete in politics today—the benchmark survey, computerized fund-raising, television advertising—each requires consultation with an expert in the field" (Luntz 1988, 42, 43).

Given the aforementioned lack of organized training for political consulting, one might ask just how it is that professional consultants become experts. Some have suggested that it is largely "instinct" or "intuition" that sets consultants apart (Sabato 1981, 5; see Levin 1962 on the inadequacy, but rather widespread use, of intuition in campaigns). While this is undoubtedly an element of the consultant's abilities—

indeed, it may be what differentiates the extraordinary consultant from the average operative—it is not sufficient, or even necessary, to make one an expert. Instead, as Marjorie Randon Hershey (1974, 116–21; 1984) has shown, campaigners (including consultants) simply learn how to run campaigns from experience. Hershey's approach is based on social-learning theory, which "directs our attention to the fact that individual actions take place within a setting" (1984, 38). A campaigner's behavior, then, is learned through an interaction between him/herself and his/her environment (39; see Hershey 1984, chapter 2, for a complete explanation of social learning theory). The information obtained from past experiences, both campaign related and not, enable political operatives to generalize to current races and innovate in new situations (60–66). Eventually, these handlers will develop models of campaigning that can be applied to any campaign (69–73).

Professional consultants, at least as defined in this study, clearly have an advantage over nonprofessional campaigners given the former's extensive learning through experience. As Hershey points out, consultants are "natural 'carriers' of innovations from one campaign to another" and are hired to "provide models of effective campaigning to their clients. Since they often work on several campaigns in a given election year, consulting firms are in a position to draw conclusions about the effects of different strategies under various circumstances, and bring their learning to the next batch of campaigns" (1984, 74).

One of the best examples of how consultants "carry" models from campaign to campaign is direct-mail fund-raising. Once a fund-raising letter has proved to be effective (i.e., has raised a great deal of money), its basic model will be used again and again, in different settings with variations made when necessary.

Other bits and pieces of the proto-theory have been offered by various people. The direct mail practitioner Richard Armstrong, for example, argues that the only thing different about today's campaigns, as opposed to those before the 1980s, is that they are faster (1988, 18). This is obviously the case for professional, as opposed to amateur, campaigns. Professionally handled campaigns have the equipment and know-how to attack, or react, almost immediately. As Armstrong notes, new video production, distribution, "free" media, media buying, and polling technologies—not to mention the Internet—mean that the real distinction between today's professionalized campaigns and older party-driven ones lies not in its negativity (as is often claimed) but in "the campaign's 'reactivity,' its sheer technological ability to respond" (18–22).[38]

Paul Smith's (1982) construction of a "cybernetic model" of campaigning (67) also contributes to the foundation of a theory of consultant influence. Smith's model emphasizes "communication and control" and posits an ideal campaign that "collects information about those parts of the political environment that can affect the outcome of the election, 'processes' this information through internal communications and decisions, and then communicates information to the political environment in order to maximize electoral support for its candidate" (67). The cybernetic model is based on information, and its version of a successful campaign is one which "steers" or controls the electoral situation through the use of relevant information (79). Smith's approach is a further development of the incremental model of decision making that he developed with Karl Lamb (49). Consultants, it seems to me, would be beneficial in the cybernetic model because they can "shorten the time it takes their [the campaign staff's] patterns of interpersonal communication to fuse into a cybernetic system" (78). Unfortunately, while it accounts for basic elements of the consultant's role in campaigns (i.e., research or polling, strategy formation, and message dissemination), it makes no mention of the voter's role. Indeed, it is not clear how the voter has anything at all to do with a cybernetically run campaign. This is obviously not, therefore, a comprehensive theory of consultant influence.

The proto-theoretical explanation of consultant influence, then, rests primarily on the fact that consultants are considered experts who can be relied on for useful advice and assistance. One view of the consultant's technical skill held that it is essential in the selection of the most effective medium of communication (Kelley), whereas another stressed the importance of resource allocation and the consultant's ability in that capacity (Nimmo). In addition, a key assumption of the expertise thesis is that professionals essentially learn effective tactics through their experiences handling campaigns (Hershey).

Of course, the consultant-as-expert approach is not the only element of the proto-theory. Consultants also shape or define the campaign environment, mediate between candidates and voters, supply campaigns with the ability to "react" effectively, and control the type of information that comes into and goes out of the campaign. As for voters, the proto-theory is considerably more vague. Citizens are seen as quite passive, and many are perceptually, though not attitudinally, vulnerable. Thus, voters are segmented according to those who are primary targets of consultants and those who are not, namely, the uninvolved/uninterested and the involved/interested, respectively.

Clearly, we are without a comprehensive theory for the phenomenon under examination. The proto-theory outlined above is insightful but incomplete. Although it accounts for what consultants do, it fails (with perhaps one exception) to explain how the campaign, as a communicative event mediated by consultants, affects the voters.

Summary

In this chapter I laid the groundwork for the theory of consultant influence that follows in chapter 3. In doing so, I addressed some of the potential barriers to the study of political consultants and discussed why they should no longer hinder a systematic, comprehensive examination of the consulting phenomenon. I also examined the idea of "professional" campaign consultants.

More important, I outlined six major functions of campaigns in American elections. That discussion was necessary for understanding the context within which consultants operate. It becomes apparent from the discussion of those functions that campaigns are primarily about communication. Thus, the theory to be developed herein is essentially a theory of political communication.

Finally, this chapter reviewed what I called the proto-theory of political consultant influence. While numerous scholars have explored political consulting, none, with the possible exception of Dan Nimmo, have offered a comprehensive theory for explaining why we might hypothesize that the presence of consultants in campaigns increases a candidate's chances of success. To do so, a theory would have to address consultant behavior, voter behavior, and the process of communication within the campaign. What follows, therefore, is a theory of consultant influence that at least attempts to engage each of these three elements of the campaign context.

· 3 ·

The Theory of Deliberate Priming

In chapter 2, I described six functions of the campaign in the American political system. While almost all campaigns exhibit each of the six roles at one time or another during the course of an election cycle, no one function captures the entire purpose of the campaign. There are two important characteristics that each of the functions share and that not only help us understand the ultimate purpose of any campaign but also serve as primary ingredients of the theory to be developed in this chapter. The first is that all campaigns are communicative events (Trent and Friedenberg 1995). This is an obvious but often neglected point and one that ought to be given more attention by political scientists interested in campaigns and elections. Whether a candidate uses symbolic expression, is fulfilling a representative function, seeks to inform or educate, hopes to persuade, or intends to activate and/or mobilize people, he/she is fundamentally engaged in communication.

Second, campaigns attempt to reorder the agendas of their targets and prime them to vote a certain way. By emphasizing certain issues (or candidate characteristics) rather than others, candidates aim to bring those issues (or characteristics) to the fore. Of course, the extent to which they are successful at doing so depends on the resources marshaled on their behalf and the psychological resources of the campaign's targets.[1] It also depends on the skill with which they frame the campaign situation (or "set the terms of debate") to their own competitive advantage.

Generally speaking, priming is a process in which issues emphasized by the news media are, in turn, used by voters to evaluate candidates (Iyengar and Kinder 1987, 63). The media's agenda-setting and priming effects are unintended consequences of reporting the news. Of course, the process of selecting the news inevitably results in focusing on some things rather than others.[2] Campaigns, on the other hand, select certain issues with the *sole purpose* of priming voters. Thus, just as all

37

campaigns are about communication, all campaigns are equally about priming.

I now turn to the development of what I will call the "theory of deliberate priming." By combining an explanation of the consultants' behavior, the cognitive activity of the voters, and communication between the two, I hope to offer a comprehensive explanation of consultant influence. Such a theory will give me and others guidance in exploring the myriad ways consultants affect elections and American democracy. Without a theory, however, there is little reason to believe that consultants influence the outcome, or perhaps even the conduct, of elections.

Schema Theory and Voting Behavior

I begin on the voter's side of the equation. Consultants confront an electorate whose individual members have various interests, experiences, and cognitive abilities. What makes them similar is the way in which they process information and reach conclusions about matters at hand. Earlier, I briefly mentioned a theory that explains how these processes work; I turn now to a more detailed description of schema theory.

The study of political psychology is a variant of work on social cognition, which itself belongs to larger (and older) fields such as cognitive (Kuklinski, Luskin, and Bolland 1991, 1341) and social psychology (Hastie 1986). Schema theory has emerged as one of the most widely applied theories in voting behavior research.[3] Though certainly not without its detractors, this theory has enjoyed success because it can reconcile voters' low levels of information with rational behavior and because it is parsimonious.

The central concept in the theory under review is, obviously, the "schema."[4] Lau (1986) describes a schema as "a knowledge structure, based on experience, that organizes people's perceptions of the world. Schemata are hierarchically structured, containing a schema label, particular instances of the schema, and generic information relevant to all or almost all of those specific instances. Schemata organize the processing and storage of incoming information, and they guide the recall and interpretation of information already in memory" (95; see also Lau and Sears 1986, 349). In other words, "A schema is a cognitive structure that contains a concept's attributes and the links among those attributes" (S. Fiske 1986, 41).

There are various types of schemas, or schemata, including person (those related to human traits, whether specifically or in general), self (those about one's identity), role (those involving social roles or classifications, including gender/sex, race, age, etc.), and event (those dealing with situational information like doctor visits, office behavior, or family interactions) (Milburn 1991, 73; Fiske and Taylor 1984). Political schemas have also been identified. For example, Lau (1986) found issue, group, personality, and party schemas while Hamill, Lodge, and Blake (1985) uncovered class, partisan, and ideological ones.

Concepts within a schema are organized into associative networks or knowledge structures (Lodge and McGraw 1991, 1360–61). These concepts, or nodes, can be superordinate or subordinate in any given schema and are characterized by two traits—strength, or "accessibility from long-term memory," and evaluation, or an "affective tag" (1361; see also Hastie 1986, 17). "Nodes become *linked* to each other in long-term memory when they are brought into working memory simultaneously, the long-term effect of such repetitions being a schematic representation of one's prior experiences" (Lodge and McGraw 1991, 1361; emphasis in original).

One accesses information from memory according to "spreading activation principles" (Hastie 1986, 22; Lodge and McGraw 1991, 1363; Anderson 1980, 1983). In short, this means that "new material is processed by being linked with previously established ideas" (Miller 1986, 211). When an individual receives a message from his/her environment, "meaning(s) of the message will be determined by what existing knowledge is activated and how it is activated" (Biocca 1991a, 33). This preexisting knowledge is important not just because it is already present but also as a result of how it happens to be configured in the mind. "The assumptions of the activation process are that activation spreads from a currently active location in a knowledge structure to other nearby locations, that the spread is rapid, that the amount of activation of proximate locations is inversely related to the number of locations (number of efferent links), and that it diminishes sharply with distance from the source of activation" (Hastie 1986, 23).

Remember that specific pieces of information are often not available to the voter. This is because information is used to modify a cumulative judgment of a known object, or to create a judgment of a previously unknown object, and then is either stored so deep in one's cognitive structure that it cannot easily be accessed or is forgotten altogether. In memory-based models of candidate evaluation, the inability to recall details about a candidate means that decisions were reached in "irrational" ways. Unless one can offer specific reasons for preferring one candidate over another, one is viewed as less than the ideal citizen. As briefly noted earlier, however, on-line models of candidate assessment characterize voters and their cognitive processes much differently, both in psychological and normative terms (Lodge, McGraw, and Stroh 1989; McGraw, Lodge, and Stroh 1990; Lodge, Steenbergen, and Brau 1995).

According to the on-line model, voters maintain impressions of candidates that were constructed from prior information obtained about those candidates. (If the candidate is unknown to the voter, the impression begins with the first exposure to that candidate; of course, the voter will have preconceived information about certain aspects of the candidate such as his/her party, gender, race, age, occupation, etc.) With each additional piece of information, the voter alters his/her overall assessment of that candidate. However, because information is evaluated based on impressions already formed, drastic change in the voter's cumulative judgment of the candidate is typically unlikely. Nevertheless, the potential for change, even if only slight, does exist. Once the new bit of information has been processed, it is stored or forgotten. This is how voters can offer evaluations of candidates without corresponding reasons for those evaluations. From an on-line approach this does not make voters irrational or, worse, stupid; it simply means they are pragmatic users of information (Conover and Feldman 1986; Jervis 1986; 329–34; Fiske and Taylor 1984; Taylor 1981).

Perhaps the most important point about schema theory for our present purpose is that while "schemata organize an individual's knowledge, . . . that same knowledge can be organized in many different ways" (Lau and Sears 1986, 350). This means, in turn, that different schema can be activated depending on which nodes are "foregrounded" (Biocca 1991a, 47) and which links are utilized. While external actors can and do influence the activation of schema, it is important to keep in mind that individuals are not passive in the process. In fact, one of the advantages of schema theory is that it posits people who "actively process and interpret incoming information according to their preexisting knowledge structures" (Lau and Sears 1986, 351) whether, I would add, purposefully or not (see Lane 1986).

How, then, are schemas cued? Again, Lau and Sears (1986) explain, "At the individual level, particular schemata are cued or brought to mind in particular instances by exposure to explicit schema labels or to a set of attributes more closely linked to one schema than another" (362). Variation in schema activation between individuals occurs along three dimensions, namely, the accessibility, availability, and development of schemas (Conover and Feldman 1986, 135). Accessibility refers to the particular schema a person taps in any given situation. During an election, for example, some people may evaluate candidates on ideological grounds while others use a partisan schema to make determinations (135).

The availability of a schema refers to whether or not a particular schema is in the possession of a person. For some people, an ideological schema does not even exist and, therefore, could not be made accessible for use in an election setting. Such people would be considered "aschematic" in that particular area, while those possessing an ideological schema would be "schematic" (Conover and Feldman 1986, 136). This does not mean, however, that those who are aschematic in one area do not possess any other schema. For example, a person who is aschematic with regard to ideology may, instead, apply class or partisan schema to politics.

Finally, schema development (or, for lack of a better term, sophistication) varies among voters. Along these lines, some people are experts on certain topics while others are novices (Fiske and Kinder 1981; Fiske, Kinder, and Larter 1983; more generally, see Lau and Erber 1985). Experts have more knowledge than novices in a given subject area and that knowledge is better organized. Furthermore, experts can activate their schemas more easily and can draw more inferences (Conover and Feldman 1986, 136; see also Lau and Sears 1986, 352–55).

Ultimately, schemas, or specific nodes within a schema, are "primed," or prompted, by "semantic frames" (Biocca 1991a, 38; Biocca 1991b). Biocca (1991a, 34) describes the semantic activation of schema during a political advertisement as follows: "Viewers automatically use social, political, and textual schema as 'grids' for the processing of television. The cells of these 'grids' are like variables. When a schema is activated, it determines what kind of information ('values' for the variables) will be sought and how the information will be organized (the 'structure' of the grid). When information (a value for a variable) is 'missing,' it may be inferred from existing knowledge and placed by default into the grid."[5] That schemas *determine* the type of information culled from memory and its usage during a campaign is crucial in understanding why and how political consultant behavior is effective (at least theoretically).

Schemata are also cued by contextual factors. Indeed, as Conover and Feldman (1986) note, "The political environment 'primes' voters to use certain schemata in their perception of candidates" (133). The political environment, which includes human actors and inanimate objects, need not exert enormous pressure to prime different schemas; a minor event is enough to activate a schema that might otherwise have remained dormant. Take the following example: "At a campaign rally . . . an antiabortion heckler might jeer 'baby killer,' thereby *priming* bystanders to use a schema that they almost certainly would not have employed otherwise" (134; my emphasis). Likewise, Miller (1991) notes that surveys conducted as part of the National Election Studies (NES) might elicit different answers from respondents by simply altering question and/or response order. "It is worth noting that the approach used in the NES studies employs a candidate-salient display rather than an attribute-salient approach (which would ask the respondent to compare the various candidates with respect to each attribute in turn). These are very different approaches. They *prime* potentially different schemas that may give rise to very different results" (1376; my emphasis). As will become clear below, attempting to activate or prime specific schemas (what I call "deliberate priming") is the central activity of political consultants.

Other contextual factors can be thought of as "given" in campaigns. Brody (1986), for example, has argued that most Americans have "candidate role" and, potentially, "incumbency-role" schema. This suggests that one of the more important elements in determining the type of schema that gets activated is whether or not the candidate under evaluation already holds the office he/she is seeking. Still another aspect of the electoral environment is the partisan climate of the district (indicated by, among other things, the party affiliation of local officeholders) and the party affiliation of the candidates. Of course, partisanship contributes to candidate evaluation only to the extent that an individual voter has a partisan schema available or has it more accessible than other political schemas. However, unlike incumbency, which is outside a candidate's control, partisanship can be "handled." A candidate can generally downplay party allegiance, accentuate his/her "independence," or, more drastically, switch parties.

Ideology can also serve as a contextual factor, again, both in terms of the district's (or state's or country's) general ideological mood and the ideologies of the candidates. But ideology is even more easily manipulated by candidates than is party affiliation. Although vote studies from ideological interest groups (e.g., Americans for Democratic Action and the American Conservative Union) are available, such information is relatively unknown by most voters and is, perhaps surprisingly, not employed very often in campaigns.[6] Therefore, candidates can—within reason—reshape their ideology during a campaign to fit the general leanings of the electorate. While this usually takes the form of more or less vague rhetorical posturing, it may also be reflected in concrete activity like changes in roll call voting patterns. Indeed, Martin Thomas (1985) has shown that roll call votes of U.S. senators become more moderate as an election approaches.

Thus, while incumbency status, partisanship, and ideology are thought to be given in most elections, they vary in the extent to which they constrain the activation of voter schemas and the candidates' role in influencing that activation. In fact, most of what is taken as contextual (or given) in a campaign is actually variable; as a result, campaigns are thoroughly dynamic events.

One last point, which is most relevant to the following section, is that according to Hastie (1986), schema activation involves "the transformation of symbolic information from one representation into another" (24). "Physical signals" in one's environment (which I will later call "signs") trigger sensory responses that get transformed into "semantic information" (24). Although Hastie claims to be "dissatisfied with the unsystematic character of . . . semiotic [among other] . . . methods" (12), we will now see that his description of the information-processing system fits nicely with the semiotic perspective on communication.

Political Communication and Semiotics

In 1972, political operative Joseph Napolitan wrote that "a political consultant is *a specialist in political communication* (2; emphasis in original). Today, communications scholar Frank Biocca (1991c) likens political consultants to "semiotic engineers" (4). What is semiotics, and what does it have to do with political communication? This section addresses that question and adds an element to the "theory of deliberate priming."

Semiotics is often referred to as "a science that studies the life of signs within society" (Saussure 1959, 16). This definition comes directly from one of the field's founders, Ferdinand de Saussure, who suggested that "semiology" (his term for semiotics) would be "a part of social psychology and consequently of general psychology" (16). Indeed, Wendy Leeds-Hurwitz (1993) suggests that "Saussure studied *behavior*" (6; emphasis in original). Thus, from its very beginning semiotics was linked to the human and social sciences. Today, one of the leading semioticians, Thomas Sebeok, believes this "doctrine" should serve as the foundation for such sciences (see Switzer, Fry, and Miller 1990, 394–95). Indeed, it has even been said that "all of human behavior is the subject matter of semiotics" (Nuessel 1996, 145).

Given the centrality of human behavior to the study of semiotics, it should be clear that the field is more than relevant to the study of political communication. As Sebeok (1994) maintains, "The subject matter of semiotics . . . is the exchange of any messages whatsoever—in a word, *communication*" (5; emphasis in original). Therefore, those interested in the way candidates communicate during campaigns might gain some insight from an understanding of semiotics.

A number of terms should be clarified before discussing the main tenants of semiotics. To begin with, a *sign* "refers to something other than itself" (Fiske 1990, 41) or is "something which stands to somebody for something in some respect or capacity" (Peirce cited in Eco 1984, 14). Similarly, after Eco (1976) says, "Semiotics is concerned with everything that can be *taken* as a sign," he adds, "A sign is everything which can be taken as significantly substituting for something else" (7; emphasis in original). Thus a sign, according to Marcel Danesi (1994), is "any mark, bodily movement, symbol, token, etc., used to indicate and to convey thoughts, information, commands, etc." and, together, signs "are the basis for human thought and communication" (xi).

According to Saussure, signs are made up of two parts, the signifier and the signified. The *signifier* is the sound or image that our minds perceive when we use language (by thinking or communicating) and the *signified* is the concept or meaning produced by the sound-image (Silverman 1983, 6). Leeds-Hurwitz (1993) describes the two elements of a sign as "the visible part" and "the absent part," respectively (9).

Of nearly equal prominence in the study of semiotics is the concept of codes. Codes can simply be seen as the rules for using, and therefore understanding, signs (see Eco 1976, 1984 for his discussion of codes). Sebeok (1994) explains that a code is "a set of unambiguous rules whereby messages are convertible from one representation to another; the code is what the two parties in the message exchange are supposed to have, in fact or by assumption, totally or in part, in common" (9). People are socialized to understand the prevailing codes of their society or culture. As an example of how a code works, Americans know that a white hat in a movie Western is a *sign* meaning the "good guy" and they know this because they understand the *codes* involved in watching Westerns.

Signs are often discussed in terms of motivation and constraint. These concepts refer to the "extent to which the signified determines the signifier" (Fiske 1990, 52). In other words, if a given signified, let us say a photograph of a man (to use Fiske's example), easily and reliably creates a signifier, in this case, the mental image of the man photographed, that sign is said to be highly motivated (52–53). If I wanted you to think of Richard Gephardt, and I drew a stick figure of a man, that sign would not be very motivated. Constraint is virtually synonymous with motivation. Indeed, "The more motivated the sign is, the more its signifier is constrained by the signified" (52). This will have important consequences for political consulting because campaigns must use highly motivated signs in order to elicit the behavioral responses they need from voters. For now, one should be able to see that motivation is closely linked to codes. As Fiske (1990) notes, "The less motivated the sign is, the more important it is for us to have learnt the conventions agreed amongst the users: without them the sign remains meaningless, or liable to wildly *aberrant decoding*" (53; emphasis in original). For our purposes, think of these conventions as codes.

Just as one might discuss the motivation or constraint of a sign, one could also discuss codes in terms of whether they are "restricted" rather than "elaborated" and "broadcast" rather than "narrowcast" (Fiske 1990, 70–77). Without getting too specific, the issue of restricted and elaborated codes relies on "the type of social relations that exist" and "the nature of the code itself." Restricted codes are premised on "a tight, closed, traditional community" while elaborated codes are produced by a "more fluid, changing, mobile, impersonal type of social relations." Narrow and broadcast codes, on the other hand, "are defined by the nature of the audience" (70, 73). Narrowcast codes are "aimed at a defined, limited audience" with specific interests and demands (76). Broadcast codes, on the other hand, are made to appeal to an undefined audience, that is, everyone (73). Signs, or messages, will be more widely understood if they rely on elaborated broadcast codes as opposed to restricted narrowcast codes. As one might guess, these distinctions have great relevance for consulting, particularly with regard to targeting.

We are now entirely situated in the realm of communication. As such, we are interested in messages and how they are formed, sent, and received. Semiotics informs our understanding of these processes in a number of ways. To begin with, Sebeok (1994) draws a link between messages and semiotics when he writes, "A message is a sign or string of signs transmitted from a sign producer, or source, to a sign receiver, or destination" (6). As for the first of our three concerns about messages (i.e., their formation), Sebeok claims, "It is unknown how most sources generate—or, to use a less overburdened term, formulate—a message" (9). What semiotics tells us, however, is that to be sent, a message is always *encoded* (i.e., created using a code). We say that a message is encoded with meaning but, according to semiological models, that meaning is not always intentional. In other words, one can send a message without intending to or with a different meaning than intended. Once sent, the message is *decoded* (i.e., interpreted according to a code) by the receiver (9). It is important to realize that in semiotics there is "no distinction between encoder and decoder" (Fiske 1990, 42). "The interpretant is the mental concept of the user of the sign, whether this user be speaker or listener, writer or reader, painter or viewer. Decoding is as active and creative as encoding" (42).

That last point is of utmost importance. In most models of communication, a sender has clear intentions with regard to a message's meaning, and if the receiver gets any other meaning from that message, it is considered miscommunication or misunderstanding. From a semiotic perspective, messages are encoded with multiple potential interpretations. A given receiver decodes a message based on the codes he/she has available. Among these codes will usually be one shared with the larger culture. Typically, that shared or conventional code is used to decode the message. But this is not always the case. Sometimes receivers get very different messages than either the sender intended or the wider society would have received. When this happens, it is called "aberrant decoding" (see Eco 1980). "Aberrant decoding," writes Fiske (1990), "results, then, when different codes are used in the encoding and decoding of the message" (78). "Aberrant," in this usage, does not necessarily mean "wrong"; it simply means "different." Of course, some decodings are so aberrant as to be essentially wrong. But semiotics does not distinguish, within a given range, between correct and incorrect interpretations. It simply posits an explanation for how communication operates.

Before exploring the act of decoding more deeply, one last concept should be introduced. *Signification*, as has been noted, is the basic subject matter of semiotics. Simply put, signification is "the relationship of the signified to reality" (Fiske 1990, 51). Roland Barthes's work addresses this topic most directly. Barthes (as detailed in Silverman 1983, 25–32; Fiske 1990, 85–92) described two "orders" of this process of signification. In the first order, *denotation*, or "the common-sense, obvious meaning of the sign," takes place (Fiske 1990, 85–86). In the second order of signification, *connotation* replaces denotation. Connotation is "the interaction that occurs when the sign meets the feelings or emotions of the users and the values of their culture. This is when meanings move toward the subjective, or at least the intersubjective" (86). Another way of explaining this is with reference to a photograph; "Denotation is *what* is photographed; connotation is *how* it is photographed" (86; emphasis in original). To use an example from American politics, the Willie Horton ad from 1988 denoted an African American male.[7] However, with its use of a cold black-and-white mug shot, it connoted for most Americans crime in general and, for many, the threat of crime committed by black men.[8] In addition, it connoted Michael Dukakis's "softness on crime" (Diamond and Bates 1992, 277–80).

With this in mind, I return now to encoding and decoding. From the semiotic perspective on communication, campaign messages, like written texts, can be understood as "writerly" (Barthes 1974) or "open" (Eco 1979; 1989, 44–83) rather than "readerly/closed." With an open text, "a reader or viewer [or voter] . . . participates in an on-going manufacture of meaning, an activity without a final goal or resting point" (Silverman 1983, 247). According to Biocca (1991a), "political messages flirt with openness by avoiding unambiguous statements of issue positions and policy" (37). As a result of their openness, campaign messages and ads are also polysemic, which means "that several interpretations coexist as potentials in any one text, and may be actualized differently by different audiences, depending on their interpretive conventions [or codes] and cultural backgrounds" (Jensen 1995, 75) as well as the configuration of their schemas (Fiske 1986, 1987). This means, for our purposes, that when a candidate issues a message of any sort, that message is open to various interpretations. Now, as has been pointed out, most people will come to a shared interpretation of the message because they are using common codes in the decoding process. The more vague the message, however, the more open it is to divergent, or aberrant, decodings. As we will see below, the role of the consultant becomes one of establishing as much "semantic closure" as possible. In other words, consultants attempt to craft messages which elicit responses that benefit their candidate. They must be aware, therefore, of which codes are predominantly in operation and how voters are going to decode their campaign messages.

Semiotics is crucial to understanding communication in general and political communication specifically. This makes it central to the purpose at hand, namely, to understand what consultants do and how they are effective.

Consultant Behavior and Deliberate Priming

Given the polysemy of messages and the open nature of signs, it should be clear that schema activation and decoding are dynamic processes and, as such, are quite difficult to control or manipulate. This, however, is precisely where political consultants enter. As "semiotic engineers," consultants are responsible for determining which campaign signs and messages will be decoded in the most advantageous manner. In the terminology of semiotics, consultants are skilled at reducing the number of aberrant decodings. I do not mean to suggest that political consultants operate with semiological concepts in mind. Most consultants, if not all, are unfamiliar with semiotics and do not think in those terms when they work. But just as voters are unaware of schema theory even as they behave in ways explained by that theory, so too consultant behavior can be explained by semiotics—at least in part—without them having any knowledge of that field.

In this section I bring schema theory together with semiotics to explain how political consultants influence elections.[9] The formulation of the "theory of deliberate priming" melds insights from a body of scholarship that explains voting behavior as well as one that accounts for the communication process. The uniqueness of the theory lies in the fact that it addresses all the elements in the campaign equation—the voters, the campaigners, and the communication processes that go on between them. Thus, it is the first comprehensive theory of political consultant behavior.

One of the ways that consultants determine which signs and messages will be most effective in an election is with the use of focus groups. While opinion polling of randomly selected samples of voters is heavily relied upon in campaigns, the use of focus groups has been increasing among consultants in recent years. This is because, as consultant Christopher Herbert (1994) suggests, a campaigner can "watch the information gathering process in action" in a way not available to the survey researcher (1). In a focus group, consultants can probe participants for the justifications behind a response. These justifications give a consultant clues about what codes are in use by voters and how those voters are likely to interpret any given sign.

The method has also been used by scholars to "investigate how people use campaign information in constructing images of candidates and arriving at a voting decision." In addition, it helps answer the question "What kinds of messages . . . are most critical in developing a candidate schema?" (Kern and Just 1995, 127; see also Kern and Just 1994). Political consultants are interested in these exact questions and are equally aware of the potential of the focus group method. Focus groups are useful in the early stages of a race, particularly for creation of the campaign theme (as well as for a basis of future polls; see Marquette 1996, 124).[10] They are also helpful in testing political advertisements, although their use late in a campaign is limited by the need for rapid reaction.

An example of how the focus group works, semiotically, is provided by Biocca (1991a). In 1984, the Reagan campaign used a commercial called "Bear in the Woods" in which a hunter stalks a bear through a forest (see Diamond and Bates 1992, 25–27, for details). Biocca explains, "A voice over mused how 'some people' were not sure whether or not there is a bear in the woods and whether he is dangerous" (60). Clearly, the ad's producers hoped that the bear would connote the Soviet Union and that the hunter would be seen as a symbol for Reagan. Drawing such links depends upon the codes viewers use to foreground particular schema. Biocca describes the response to this ad as follows:

> When Republican strategists tested the "Bear in the Woods" commercial in focus groups, it became immediately apparent that the key metaphorical connection was not activated in the minds of many viewers. This failure led to the instantiation of a variety of aberrant decodings. Some viewers inferred the discursive topic of "environmentalism" by making the wrong metaphoric link between actantial role and actant (represented bear—"Smokey Bear"). Others decoded it by using the representation of a gun to infer a discursive frame of "gun control laws" and, by foregrounding this value, read the ad as a defense of the right to bear arms (no pun intended, of course). Nonetheless, the commercial was aired. It benefitted from repeated exposure. Its metaphorical structure led many viewers to pay more attention upon second and third exposures. This additional attention may have led to deep processing of its structure and, subsequently, to high recall for the ad and its macropropositions regarding danger, safety, and defense. (61)[11]

West (1993) reports that "Bear in the Woods" was, indeed, remembered by more people than any other Reagan ad in 1984 (111). Nevertheless, "this commercial had no significant effect on either of the concerns noted [in the ad]: peace and arms control or restoring pride in the United States" (112). He explains, "Although the Reagan campaign was apparently confident of the public's ability to understand this ad, the spot contained abstract allusions both to dovishness—the bear may not be dangerous—and hawkishness—we need to be strong. The complexity of this ad may have limited its effect on the agenda" (112).

Diamond and Bates (1992) are more positive about this ad's effectiveness. According to them, "Many viewers missed the allegory but got the message of peace through strength. According to [Douglas] Watts [Reagan's media director], the ad attracted two demographic groups whose views often diverge: women liked the peace-through-strength appeal, and blue-collar men warmed to the macho theme" (26).

In sum, then, this example shows how consultants glean interpretations of campaign messages from the participants in focus groups. That information is of enormous importance for determining which messages will be most effective at priming voters, the central activity of my theory of consultant behavior.

Before turning to "deliberate priming," I should briefly explain how consultants function in a campaign. In the early stages of the campaign, the consultant most crucial to an effective operation is the pollster (which is not to say that they are not essential at all stages of the campaign). Pollsters conduct both polls and focus groups (the latter are also undertaken by media specialists). Very crudely, the early round of a professionally run campaign might go as follows: Pollsters use surveys not only to gather information about the candidates (name identification, approval/disapproval, likes/dislikes, etc.) but also to determine which issues are most salient, both actually and potentially, to voters. Then, through focus groups (or surveys), they ascertain which image of the candidate elicits more favorable responses from voters (i.e., which actant role is most effective). They also uncover potential weak spots in the candidate's record or character and the best way to "defuse" those weaknesses (see discussion below and West 1993, chapter 7). In addition, they test various messages and issues for salience. This might consist of determining which phrases produce the best responses (e.g., "read my lips, no new taxes") or it may entail further exploration into the proper approach to take on the most salient issues.

The last point does not mean, however, that consultants simply find the "best" spot on an imaginary spectrum and place their candidates in that spot. Despite cynical suggestions to the contrary, candidates are not puppets. Even if they were willing to ignore their personal preferences and take only popular positions, there are structural constraints that would not allow it. These constraints, highlighted by what has been called the "party cleavage theory" of elections, include the prior policy positions of the candidate, nomination activists (including the primary electorate), campaign volunteers, and, not least, financial contributors (Page 1978). Most Republicans, for example, would have a difficult time being in favor of abortion, gay rights, affirmative action, and considerable regulation of business. Republican primary voters in virtually all districts in the country would reject such a candidate. Furthermore, candidates cannot snub influential interest groups in either party. A Democrat would have difficulty winning an election without the help of labor, which provides money and volunteers to many Democratic campaigns. Even if a given district is anti-union, odds are the Democrat will culti-vate ties, albeit not highly visible ones, with local unions. This means he/she will not be able to take many anti-labor positions, regardless of public opinion.[12]

Therefore, consultants in the early stages of a campaign help candi-dates understand how, but not where, to position themselves. As a hypo-thetical example, suppose a candidate opposed the death penalty and polls in her district determined that a clear majority favored that form of punishment. Rather than change her opinion, the candidate is likely to either ignore or downplay the issue or, if possible, find a way to use her position to her advantage. If that majority, while favoring the death penalty in the abstract, was uncomfortable with, say, the racial disparity on death row (something which could be determined through focus groups), the candidate could use this discomfort by addressing that aspect in the explanation of her opposition to capital punishment. By doing so, she might be able to "defuse" an issue that otherwise could have been used against her.

Keep in mind that the pollster's role in the early stages of a campaign, as I have outlined it, is ideal. A minority of campaigns operate in pre-cisely that manner, in part because not all candidates hire pollsters. Even when pollsters are in use, financial constraints may require that they only conduct surveys and not use focus groups to hone their polling in-formation. Nevertheless, for theoretical purposes I am offering a model of consultant behavior at the outset of a campaign.

Besides pollsters, general consultants are crucial in a campaign's planning stage. Earlier I discussed the specialized role of generalists in today's campaigns. Where once they were considered jacks-of-all-trades, now generalists specialize in message construction. While many still offer full campaign services, their ability to run every aspect of the cam-paign centers on their expertise in message formulation (as well as strat-egy and tactics, two areas requiring more specialized skill than general knowledge). It is true that in large-scale campaigns, such as those at the senatorial or presidential level, generalists are often used as managers. In House races, however, most generalists are used as message and strategy gurus. In order to create a message, the consultant must rely on information obtained by the pollster. Polling and focus groups should have identified the most salient issues in the election, as well as issues of potential salience, and should have uncovered the effects of the various ways that those issues could be framed. In addition, the best (and worst) characteristics of the candidate should have been explored and the weaknesses of the opponent pinpointed (the latter can also be done, to some extent, with basic opposition research). At this point, the consultants working on message creation combine polling data and focus group analyses with other substantive information (voting records of the candidates, past voting behavior of the district, etc.) to identify a working campaign theme (Shea 1996, 150). That theme has one objective, and it lies at the heart of the present theory of consultant behavior.

The campaign theme seeks to deliberately prime voters. By "deliberate priming," I mean that campaigns emphasize certain topics with the intention of altering the criteria that voters use for candidate evaluation. Jarol Manheim (1975) described this campaign strategy when he wrote, "Each candidate must emphasize his assets and de-emphasize his liabilities in what amounts to the 'selective projection' of a campaign image" (94; see also Salmore and Salmore 1989, 112). Indeed, many scholars have recognized the common use of a selective emphasis campaign strategy. According to the "emphasis allocation theory" of Benjamin Page (1976), "Candidates must allocate their emphasis (in time, energy, and money) among policy stands and other sorts of campaign appeals" (748). Under Page's theory, candidates are likely to keep policy stands vague, choosing instead to emphasize those things that create a positive personal image.

In addition, "saliency theory" (Budge and Farlie 1983) suggests that parties emphasize only those issues upon which they have an advantage over their opponents (see also Aldrich 1980). The theory rests on the recognition that voters have established perceptions, based on accumulated knowledge of party priorities and performances in office, about the issues that parties (or candidates) are better suited to handle. John Aldrich (1996) calls this phenomenon "issue ownership." As Aldrich explains, "The critical constants are the issue handling reputations of the parties and the voters' bias toward the party advantaged by the issue agenda. . . . The campaigns waged by the candidates increase the salience of some problems and, in doing so, cause voters to use their party linked perception of the issue handling ability of the candidates to choose between (or among) them" (826–27). For example, Byron Shafer and William Claggett (1995) argue that in contemporary American elections

Democrats are generally advantaged when the issue agenda centers on an economic/welfare principle (including social welfare, social insurance, and civil rights) and Republicans have the upper hand when the focus is on a cultural/national principle (including basic cultural values, civil liberties, and foreign affairs).

While the work of the aforementioned scholars deeply informs and shapes the theory developed herein, I suggest that we continue to lack a complete picture of how a selective emphasis strategy operates (although clearly Aldrich incorporates framing and priming into his research). In particular, as I have indicated, a comprehensive theory should address not only candidate and consultant activity but also the behavior of voters and the communication processes that link the two. A theory of deliberate priming seeks to integrate all three elements.

It is, perhaps, important to remind ourselves that priming is most often used to refer to a media-driven process (as is agenda setting; Iyengar and Kinder 1987). When referring to the media, these processes are "unintentional by-products of news coverage managed with other ends in mind" (Buchanan 1991, 129). Few scholars have distinguished between the intentional (or deliberate) priming of campaigns and the unintentional priming that occurs as a result of reporting the news. Darrell West (1993), for one, recognizes the difference between electoral and nonelectoral priming, but does not develop that difference for any broader theoretical purpose (128). Lawrence Jacobs and Robert Shapiro (1994), on the other hand, clearly differentiate intentional from unintentional priming (528). Because their work on issues, images, and polling in the 1960 presidential election focuses on the notion of a priming strategy, I will briefly explain their assumptions.

Jacobs and Shapiro point to "three analytical obstacles to incorporating policy issues into campaign strategy: multiple issue dimensions, incomplete or imperfect information, and image-oriented campaign strategy" (1994, 528). When scholars study priming, they can address each of these obstacles in a meaningful way. To begin with, voters do not take every possible issue into consideration when they vote. When they take issues into account at all, they are likely to focus on only a few. As a result, candidates need not emphasize, or even take, issue positions in all policy areas. This is especially true at the congressional level. Thus, "campaign strategy involves the manageable task of influencing the weights voters attach to a few issues" (528).

Because voters do not have complete information, candidates are likely to introduce new bits of information to voters, thereby stimulating schemas that the candidate did not intend to activate. In keeping with the role of pollsters that I outlined above, Jacobs and Shapiro (1994) note that polling data enable candidates to better pursue a priming strategy

(528). "The priming concept is consistent with the information available to modern campaign organizations: extensive and sophisticated polling lowers a campaign's risk and enhances its skill in taking issue positions" (529). In other words, the chance that widespread aberrant decodings of the campaign message will occur is reduced when professional consultants (pollsters, generalists, and, as we will see, media specialists and direct mail consultants, too) are employed by a candidate.

Finally, priming deals with the much commented upon "image-oriented" campaigns that seem to be ubiquitous in contemporary American politics. A candidate's image is simply the combination of perceptions an individual voter has of that candidate (for an alternative definition, see Nimmo and Savage 1976, 8).[13] In reality, a candidate's issue positions, his/her personal traits (i.e., honesty, strength, dignity, etc.), and his/her image are intimately linked (see Page 1978, chapter 8; Rahn et al. 1990; Popkin 1994). Jacobs and Shapiro (1994) claim that "when office seekers announce their positions, they 'signal' or increase the perception of favorable nonpolicy characteristics" (529). Voters' perceptions of candidates' images are influenced, therefore, whether the candidates emphasize personal traits or their issue stances. This is one of two places where semiotics is of major relevance. When Jacobs and Shapiro say that candidates "signal" certain responses in voters, it is another way of saying that they have used certain signs that "signify" the types of images they want the voters to have of them. To round out the equation, we account for the voters' behavior by arguing that the reception of specific signs activates relevant schema which will produce an evaluation of the candidate on the desired grounds. As the centerpiece of the theory of deliberate priming, this connection between semiotics and schema theory deserves more attention.

After analyzing 669 political advertisements from 1984 and 1986, Montague Kern (1989) concluded that contemporary campaigning "requires the development of a limited number of readily comprehensible messages, suitable for the short 'take,' messages in which candidate character and issues blend, or dovetail for maximum impact" (207–8). This dovetailing, according to Kern, occurs as a result of "the interaction between issues and visual and aural effects in ads" (209). These visual and aural effects "personify" issues so that "the crime issue *becomes* Willie Horton" (209; emphasis in original). Kern acknowledges, however, that more research is needed to understand that process.

Theoretically, semiotics would explain the dovetailing of issues and affect in the following way. Rather than personification, semiotics suggests that campaign ads are engaged in signification. Crime "becomes" Willie Horton not because voters best understand issues when they are embodied by a real person but because voters understand campaign messages through signs. Willie Horton, then, simply becomes a sign of (i.e., stands for) crime. An ad like George Bush's 1988 "Tank" spot does not personify an issue. That commercial, which used footage of an awkward Mike Dukakis riding in a tank, questioned the Democrat's ability to serve competently as commander-in-chief (see Diamond and Bates 1992, 31 and 328–29 for details of the ad). It may have done so by making Dukakis look "goofy" in a military setting (and thereby questioning his leadership), but the tank in the ad served as a sign that tapped many people's "foreign policy" schema. And polls indicate that most voters think Republicans handle foreign policy better than Democrats. By using a tank in order to signify defense issues, Bush hoped to prime voters into using foreign policy as an issue on which to judge the candidates and on which Bush had a clear advantage over Dukakis.

For another example of how signification works in the creation of candidate images in voters' minds, I turn to a study by Kern and Marion Just (1994). Kern and Just showed a focus group a series of political ads and news stories from the 1990 North Carolina Senate race between Harvey Gantt and Jesse Helms. The focus group participants were New Jersey residents who had no real impression of Gantt and only a sketchy one of Helms (6–7). One ad in particular that was shown to the group, Gantt's "SAT Scores Worst" spot, described the poor shape of North Carolina schools and suggested that Helms had "voted against education" (8). The authors explain the impact of this one ad on some of the focus group participants: "Two voters, who expressed their own concern about education, . . . used 'SAT Scores Worst' to help construct a positive image of Gantt. The positive image construction survived a challenge from one voter, Ken, who based it first on the value of 'needing more information' and subsequently on the emotion 'distrust of politicians.' It also survived a challenge from another voter, Ralph, who drew from his own experience with the unpopular Governor Florio of New Jersey" (9). Thus, the ad used education as a sign of Gantt's primary policy concern, namely, his support of education, and that sign easily tapped the schemas of two voters who already placed emphasis on that issue.[14] For two other voters, schemas of distrust were activated, and in one case the activation was based on concrete experience. The specifics of the ad seem almost immediately lost on the voters; even among those who liked the spot it was reduced to the idea that "he's doing education" and "he's tryin' for education" (9).[15] Equally important is the fact that Gantt built a positive image with at least two voters in the group by priming them on an issue with which they were likely to evaluate him positively. Had he used affirmative action, on the other hand, these same two voters may very well have constructed a negative image of Gantt, one which would have been difficult (if not impossible, given the limited amount of time in a campaign) to reverse.[16]

The Gantt example illustrates that "[i]ndividuals actively participate in the process" of candidate image building (Kern and Just 1994, 6). That is what semiotics and schema theory would predict. The decoder of any message uses the codes at their disposal to interpret a sign while that sign is activating a specific schema arrangement. By running an ad about education, Gantt hoped that the sign of an education-friendly candidate, regardless of the specifics of that friendliness, would trigger an issue schema upon which most voters would evaluate him positively (because few voters favor candidates who are "enemies" of education). Gantt's choice of education, like Bill Clinton's in 1996, was an effort to deliberately prime voters using specific signs chosen to foreground the intended schemas. Thus, the theory of deliberate priming explains the candidate's and the consultant's behavior, the voters' role in the election, and the message's communication function. Yet deliberate priming doesn't seem entirely successful. Some members of the focus group were not influenced by the education ad in the way Gantt had hoped. Another example illustrates how aberrant decodings operate even in finely crafted campaign spots.

In 1986, Wyche Fowler of Georgia thought it important that the voters of his state recognize him by his first name (Kern 1989, 40). In order to prime voters along name identification lines, Fowler's consultants created and placed an ad featuring a classroom of students who have just finished the Pledge of Allegiance. The students are asked to name the Democratic candidate for the Senate, and one child says, "Senator Fowler." The teacher corrects her (saying, "He's not Senator—yet") and the student continues, explaining that Fowler's "first name is Wyche. Y-ch as in CHURCH. Wyche Fowler" to which another student replies, "Senator Wyche Fowler. [Pause to reflect] And *my* Dad said he's the best." Frank Greer, the ad's producer, later told of a focus group in rural Georgia that was asked to comment on the message of the ad. According to Greer's summary, the participants said, "Belief in parental discipline. Because that little girl says people should listen to her daddy when he talks. And that Wyche Fowler believes in school prayer, when [in fact] he doesn't." Greer added, "How much people can read into *symbolism*. . . . People read a lot more into television spots than we give them credit for" (40–41). For the focus group participants, the word *church* was a sign meant to stand for Fowler's support of prayer in school. The girl's comment that her Dad said Fowler is the best signified her obedience to her parents. The campaign intended to prime voters on Fowler's name, but even such a seemingly direct, semantically closed spot stimulated aberrant decodings. The Gantt and Fowler examples raise the question of the effectiveness of deliberate priming. Is that strategy successful? If not, why does it fail?

Given the millions of dollars spent on polling annually, one would think that consultants would know exactly which issues most benefit their clients and, as communication experts, would be able to create campaign themes that are highly effective. However, there is at least one barrier to the success of deliberate priming. Semiotics suggests that no matter how constrained a sign may be, a message cannot arrive exactly as it may have been intended. As Biocca (1991a) argues, "Communication always fails to some degree" (39). Each individual will decode a sign (message) in their own unique way. Additionally, every individual has different schemas and schema networks, which are formed as a result of their own personal experiences. When individualized schemas and the inevitability of unique decoding are taken together, we might ask ourselves not "Why does deliberate priming sometimes fail" but, instead, "How can it ever succeed?"

Semiotics actually answers both questions at once. Deliberate priming often fails, as I have explained, because of the uniqueness of the decoding process for each voter and as a result of the polysemy of signs. Recall that aberrant decoding occurs when the receiver uses different codes in his/her decoding than the sender used for encoding. Yet convention, the factor that dictates for most people which codes to use in interpreting a message, ensures that the majority of people will arrive at the sender's intended meaning. Only semiotics explains how the communication process can simultaneously be similar yet unique among various people. And only semiotics clarifies the success and failure of deliberate priming.

Furthermore, semiotics accounts nicely for the fact that campaign themes need to be broad enough to be used for mass campaigning yet specific enough to appeal to subgroups of voters through narrowcasting. Here, the difference between a theme and a message should be elucidated. The two are not usually considered different by practitioners (see the discussion of "single theme-ism" in chapter 2), but distinguishing between these concepts will be insightful for present purposes. I consider a campaign theme to be the answer to the question of why a candidate is running for office and why he/she should be elected. There are a number of ways to answer that question, however, and those ways take the form of campaign messages or "thematic statements" (Shea 1996, 153). Campaigns seek, in keeping with the "single theme" strategy, to say the same thing in different ways. Take a hypothetical example: If a candidate runs on getting the economy moving again (the theme), she might explain that proposition for working-class voters by promising to create more jobs (a message) while talking about lower taxes, and thus increased profits, to business leaders (another message). The consultants' role, then, is to create consistent, though distinct, messages that can appeal to various groups of voters based on the campaign's theme. My earlier statement about the objective of a campaign theme could be amended to read: *The campaign theme seeks to deliberately prime voters through various campaign messages.*

It remains to be seen, however, whether deliberate priming, on the whole, is successful. In general, studies in psychology have shown that priming "makes items more readily available and faster to respond to" (Schunn and Dunbar 1996, 272). The implication is that an item is more accessible to a person when it has been primed, presumably because priming foregrounds the schema related to that particular item. With regard to politics specifically, it has been shown that "focusing voters' attention on a few particular issues influences the importance that the electorate as a whole attaches to them" (Jacobs and Shapiro 1994, 528; see also Nie, Verba, and Petrocik 1976). To this, Kern and Just (1994) add, "The extent to which public discourse during a campaign centers on issues favoring one candidate as opposed to another is considered a good predictor of recent election outcomes" (1). While the empirical results of the aforementioned studies indicate that deliberate priming would be successful, none of them directly examine a campaign's efforts to prime voters and/or the extent to which those efforts are successful. To my knowledge, only two such studies address these matters.

One of those studies, which I have already discussed, deals empirically with the deliberate priming strategy. Jacobs and Shapiro (1994, 532) used policy statements from John F. Kennedy in 1960 along with private polling results archived at the Kennedy Library to analyze the responsiveness of the Kennedy campaign to public opinion (i.e., the extent to which Kennedy made statements on policies determined by the public to be salient). That Kennedy's policy statements were chosen on the basis of polling data is important. As Jacobs and Shapiro note, "Our quantitative analysis confirms that Kennedy's positions responded to public opinion: the issues that were raised in Louis Harris's polls were persistently mentioned by Kennedy in his subsequent public statements" (532; see also 536).[17] Furthermore, the study revealed that "Kennedy's responsiveness coexisted with his attempt to manipulate voters' evaluations of his *personal character*" (532; emphasis in original). What Jacobs and Shapiro do not examine, however, is the effectiveness of the Kennedy campaign's deliberate priming strategy.[18] Nevertheless, their study lends considerable support to the theory developed herein, and the findings confirm that at least one prominent campaign that employed professional political consultants attempted to prime voters deliberately. To that extent, the 1960

Kennedy campaign is a "real-world" model of the deliberate priming theory.

The second study is one that attempts to determine the effectiveness of deliberate priming. In order to search for priming effects, Darrell West (1993) narrowed his broader project of analyzing television advertising in political campaigns since 1952 to specific campaigns between 1972 and 1992. His results are mixed but tend to suggest that deliberate priming works more often than not. For the presidential race of 1984, West finds "significant evidence of priming," whereas in 1988 there was little such evidence (131). In 1972, Nixon was able to prime voters on personal characteristics and his electability but not on foreign affairs or the economy (132–33). In addition, there seems to be some evidence for Jesse Helms's ability to prime voters on abortion in his 1990 Senate race with Harvey Gantt (136–37).[19] Finally, Bill Clinton was successful in focusing "public attention on the economy and his own ability to improve economic performance" (139).

West also examines the impact of what he calls "defusing." This concept "refers to efforts on the part of candidates to decrease the importance of particular standards of evaluation." He suggests that this can be done by lowering the salience of a given topic or by blurring distinctions between the candidates on that matter (125–26). He does not offer much in the way of a theoretical explanation for how this is done, and it seems difficult to me for a candidate to be able to decrease the salience of an issue by actively addressing it. More likely is an attempt either to narrow the perceptual gap between the two candidates or to ignore the matter altogether. For most congressional candidates, given the sparse amount of exposure to their campaigns, the latter would seem to be the strategy of choice for defusion of an issue. Nevertheless, West finds some evidence for a defusion effect of campaign ads (see 132–40, esp. 134–36). The results of West's research suggest that candidates do have some ability to prime (and/or defuse) voters but that such a strategy is not a guarantor of success.

West's priming study examined political advertisements, which brings us to the next stage in our ideal campaign. Once pollsters gather the initial information needed to create a campaign theme, and after generalists formulate the messages that correspond to that theme, media specialists and direct mail consultants are brought in to disseminate those messages (Shea 1996, 205). The aim of media and mail consultants is the same—to use images (video for media specialists and photographs for direct mail handlers) and text (spoken and written for television and written for mail) to signify a given theme. Media consultants have the added benefit of using aural effects in their ads. The images, text, and sounds used by these consultants are signs, and their proper selection is a crucial step in the priming process.

As Reagan's "Bear in the Woods" ad suggests, sign selection is difficult, and the cleverest ads can miss the mark because the producer had one thing in mind while the voters saw something else. Of course, given the polysemy of any message, ads are decoded in numerous ways. Thus, it is often possible for people to reach the same conclusion via different routes. The "Bear in the Woods" ad was meant to signify Reagan's strength in dealing with the Soviet Union. Although many people, if not most, missed the metaphorical use of the bear, Reagan's media director realized that the message of the ad came through, for different reasons, to the targeted audiences. As I have noted, this is why the Reagan campaign ran the ad even though it was likely to be "misinterpreted."[20]

The difficulty of selecting the best (i.e., the most highly "motivated") sign for one's message can be illustrated by an example from the 1994 Vermont Senate race. Although surveys indicated that crime was a salient issue to Vermonters, a statewide direct mail piece from the Jim Jeffords campaign mistakenly signified the general issue with a signifier indicating violent crime specifically (Liley 1994). The front of the flyer pictured "a man in a body stocking with a gun." Controversy erupted when some recipients of the piece failed to recognize the crime portrayed in the mailing as one of concern to them. As one voter said, "We do not have this type of crime in Vermont." Although crime was an issue that might have worked to Jeffords's advantage, the sign selection for that particular direct mail ad evoked a specific kind of crime unfamiliar to many residents of the state. Thus, in selecting signs to be used in advertising, consultants must recognize the open nature of signs as well as their level of motivation and constraint. Signs that are less constrained when specific information is to be conveyed, or ones that are highly motivated when the goal is to disseminate the campaign message broadly, are likely to be less effective.

In addition to sign selection, message dissemination requires decisions about balancing issues and images as well as the use of affect. Kern (1989, 24–25) outlined three "schools of consulting" that could be applied to political advertising in the 1980s. The emotional, the new informational, and the quick response approaches to producing campaign spots grew out of older models established in the late 1960s and the 1970s. While the schools differ in certain ways, they have a few things in common. For one, each blends issues and candidate character through "dovetailing" or having "both sides of the advertising message . . . reinforce each other." Each also uses "projective" polling techniques (essentially described above). Finally, the different approaches increasingly rely on the use of affective appeals.

"Referential advertising" is one way of using affect in political com-mercials.[21] Interestingly, Kern relies on a semiotician to describe this type of advertising. Explaining Judith Williamson's work, Kern argues, "The basic premise of advertising . . . is that of transferring meaning from an affect-laden symbol, such as a child, place, or object, to a product. . . . The idea is to use symbols toward which the viewer holds positive feelings and 'associate these with the product in the marketing process'" (Kern 1989, 30). The "product" in this case is the candidate and the "marketing process" is the campaign. During the campaign, "symbols," or signs, stand for the candidate as meaning gets transferred from the lat-ter to the former. This transfer, in turn, forms an association between the voters and the candidate. In order to make that association, I maintain that candidates have to prime voters by foregrounding certain schemas. If a candidate hopes to be viewed as patriotic, he/she must stimulate voters to think in these terms. The candidate can do so by being associated with, for example, the American flag. A simple picture of the flag for many people conjures up nostalgic thoughts of the Fourth of July and the Pledge of Allegiance. Once on this train of thought, voters are more likely to evaluate the candidates on their patriotism. Such a strategy was used effectively by George Bush against Michael Dukakis in 1988 (see Jamieson 1992, 152–53). Thus, according to Kern's description of the dominant political advertising schools, media consultants clearly have a role in deliberate priming. I should add that direct mail consultants en-gage in similar behavior in producing "flats" or direct mail advertising.

Finally, the candidate him/herself has a role in priming. On the cam-paign trail, the candidate gives speeches and shakes hands in hundreds if not thousands of places. At each stop, the office seeker must reinforce the theme of the campaign by drawing a link from the theme to the con-cerns of a particular audience (see Bradshaw 1995, 44–45). Consultants call this "staying on message" or having "message discipline"—that is, they must reiterate what I have been calling the theme as much as possible, weaving answers to each question back to that theme. Here, consultants have less control over how the campaign operates. While they may write important speeches and instruct the candidate on how to incorporate the campaign theme into his/her public statements, consul-tants cannot script every remark made by a candidate nor can they pre-pare the candidate for every question from a reporter or voter.

Gaffes and inappropriate behavior plague many a campaign and frus-trate the efforts of handlers. When candidates make mistakes on the hus-tings, their words or deeds are not simply embarrassments; a faux pas is a sign that signifies latent attitudes, insensitivity, or incompetence. A number of famous blunders illustrate the point. While courting the Jew-ish vote in New York City during the 1972 primaries, Senator George

McGovern ordered a kosher hot dog and a glass of milk. Later, the McGovern campaign attempted to give a speech in a synagogue on the Jewish Sabbath (Popkin 1994, 2). In the midst of the 1976 primaries, President Gerald Ford was campaigning among Mexican American voters in Texas when he bit into a tamale, "corn husk and all" (1). His hosts had to stop the president to shuck the tamale. Other examples include Ford's 1976 comment during a general election debate that Eastern Europe was not under Soviet influence at the time (Boller 1984, 346) and Dukakis's emotionless, policy-wonkish response in 1988 to a hypothetical question about whether he would want the death penalty for someone who raped and murdered his wife (Taylor 1990, 208). Samuel Popkin (1994, 3) argues that incidents like these "illustrate the kinds of *cues* that voters use to make judgments on the fly—judgments . . . that need to be taken seriously in order to understand voters and campaigns." Mexican American voters evaluating Ford, or Jewish voters considering McGovern, may very well have taken such cues, which I have been calling signs, as serious indications that the candidates were unfamiliar not only with their cultures but also with their concerns. Similarly, voters who were most interested in foreign policy and those concerned about crime might take the Ford debate comment and the Dukakis incident, respectively, as signs that those candidates were not the best choices to address their interests.

Of course, campaign appearances, and statements made at them, can be beneficial as well. In a 1980 New Hampshire Republican primary debate, Ronald Reagan signified his toughness when, in a heated discussion with the moderator, he shouted, "I'm paying for this microphone, Mr. Green" (Taylor 1990, 196). That remark, having been replayed over and over through the media as a sound bite, became a sign of Reagan's unwillingness to be pushed around. It primed voters to evaluate him (and the other candidates, including George Bush, who was widely perceived to lack fortitude) on a specific characteristic, namely, fearlessness. In fact, Bush defused the "wimp factor" in 1988 largely by using a direct confrontation with Dan Rather on live national television as a sign of his "real" mettle. Again, repeated discussion of the incident in the media served to defuse the perceived character flaw as an issue on which voters would have evaluated Bush.

In fact, the Bush-Rather incident provides a case where consultants did have some control over a candidate's behavior on the campaign trail. It was the theory of Bush's handlers (Lee Atwater and Roger Ailes) that "Bush's good manners were misconstrued by voters as a lack of spine" (Taylor 1990, 196). With this in mind, they had been looking for a defining moment to reverse, or at least neutralize, Bush's weak image. Far from being a spontaneous event, Taylor reports that the entire episode was planned by both parties in the affair. Evidently, Atwater and Ailes got word of a likely "ambush" by Rather and crafted a response ahead of time (197; see also Brady 1997, 161–62).

If the importance of signs at campaign appearances was ever in doubt, Bill Clinton's 1996 stop at the Grand Canyon should have been enough to convince skeptics. Although technically not a campaign event, the Grand Canyon appearance at which Clinton signed an order creating the Grand Staircase–Escalante National Monument was interpreted as an election year reminder that the Clinton administration was committed to protecting the environment (Achenbach 1996). What better way to prime voters on the environment than using the Grand Canyon, even if the national monument this particular order produced is in Utah and not Arizona?

These examples reveal how campaign appearances can prime voters by using signs to cue specific schema. Whether the candidates themselves, the backdrop to an appearance, or a prop at such an event, signs are an omnipresent part of the campaign landscape and they are the vehicles by which candidates prime voters.

Summary

The picture that emerges here is of a well-oiled machine, making decisions based on reliable information and creating effective vehicles (e.g., political advertisements, speeches) for carrying the campaign theme to the voters. Such a machine requires pollsters, general consultants, media handlers, and direct mail specialists.[22] Of course, as I have noted, all campaigns do not operate in this manner. Nevertheless, some do even though acquiring an entirely professional line-up is an expensive proposition, especially for nonincumbents. The closer a campaign comes to the model, however, the more effective that campaign should be. The chapters to follow seek to determine if that statement holds empirically.

As for the theory of deliberate priming, one could summarize it as follows: Campaigns attempt to disseminate a theme by using various messages to appeal to distinct groups of voters. The theme and its messages have one goal, and that is to prime voters to evaluate the candidate on his/her terms; that is, certain issues (whether of a character or policy nature) play to the advantage of some candidates while other issues benefit other candidates. Campaign consultants are brought in to determine which issues their client should emphasize and how those issues should be framed. Voters, for their part, take an active role in decoding messages. While consultants attempt to foreground specific schema, they are never totally successful because messages (i.e., strings of signs) are always interpreted in a slightly different way by the messages' receivers; for this reason, consultants have to be aware of the numerous potential decodings of any message they create, and they are primarily concerned with reducing the number of aberrant decodings that occur. Thus, the more consultants a candidate hires, the less risk of misinterpretation.

There is another limit to the ability of a candidate to deliberately prime voters (besides the open nature of signs and messages). If one wishes, this limitation could be called a "real-world" constraint on deliberate priming. Candidates can only prime voters along relatively believable lines. For example, Bob Dole would have had a difficult time convincing voters that he was youthful and energetic. Popular culture, from late night talk shows to *Saturday Night Live,* was full of references to Dole's age. He could spin this in his favor, by suggesting that he was "experienced," but he could not change what had become a basic fact in the American mind. Even the aforementioned Bush-Rather incident, which seems to be a case of a candidate reshaping his image, may have had less of an impact than it first appeared. As Roderick Hart (1994) maintains, "American viewers did not experience that confrontation newly born. They came equipped with a wealth of assumptions about reporters and presidents, about political propriety, about newsworthiness, about perfidy" (117).[23] The point is that our interaction with the world is premised on prior constructions of that world that were formed by past experiences (see Neuman, Just, and Crigler 1992). This means that while candidates can assist in creating people's constructions of themselves and their opponents, they are limited to the extent that prior images of the candidates are already available. Still, in most races, including congressional elections, preconceived images of at least one of the candidates are nonexistent. Thus, consultants usually have some latitude in crafting campaign strategy.

The theory developed in this chapter is going to be tested in the following chapters. To do so, I analyze the impact that consultants have on the outcome of elections. This is, admittedly, a rather indirect approach. Nevertheless, I chose this route because a systematic quantitative examination of consultant influence had not yet been undertaken. To be sure, there are many other ways the theory could be tested. Using campaign documents, one could determine the extent to which candidates pursue a priming strategy (following Jacobs and Shapiro 1994) and/or examine the signs employed by candidates in a variety of settings. Experimental research on the reaction of voters to priming is yet another way to study the theory. Finally, consultants could be observed "in the field" as they work on a typical campaign.

It seems to me, however, that the quantitative approach is a necessary starting point in the study of campaigns, consultants, and deliberate priming. If consultants do not appear to matter to a candidate's electoral success, serious questions about the theory emerge. Yet if consultants are influential in elections, further work in this area will be well justified in exploring whether or not the theory of deliberate priming explains that success. Either way, determining the impact of consultants on elections is a first step in understanding the phenomenon of consulting in general and deliberate priming in particular.

I turn now to a statistical description of the level of consultant use in congressional elections. At best, only one reliable census of the number of consultants active in House races exists. Chapter 4, therefore, provides us with a much needed estimate of the breadth and depth of political consulting in American politics.

· 4 ·

The Use of Consultants in Congressional Elections

Determining the extent to which professional political consultants are hired by congressional candidates has never been an easy task. Before the early 1970s, the allocation of campaign resources was a relatively mysterious activity. However, beginning in 1974, as a result of the passage of some amendments to the Federal Election Campaign Act (FECA), candidates were required to officially disclose who gave them money and how they spent it.[1] Since then, we have learned a great deal about the effects of campaign spending in congressional races (see Abramowitz 1991; Green and Krasno 1988, 1990; Jacobson 1978, 1980, 1985, 1990a). Nevertheless, due to the enormous amount of work involved in combing through FEC reports, we have only recently gained access to the specifics of campaign spending. Of particular relevance to this study is the extent to which congressional candidates purchase the services of political consultants.

The data set employed herein enables us to explore that issue for the first time in a comprehensive way. This chapter offers an empirical account of the extent to which consultants are used. First, I explain the data set I have created for this book. A review of past estimates of consultant activity in congressional elections follows the explanation of data. Finally, I present the levels of use of campaign professionals in 1990 and 1992 House races.

The Data

In chapter 2, I briefly discussed what had been seen as a barrier to studying political consultants. Specifically, a lack of data made it difficult to examine the activities of the consulting industry. This particular problem has been overcome by the publication of two data sets dealing with consultant use in congressional elections. The first source comes from *Campaigns and Elections* magazine (see Beiler 1991 and Brown and Kruse 1993, specifically, for consultant activity data). A trade magazine, *C&E* has compiled a "Campaign Scorecard" for each election cycle since 1986, but began employing a reliable and valid methodology in 1990. As was explained in chapter 2, the scorecard lists the nation's top political consulting firms, the type of consulting they do, and the clients who hired them. The scorecard for 1990 (and the years following) relied on Federal Election Commission disbursement forms as well as follow-up calls to campaign staffs and local reporters when necessary to report the client lists for over three hundred firms (Beiler 1991, 27).

In addition to the *C&E* data, the *Handbook of Campaign Spending* for 1990 and 1992 (Fritz and Morris 1992; Morris and Gamache 1994) offered substantive reports for all 435 congressional races that included, in virtually every race, the names of consultants hired by both candidates. This information is offered in conjunction with extensive campaign spending data listed for each race. Again as noted in chapter 2, the *Handbooks* itemize the finances of all House (and Senate) candidates according to eight categories. The information provided by the *Handbook* was also taken from FEC reports.

In compiling the information from *C&E* and the *Handbooks* into my data set, I included only general election use of consultants unless work done for the primary was also used in the fall campaign. For example, if a candidate used brochures or television spots in the general election that were made during the primary, I coded that candidate as having hired a consultant. Such detailed information came exclusively from the *Handbooks*.[2] Thus, to record whether or not a candidate had a "professionalized campaign," I created a dichotomous variable—coded as one if he/she hired a consultant and as zero if he/she did not.[3] To be included in the data set, a consultant had to work on at least two congressional races in a given cycle (1990 or 1992). I would have also considered a consultant who had worked on only one congressional race and at least one statewide race (e.g., governor, attorney general, etc.), although none of the handlers I eventually included qualified in this way. The only exceptions to the two congressional race requirement were for consultants who were among the highest grossing consultants in their fields (as determined by the *Handbooks of Campaign Spending*) or were members of the American Association of Political Consultants (for lists of AAPC members, see Hess 1989 and 1992). Consultants in either of these two categories were included in the data set even if they ran only one congressional race.

The justification for requiring a consultant to have run two races is that many amateur campaigners work on a single congressional race particularly for candidates who are relatives or friends. But professionals, as I have suggested, consult on a more or less full-time basis and handle more than one campaign per election cycle (see Sabato 1981, 8). Furthermore, only those committed to political consulting as a career (in other words, professionals) are apt to be members of the AAPC, whose membership fee in 1993—$150 for an individual—was an amount likely to deter amateurs from joining. Finally, the top moneymakers in any industry are professional in any sense of the word. Therefore, the operational definition of a political consultant, for my purposes, is someone who worked in two or more congressional campaigns, was among the highest grossing consultants in their field, or was a member of the American Association of Political Consultants.

Besides creating a variable accounting for the presence of a political consultant, I also included seven categories of consultant types (following *C&E*). Those dichotomous categories (coded as a one if the candidate hired that specific type of consultant and zero if he/she did not) are as follows: Generalist, Pollster, Media Specialist, Fund-raising Consultant (both events and telemarketing), Fund-raising Mail Consultant, Persuasion Mail Consultant, and Direct Mail Specialist (i.e., someone offering both fund-raising and persuasion mail services). Persuasion mail specialists handled not only persuasive direct mail but also voter contact (e.g., get-out-the-vote efforts), which is often performed through phonebanking. Likewise, the generalist category includes consultants who were hired for management purposes. Some generalists provided a number of services for a campaign. When it was clear that they did one in particular, they were coded in that category; when it was not obvious, they were counted as generalists. In addition, some of the work undertaken by consultants on behalf of a candidate was paid for by the parties or an interest group. In such cases, this did not count as having hired a consultant for the purposes of this data set.[4]

If a candidate hired more than one consultant of a certain type, it counted as having used only one consultant. For example, hiring two pollsters and one media consultant would count as having employed two types of consultants instead of three individual consultants. In other words, my data set does not account for the actual number of consultants employed but rather for the number of different types of consultants hired.

Beyond the consultant variables, I also included contextual (i.e., candidate and district) data. This includes the party of the candidates, their incumbency status and sex, a candidate quality measure (zero if he/she had not held past elective office, one if he/she had), a district's presidential vote for 1988 and 1992 as well as the previous vote for the Democratic candidate for the House, the *Congressional Quarterly* assessment of the vulnerability of the seat, the actual number of votes cast per candidate, the total votes cast in the district, and the voting age population. Other information in the data set includes a candidate's percentage of the vote, whether the candidate won or lost (one for a win, zero for a loss), expenditures and receipts for the candidates as well as specific spending categories (e.g., the amount of money spent on fund-raising, polling, advertising, etc.), contributions from the parties and PACs, expenditures by the parties and PACs, and independent expenditures for and against the candidates.

In future chapters I will explain which races were included for analysis and which were not and the reasons for inclusion/exclusion. For example, many races in Louisiana were excluded because the election was decided after the primary.[5] Furthermore, the unit of analysis in later chapters will usually be the district race, unless otherwise specified. In this chapter, however, the unit of analysis is the individual candidate. Here, all candidates were included except where noted in footnotes accompanying the tables.

Past Estimates of Consultant Use

Estimates of consultant use in congressional campaigns date to the 1950s. Alexander Heard's (1960) classic *The Costs of Democracy* contained a brief discussion of "public relations counseling firms" and their activities in political campaigns (413–24). Therein one can find the results of a questionnaire given to 130 members of the Public Relations Society of America. According to their responses, Heard found that between 1952 and 1957 nineteen firms rendered at least partial services to thirty-one nomination and thirty-two general election campaigns for the House of Representatives. Furthermore, ten firms claimed to have given full-service management assistance to nineteen House campaigns during that period (417). Of course, it is possible that some of the paid consultants working on congressional campaigns in the 1950s were not members of the PRSA and therefore were overlooked by Heard. Using professional public relations firms as the source of information on political consulting, however, was justified by the fact that most political consultants at that time were from public relations or advertising agencies (Pitchell 1958, 280), and one can assume that most were members of the PRSA. If Heard's numbers are at all accurate, it would appear that by the end of the 1950s professional consulting had yet to become a widespread phenomenon in congressional elections.[6]

In a 1963 article in *Public Opinion Quarterly*, pollster Louis Harris estimated that 10 percent of congressional candidates used a professional pollster during their election bids in 1962 (3). For the same campaign season, Robert Huckshorn and Robert Spencer (1971) found that 4 percent of all losing candidates and 22 percent of those who had run marginal campaigns hired professional managers (95). In addition, they noted that 47 percent of the losing candidates and 61 percent of the marginals employed advertising or public relations firms (106). Huckshorn and Spencer's interest was in campaigns that lost and, therefore, they could make no general claim about the use of consultants among all candidates. Nevertheless, these figures suggest that professional consultants were beginning to be quite active in congressional elections in the early 1960s.

Robert King and Martin Schnitzer (1968) reported that roughly 44 percent of the congressmen they surveyed used professional pollsters in 1966 and that Republicans used them to a much greater extent than did Democrats (434–35).[7] As with Huckshorn and Spencer's study, the generalizability of King and Schnitzer's survey is limited by the fact that they only questioned winners who were involved in competitive races, that is, where the losing candidate received more than 40 percent of the vote (431). David Rosenbloom's (1973) work on professional campaign managers is somewhat more systematic but still relies on a survey of campaign management firms. Beginning with Heard's original estimates, Rosenbloom found an 842 percent increase in the campaign management services performed in House races between the periods 1952–57 and 1964–69 (51). "Full management was offered more than eight times more frequently for House races in the 1960s than in the 1950s" (52). For 1970, Rosenbloom estimated that professional management firms were hired by no fewer than 150 House candidates (53). In the 1970s, it seems, the use of professional consultants in House races was on the verge of becoming widespread.

In their study of eighty-six congressional campaigns from 1978, Goldenberg and Traugott (1984) found that 9 percent of the campaigns had a professional campaign manager and 39 percent hired a media consultant (20). As for polling, 74 percent of incumbents, 61 percent of challengers, and 80 percent of open seat candidates relied either "very much" or "quite a bit" on polls as a source of campaign information (55). Although it is not clear what percentage of these polls was conducted by professionals, and particularly those hired directly by the candidate rather than the parties, Goldenberg and Traugott claim these findings indicate a significant increase over past studies. Such levels of polling are "a sign of the increasing professionalism and sophistication of congressional campaign techniques" (56). Notwithstanding the results for polling, the use of professional consultants in the late 1970s does not appear to have increased as expected.

By the 1980s, *National Journal* would declare that "the consulting revolution is nearly complete" (Hagstrom 1984, 1976; see also Hagstrom and Guskind 1986, 2433). Such a declaration, however, was made about statewide races for Senate and governor. There are few good estimates of consultant use in House races for the 1980s. Although C&E produced a consultant scorecard for those firms that worked for House candidates in 1986, they included only polling and media consultants. Their list, therefore, overlooks a great deal of professional activity in House races. It is also not clear the extent to which C&E relied on FEC reports for this scorecard. Nevertheless, their report shows that 87 House candidates hired media specialists and 118 used pollsters (O'Donnell 1986, 33–40). Thus, as many as 25 percent of the 815 major party House candidates in 1986 employed professional assistance (10.7 percent having hired media consultants and 14.5 percent pollsters), although the overall figure is likely to be lower due to candidates who hired both types of consultants.

Mark Petracca and Courtney Wiercioch's 1987 survey of professional political consultants does not include figures for House campaigns per se, but it does give us an idea as to how the industry grew in the 1980s. According to their findings, half of the firms in existence in 1987 were created after 1980 and 28 percent had been created between 1981 and 1983 (Petracca and Wiercioch 1988, 12, table 1). In addition, Joe Cerrell, former president of the American Association of Political Consultants, claimed that in late 1984 membership in the association was five times larger than it had been in 1980 (Pressman 1984, 3151). We might assume that the use of consultants by House candidates paralleled this growth, but we cannot be sure without specific data for those elections.

Finally, Paul Herrnson's (1995) recent work on congressional elections reveals that 19 percent of the campaigns that responded to his survey (N = 334) hired a professional campaign manager, 22 percent employed the services of an issue and/or opposition research consultant, 24 percent used a fund-raising consultant, 60 percent hired a pollster, and 61 percent relied on a media consultant (66–67). Herrnson's findings are the best evidence we have on the level of consultant activity in House races. Nevertheless, problems exist with all of the aforementioned estimates.

The primary problem with these estimates is that virtually all of them rely on surveys of either candidates, staff, or consultants. To begin with, candidates (as well as staff members) are likely to have vastly different conceptions of what constitutes having hired a "professional" consultant. As noted earlier, it makes little sense to call any hired hand a professional. To many candidates, however, having paid a staff member may mean having had a professionally run campaign. Furthermore, none of the surveys was able to question all House candidates (although Herrnson's survey is remarkably representative; see 271). Some used losing candidates (Huckshorn and Spencer) and others marginal winners (King and Schnitzer), but few included all of the more than eight hundred campaigns that are run for the House in any given cycle. In addition, consultants themselves are apt to exaggerate the number of campaigns they work on during an election season (see Mundy 1993). This is because consultants often "forget" to mention the losing campaigns for which they worked or, conversely, they claim to have worked for a winning candidate for whom, in fact, they did not consult. Finally, the functions of consultants changed greatly over time, making it impossible to meaningfully compare the managers of the 1950s (a catch-all phrase) to the managers of the 1990s (a specific, well-defined role).

The rest of this chapter will report frequencies and some descriptive statistics for the level of consultant use among House candidates in 1990 and 1992. This marks the first time that an accurate count of the number of consultants at work in congressional campaigns has been offered based on nonsurvey data for all the campaigns run in a year.

The 1990 and 1992 Congressional Elections in Context

The 1992 congressional elections differed in a number of ways from the 1990 elections. To begin with, 1992 was a presidential election year and, as expected, voter turnout was greater in that year than in 1990. Furthermore, the 1992 elections followed congressional reapportionment and redistricting. As in all such years (those ending in a "2"), a relatively large number of incumbents decided to retire before the 1992 election. In fact, a post–World War II record was set, according to Herrnson (1995, 33), when 15 percent of all House members retired in 1992. As a result, the number of open seats rose from 30 in 1990 to 91 in 1992, and the number of uncontested seats was more than halved, from 85 to 34 (Jacobson 1993a, 167). Thus, the 1992 elections produced 110 new members of the House of Representatives, a forty-year high (153).

The elections of 1992 were also unique because of the number of women who ran for Congress. Although the 1990 elections had 69 women running for office, a record-breaking number, the 1992 races shattered that mark as 106 women ran as major party candidates in the general election (Jacobson 1993a, 171). Additionally, the House banking scandal and Ross Perot's maverick candidacy for president created an "anti-incumbent" mood throughout the nation in 1992 (on the House banking scandal and its effect, see Alford et al. 1994; Banducci and Karp 1994; Groseclose and Krehbiel 1994; Jacobson and Dimock 1994; Stewart 1994; Dimock and Jacobson 1995). That mood, among other things, attracted a large number of "quality" challengers in 1992 (Herrnson 1995, 21; Jacobson 1993a, 168).

The Use of Consultants in House Races, 1990 and 1992

I turn now to the level of professionalization of House campaigns in 1990
and 1992. Given the "unusually competitive" nature of the 1992 elections (Jacobson 1993a, 153), one might expect a greater level of professionalization in that year as compared with 1990. When candidates are
uncertain of their electoral fate, they tend to increase their campaigning
efforts in all areas (Kingdon 1966, 89; Hershey 1974, 24–28; Goldenberg
and Traugott 1984, 181; Jacobson 1992, 97). Tables 4.1 and 4.2 show
the level of consultant use by incumbency status for 1990 and 1992,
respectively.

In 1990, 45.6 percent of all candidates hired at least one political consultant. In the following election cycle, however, 62.6 percent employed
professional assistance, a significantly higher number (χ^2 = 48.478, df = 1,
p = .000). One might argue that the general increase in consultant use
among all candidates is due to the presidential race of 1992. With presidential candidates on the air (via television ads) and in the news, congressional candidates have to compete harder for the voters' attention. In
such a situation, candidates may purposely turn to consultants to help
them disseminate their messages.

On the other hand, the explanation could lie in the heightened level
of competition in 1992. With more open seat races, and more incumbents
facing strong challenges, the outcome of an unusually large number of
races was uncertain. As noted above, in such circumstances, candidates
will attempt to reduce the level of uncertainty by mounting more sophisticated campaigns. Hiring consultants is one of the best ways to do that.

Perhaps more likely is an explanation that takes into account the pe-
culiarities surrounding election years ending in "2." In those years, most
incumbents are running for reelection in districts that have been redrawn
after reapportionment. Having to run in essentially new districts makes
incumbents nervous (as do any number of other "threats" to their safety;
see Fenno 1978, 10–18; King 1997). One result, as has been noted, is that
larger numbers of members of Congress retire in years ending in "2." Another consequence is that incumbents overcompensate for their uncertainty by mounting serious reelection efforts. In addition, challengers
may respond, to the extent that they can, by putting together professionalized campaigns to try to take advantage of the new electoral context.

As one can see from the top section of tables 4.1 and 4.2, incumbent
use of consultants did, indeed, increase in 1992. But the increase in challenger use of campaign professionals was even greater. In fact, challenger
use more than doubled from 1990 to 1992. Of course, the overall level of
incumbent use of professional handlers is considerably greater than that of
challengers. Nonetheless, the data suggest that it is not only incumbent

Table 4.1

Use of Consultants by 1990 House Candidates (by Incumbency Status)

	Incumbents (406)	Challengers (341)	Open Seats (58)	Total* (805)
Hired at least one consultant				
Winners	65.5% (256)	80.0% (12)	93.1% (27)	67.8% (295)
Losers	86.7% (13)	12.9% (42)	58.6% (17)	19.5% (72)
All	66.3% (269)	15.8% (54)	75.9% (44)	45.6% (367)
No. of different types of consultants				
0	33.7% (137)	84.2% (287)	24.1% (14)	54.4% (438)
1	25.4% (103)	5.9% (20)	27.6% (16)	17.3% (139)
2	21.4% (87)	6.2% (21)	15.5% (9)	14.5% (117)
3	14.3% (58)	2.3% (8)	17.2% (10)	9.4% (76)
4	4.4% (18)	1.5% (5)	15.5% (9)	4.0% (32)
5	0.7% (3)			0.4% (3)
Mean no. of consultants employed				
Winners	1.3 (391)	1.8 (15)	2.0 (29)	1.4 (435)
Losers	2.1 (15)	0.2 (326)	1.4 (29)	0.4 (370)
All	1.3 (406)	0.3 (341)	1.7 (58)	0.9 (805)

Note: Numbers in parentheses are *N*s.

*This total includes third party candidates in those races where only one of the two major parties had a candidate in the race. There were 19 such candidates in 1990 and 18 in 1992.

Table 4.2
Use of Consultants by 1992 House Candidates (by Incumbency Status)

	Incumbents (349)	Challengers (327)	Open Seats (180)	Total* (856)
Hired at least one consultant				
Winners	84.9% (276)	89.5% (17)	89.0% (81)	86.0% (374)
Losers	95.8% (23)	31.5% (97)	47.2% (42)	38.5% (162)
All	85.7% (299)	34.9% (114)	68.3% (123)	62.6% (536)
No. of different types of consultants				
0	14.3% (50)	65.1% (213)	31.7% (57)	37.4% (320)
1	19.8% (69)	17.7% (58)	13.9% (25)	17.8% (152)
2	27.8% (97)	8.6% (28)	23.9% (43)	19.6% (168)
3	22.1% (77)	7.0% (23)	20.6% (37)	16.0% (137)
4	14.9% (52)	1.2% (4)	7.8% (14)	8.2% (70)
5	1.1% (4)	0.3% (1)	1.1% (2)	0.8% (7)
6			1.1% (2)	0.2% (2)
Mean no. of consultants employed				
Winners	2.1 (325)	2.0 (19)	2.4 (91)	2.1 (435)
Losers	2.3 (24)	0.5 (308)	1.0 (89)	0.7 (421)
All	2.1 (349)	0.6 (327)	1.7 (180)	1.4 (856)

Note: Numbers in parentheses are *N*s.
*This total includes third party candidates in those races where only one of the two major parties had a candidate in the race. There were 19 such candidates in 1990 and 18 in 1992.

behavior driving the increase in consultant use from 1990 to 1992; challengers seem to have been reacting to an opportunity that would not present itself again for ten years.

Open seat use of professionals decreased from 1990 to 1992. In 1990, a greater percentage of open seat candidates hired consultants than did incumbents. In 1992, however, the level of consultant use by these candidates fell behind that of incumbents, although it remained twice that of challengers.[8] At this point, there is no good explanation for the decline in consultant use among open seat candidates, although we will see later that candidate quality may account for it. Nevertheless, the numbers indicate that the need to hire consultants to cut through the "noise" of a presidential election is not part of the congressional candidates' calculus.

Of further note in these tables is the fact that while challenger and open seat winners are much more likely than losers to hire consultants, incumbent *losers* use consultants at a higher rate than incumbent winners. This is explained by findings that suggest vulnerable incumbents use more campaign resources (particularly money) than do safe ones (see Leuthold 1968, 74–75; Glantz, Abramowitz, and Burkart 1976; Jacobson 1980, 113–24; 1992, 53; Hinckley 1981, 29; Goldenberg and Traugott 1984, 83; Krasno, Green, and Cowden 1994; Herrnson 1995, 209–10).[9] In other words, incumbent use of campaign resources, including political consultants, is reactive; more resources are used in response to greater threats to reelection.

Moving to the second section of tables 4.1 and 4.2, we see the number of types of consultants used. It should be noted that these results indicate not the total number of consultants hired but simply the number of campaign functions performed by professionals. No candidate in 1990 used more than five types of consultants (and only three incumbents used that many). In 1992, however, two open seat candidates used six consultant types, and seven candidates used five. The bottom section of the tables, which provides means for the number of types of consultants hired, indicates that an average of just under 1 consultant type was hired per candidate in 1990 while 1.4 consultant types were used per campaign in 1992. Again, this is evidence for an increase in the professionalization of House campaigns from 1990 to 1992 (t = 7.88, df = 1659, p = .000). In addition, except for incumbents, winners are more highly professionalized than losers, although the difference was more pronounced in 1992. Furthermore, in 1990, open seat candidates were the most professionalized, hiring an average of 1.7 consultant types, while incumbents, many of whom were feeling particularly vulnerable, hired the most types of consultants in 1992, averaging 2.1 per campaign. Of note is the paltry level of professionalization among losing challengers. This surely reflects the inability of such candidates to raise decent amounts of money, making it difficult if not impossible for them to purchase the services of professional handlers (Jacobson 1980, 105–13). The paradox for challengers is that hiring professionals would enable them to raise money (by making them appear to be serious candidates; Herrnson 1992). But in order to hire professionals, a candidate must first raise a sufficient amount of money (Salmore and Salmore 1989, 96).[10] Few House challengers ever overcome this problem, and therefore few have professionally run campaigns.[11]

Tables 4.3 and 4.4 focus on the various types of consultants hired by House candidates in 1990 and 1992. In both years, pollsters were the most widely used type of consultants, followed closely in 1990, and not so closely in 1992, by media specialists (see Herrnson 1995, 67). This order holds by incumbency status as well, save for open seat candidates in 1990 who hired more media specialists than pollsters (although only by one). The least used type of professional was the fund-raising specialist. Of course, many campaigns used direct mail specialists to both raise money and send persuasion mail. Nevertheless, when fund-raising mail and direct mail specialists are combined, it remains the least used category of consultants.

Table 4.3
Types of Consultants Hired by 1990 House Candidates (by Incumbency Status)

Types of Consultants Hired	Incumbents (406)	Challengers (341)	Open Seats (58)	Total* (805)
Pollsters	35.7% (145)	10.6% (36)	48.3% (28)	26.0% (209)
Media specialists	35.5% (144)	8.2% (28)	50.0% (29)	25.0% (201)
Generalists	11.1% (45)	4.7% (16)	25.9% (15)	9.4% (76)
Fund-raisers	30.3% (123)	3.5% (12)	22.4% (13)	18.4% (148)
Fund-raising mail specialists	4.9% (20)		1.7% (1)	2.6% (21)
Persuasion mail specialists	11.6% (47)	2.6% (9)	13.8% (8)	8.0% (64)
Direct mail specialists	3.4% (14)	1.5% (5)	10.3% (6)	3.1% (25)

Note: Numbers in parentheses are *N*s.
*This total includes third party candidates in those races where only one of the two major parties had a candidate in the race. There were 19 such candidates in 1990 and 18 in 1992.

Table 4.4

Types of Consultants Hired by 1992 House Candidates (by Incumbency Status)

Types of Consultants Hired	Incumbents (349)	Challengers (327)	Open Seats (180)	Total* (856)
Pollsters	67.7% (236)	21.1% (69)	50.6% (91)	46.3% (396)
Media specialists	53.3% (186)	19.3% (63)	45.0% (81)	38.6% (330)
Generalists	15.8% (55)	7.0% (23)	16.7% (30)	12.6% (108)
Fund-raisers	35.2% (123)	9.2% (30)	29.4% (53)	24.1% (206)
Fund-raising mail specialists	4.6% (16)	0.3% (1)		2.0% (17)
Persuasion mail specialists	22.6% (79)	3.7% (12)	18.9% (34)	14.6% (125)
Direct mail specialists	7.7% (27)	1.8% (6)	6.1% (11)	5.1% (44)

Note: Numbers in parentheses are Ns.

*This total includes third party candidates in those races where only one of the two major parties had a candidate in the race. There were 19 such candidates in 1990 and 18 in 1992.

A greater percentage of open seat candidates than incumbents hired each type of consultant in 1990 except for fund-raisers and fund-raising mail specialists. This result follows the pattern for basic level of consultant use found in table 4.1. As expected, given table 4.2, the results were reversed in 1992. Table 4.4 indicates that use of each type of consultant, with the exception of generalists, is greater for incumbents than for open seat candidates in 1992.

Differences in consultant use by party are not reported in tables, but the general pattern in 1990 reveals that Democrats were significantly more likely than Republicans to hire at least one consultant.[12] Of the Democrats, 52.5 percent employed consultants, while just over 40 percent of Republicans did (χ^2 = 11.531, df = 1, p = .000). When looking at party and incumbency status, we see that more Democratic challengers (20.5 percent) used professionals than did Republican challengers (14 percent). The difference among challengers is accounted for by winners; all the Democratic challengers who won in 1990 used a consultant, while exactly half of successful Republican challengers did the same. There were no overall differences between the parties in the use of consultants by incumbents and open seat candidates. Nevertheless, every Republican incumbent who lost hired a consultant, considerably more than the two-thirds of unsuccessful Democratic incumbents who did so. Finally, more Republican open seat winners hired consultants than did their Democratic counterparts, although the difference was not great (100 percent to 88.2 percent, respectively).[13]

In 1992, the picture is similar, with some notable exceptions. As in 1990, more Democrats than Republicans hired at least one consultant, with 71.1 percent of the former and 56.7 percent of the latter using professionals (χ^2 = 18.739, df = 1, p = .000). More than 80 percent of winners in both parties used handlers in 1992, but a larger percentage of Democratic losers employed professionals than did Republican losers (50 percent to 40.1 percent). With regard to the use of consultants by party and incumbency status in 1992, I find that, as in 1990, incumbents of both parties hired professionals at similar rates but that, unlike in 1990, so did challengers of the two parties. On the other hand, in 1992 differences in consultant use could be found among open seat candidates; while 84.4 percent of all Democratic open seat candidates hired at least one professional, only 54.7 percent of their Republican opponents did so. In fact, Republicans vying for open seats were the only category of candidates who decreased their consultant use from 1990 to 1992. Thus, the decrease in consultant use among open seat candidates is the result of a decrease among Republican open seat candidates specifically.

The apparently low level of Republican professionalization, at least relative to Democratic campaigns, is probably masking a more sophisticated party effort on behalf of GOP candidates. In the 1970s and 1980s, the Republican Party undertook a massive effort to revitalize its campaign operations (Bibby 1981; Herrnson 1988). In so doing, it produced an in-house, "full-service campaign consulting organization for Republican candidates" (Maisel 1993, 69). Thus, while Republicans could turn to the party for professional campaign assistance, Democrats had to build a professional organization on their own.

Returning to the numbers, a closer look reveals that open seat winners of both parties were highly likely to use a consultant; nearly 90 percent of both parties' open seat winners employed professional assistance. The differences between the parties in this category can be found among losers. While half of the unsuccessful Democratic bids for open seats were professionally run, only 32.7 percent of the losing Republican open seat campaigns were professional. The relatively low number of professionally run Republican open seat campaigns may account, in part, for the fact that Republicans did not do as well in the 1992 congressional races as was expected given reapportionment, the House banking scandal, and the resulting high Democratic retirement rate (see Jacobson 1993a, 174–76).

One of the glaring patterns to be found in the data (including those reflected in tables 4.1 and 4.2) is that challengers of both parties who win are considerably more likely to hire consultants than challengers who lose. This is true even of Republican challengers in 1990. While only 50 percent of successful GOP challengers hired consultants in that year, an even smaller 12.9 percent of Republican challengers who lost had professionals. In addition, every Democratic challenger who won, both in 1990 and 1992, hired at least one consultant. Conversely, only 14.9 and 36.5 percent of unsuccessful Democratic challengers hired handlers in those years. Clearly, hiring a consultant is evidence of other factors that matter for victory, namely, money and experience. Nevertheless, the disparity with respect to hiring consultants among challengers who win and those who lose is considerable. It should be noted that a divergence on this score between successful and unsuccessful open seat candidates also exists, although not nearly to the extent seen among challengers.

In addition to simple consultant use, incumbents of both parties increased their levels of professionalization (that is, the number of types of consultants hired) from 1990 to 1992. In 1990, 5.2 percent of Democratic incumbents and 5.1 percent of their Republican counterparts hired at least four types of political consultants, a level that I consider highly professionalized. During the following election cycle, those numbers rose to 18 and 13.2 percent, respectively. Clearly, incumbents in 1992 brought more consultants on board in response to the heightened level of competition they faced (or at least sensed) from challengers. The overall percentage of highly professionalized campaigns rose between the two years from 4.5 percent to 9.4 percent. Such an increase is to be expected given the general rise in the number of professionally run campaigns from 1990 to 1992. Interestingly, however, the percentage of Democratic open seat candidates who had highly professionalized campaigns fell from 16.7 for Democrats in 1990 to 11.1 in 1992, even though the overall number of professionally run Democratic open seat campaigns increased over that period. (The percentage of highly professionalized Republican open seat campaigns dropped from 14.3 to 9.3 in those two years, mirroring the fall in general professionalization among such candidates.)

Finally, in terms of the various types of consultants used by candidates of both parties, Democrats made more use of media specialists than any other type of consultant in 1990, while Republicans relied most heavily on pollsters. This changed slightly in 1992 as Democrats joined Republicans in using pollsters more than other kinds of professionals. Their tendency to hire media handlers in 1990 notwithstanding, Democrats still hired more pollsters than did Republicans in both years. This difference may be the result of the National Republican Congressional

Committee's greater willingness to provide its candidates with polls than its Democratic counterpart (see Herrnson 1995, 69).

As mentioned above, the 1992 congressional elections attracted a larger number of quality challengers than usual. Determining what it takes to be a quality candidate, however, is not easy. Clearly, such candidates possess those attributes which make them electorally competitive. Yet political scientists are not in agreement on exactly which attributes make someone a competitive candidate.[14] Nevertheless, as Peverill Squire (1995) notes, "There is strong agreement that whatever those qualities are they are measured in substantial part by a candidate's previous political experience" (893). Perhaps the most popular way of tapping a candidate's experience, and therefore quality, is with a dichotomous measure of whether or not that candidate has held past elected office (Jacobson and Kernell 1983; for examples of the use of this measure, see Bianco 1984; Born 1986; Ragsdale and Cook 1987; Abramowitz 1988; Jacobson 1989; Biersack, Herrnson, and Wilcox 1993; Jacobson and Dimock 1994). This operationalization, though simplistic, works as well as any other as a control for candidate quality (Squire 1995, 896). Of course, incumbents are considered quality candidates *by definition* according to such an approach. The measure is particularly appropriate, however, for nonincumbents, and its relevance for this study lies in the fact that, as Herrnson points out, "Nonincumbents who have held an elective post usually possess advantages over those who have not in assembling a campaign organization" (1995, 64). This includes, I would argue, the wherewithal to obtain professional consultants. Thus, past electoral success is a useful variable, at least for challengers and open seat candidates, in a study of campaign professionalization.

In 1990, 11.7 percent of all challengers were quality candidates whereas 67.2 percent of open seat candidates met such a description; overall 19.8 percent of nonincumbents had held past elected office.[15] The level of challenger quality increased in 1992, such that 21.1 percent qualified as quality candidates. In the same year, 55 percent of open seat candidates had held prior elected office, a 12.2 percentage point decrease from 1990. (Incidentally, this may account for the drop in consultant use among open seat candidates from 1990 to 1992.) Overall, one-third of all nonincumbent candidates were quality candidates in 1992.

We might guess, as argued above, that quality challengers and open seat candidates would be more likely to hire a consultant than would nonquality candidates. Such an assumption is based on the fact that, having held elected office in the past, quality candidates know what is necessary to run a competitive race. If we assume further that politicians think consultants are an integral part of a serious campaign, then our initial supposition is well grounded.[16] In fact, the data offer support for our conjecture in all categories. The gap between professionalized quality and nonquality candidates was narrow only for open seat candidates in 1990. Roughly three-fourths of those candidates hired at least one consultant whether they had held past elected office or not (76.9 percent and 73.7 percent, respectively). In 1992, however, quality open seat candidates were considerably more likely to hire a consultant than their nonquality counterparts (83.8 percent to 49.4 percent). Furthermore, quality challengers were more than twice as likely as nonquality challengers to hire professionals in both years.[17] Of course, it is conceivable that those things that make a candidate likely to have won a past election also make him/her more likely to hire a consultant. The high correlation between being a quality candidate and hiring a consultant will be dealt with as I undertake more extensive statistical analyses in later chapters.

Another aspect of the 1990 and 1992 congressional elections that should be examined is the extent to which male and female candidates relied on political consultants. As discussed above, a relatively large number of women ran for Congress in 1992, causing many to dub that election cycle the "Year of the Woman" (Cook 1992, 3265).[18] Were the campaigns of these women different than those of men? Specifically, were they more professionalized? Women undoubtedly face distinct obstacles to election (see Witt, Paget, and Matthews 1994, 9–10) and, in general, they emphasize different, or at least additional, issues in campaigns and in office (Herrnson and Andersen 1995; Conover 1988). Nevertheless, there is little theoretical reason to believe that there are differences in the campaign organizations, or even in the campaign strategies, of men and women (Darcy and Schram 1977; Darcy, Welch, and Clark 1987; Burrell 1994; Witt, Paget, and Matthews 1994; Herrnson and Andersen 1995).[19] On the other hand, one might argue that, because women as candidates have come to politics somewhat recently, they tap newly formed campaign networks that are thoroughly versed in the "new politics" of consultants as opposed to the old-style efforts of party organizations that have been more accessible to men over the years (Carroll 1994).[20]

There are, of course, many male candidates who are new to politics and thus also rely on newly formed campaign styles and electoral networks, especially ideological ones (particularly on the right). Furthermore, I would argue that it is quite possible that men, even long-serving incumbents, have adapted their campaign styles to meet the challenges posed by these new campaign techniques and the organizations that utilize them. Consequently, there should be few, if any, differences between men and women in campaign professionalization. The following exploration, then, is a small step in understanding professionalism and gender in House elections.

Table 4.5
Use of Consultants by the Sex and Incumbency Status of House Candidates

	Male*				Female*			
	Inc. (705)	*Chal.* (588)	*Open* (191)	*Total* (1484)	*Inc.* (50)	*Chal.* (80)	*Open* (47)	*Total* (177)
Hired at least one consultant								
Overall	74.8% (527)	24.1% (142)	71.2% (136)	54.2% (805)	82.0% (41)	32.5% (26)	66.0% (31)	55.3% (98)
1990	(382) 65.4% (250)	(304) 15.5% (47)	(50) 80.0% (40)	(736) 45.8% (337)	(24) 79.2% (19)	(37) 18.9% (7)	(8) 50.0% (4)	(69) 43.5% (30)
1992	(323) 85.8% (277)	(284) 33.5% (95)	(141) 68.1% (96)	(748) 62.6% (468)	(26) 84.6% (22)	(43) 44.2% (19)	(39) 69.2% (27)	(108) 63.0% (68)

Note: Numbers in parentheses are *N*s.
*The totals for these categories include third party candidates in those races where only one of the two major parties had a candidate in the race. There were 19 such candidates in 1990 and 18 in 1992.

Table 4.5 shows the level of consultant use by male and female candidates. There appears to be no difference in the general professionalization of men's and women's campaigns. Overall, 54.2 percent of male candidates hired at least one consultant, as did 55.3 percent of female candidates. The differences by specific election year were also slight. More men than women hired consultants in 1990 (45.8 percent to 43.5 percent, respectively), but the opposite was true in 1992 (63 percent of women hired at least one consultant compared with 62.6 percent of men). None of these differences approaches statistical significance.

One can also look at consultant use by men and women according to the incumbency status of the candidates. It could be that while there are few differences between male and female campaigns in the aggregate, nonincumbent women are more likely to hire consultants than are male challengers and open seat candidates (or vice versa). In fact, table 4.5 reveals that female incumbents and challengers are more likely to hire at least one consultant than are their male counterparts. Overall, 82 percent of female incumbents and 32.5 percent of female challengers hired consultants, whereas 74.8 percent of male incumbents and 24.1 percent of male challengers employed professionals. Male open seat candidates, however, were slightly more likely than women to hire consultants (71.2

to 66 percent, respectively).[21] When comparing by year, we can see that, for the most part, these patterns hold. In 1992, however, a slightly higher percentage of male incumbents relied on consultants than did women who were running for reelection (85.8 percent to 84.6 percent, respectively). The pattern in open seat races of men being more likely to use consultants than women also reversed to some degree in 1992 as 69.2 percent of women employed handlers in these races compared with 68.1 percent of men.

Turning to the number of types of consultants employed, which is not included in the table, I find a somewhat different pattern emerging. Female candidates seem more likely than their male counterparts to hire more than one type of professional. This finding is particularly pronounced in 1990. Whereas 18.6 percent of men hired just one type of consultant, only 2.9 percent of women did so. On the other hand, 40.6 percent of women hired two or more types of professionals, while only 27.2 percent of men employed as many consultant types. In 1992, the difference on this score is not as great, but again a greater percentage of women hired multiple consultant types than did men (by 50 to 44.1 percent).

In terms of the mean number of consultant types hired, however, any differences between male and female candidates disappear. Men hired an average of .9 consultant types in 1990 and 1.4 in 1992. For the same years, women used an average of 1 and 1.5 consultant services. Even though women tended to hire two or more consultant types at a higher level than men, the means are similar due to the larger number of men hiring a considerable number of consultants. For example, no women hired six consultant types and only one used five. Thus, women are more likely than men to use two, and perhaps three, consultant services, but the reverse is true for levels of professionalization higher than that. (But keep in mind that very few candidates of either sex employ more than four consultant types.)

From this discussion one can conclude that male and female candidates are relatively similar in their use of consultants. My findings suggest that the same percentage of men and women hire at least one consultant, and the mean numbers of consultant types employed by them are virtually identical. In terms of the level of professionalization (by which I mean the number of consultant types hired), however, some differences do occur. Female candidates who hire consultants tend, to a greater degree than male candidates, to hire more than one professional. There seems to be an upper limit to how many consultants they use, however, as men are more likely to hire five or six consultants. Differences also show up between men and women candidates according to incumbency status. In general, female incumbents and challengers are more likely to hire consultants than are men, although male open seat candidates use professionals to a greater extent than do women. Nevertheless, one could argue that there are no major differences in consultant use between men and women House candidates.

These conclusions are consistent with the findings of other congressional election scholars. As Herrnson and Andersen (1995) found, "The major differences in the professionalization of congressional campaigns are attributable to incumbency, party affiliation, and electoral competition rather than gender" (9). Furthermore, according to Witt, Paget, and Matthews (1994), "As more women are considered viable candidates, or become incumbents, the differences generally between women's and men's campaigns recede" (145). This was particularly evident in 1992. Although women were not much more successful in that year than they had been over the last two decades, they did pick up nineteen seats. Jacobson argues that nearly all of these gains were the result of women winning open seats (1993a, 154, 171). The fact that a higher percentage of women open seat candidates were professionalized in 1992 than their male counterparts, and considerably more than women open seat candidates were in 1990, may explain their having picked up these seats.

The final factor to be considered in this chapter is the level of consultant use by candidate competitiveness.[22] Table 4.6 reveals, not surprisingly, that candidates in competitive races are more likely to hire consultants than those without much competition. Whereas 77.2 percent of all candidates who had serious competition hired at least one professional, only 41.2 percent of those in noncompetitive races did so (χ^2 = 201.018, df = 1, p = .000). This general pattern holds both in 1990 and 1992.

The pattern also holds when we take incumbency status into consideration. Incumbents in close races are significantly more likely to hire consultants than those who are safe, with 89.4 percent of the former using professionals and 67.7 percent of the latter doing so (χ^2 = 43.194, df = 1, p = .000). We find a similar difference among safe and vulnerable incumbents in 1990, but in 1992, even safe incumbents hired consultants at the rate of 81.5 percent (although the difference here remains significant; χ^2 = 7.174, df = 1, p = .007). As for open seat candidates, their use of consultants mimics that of incumbents. In fact, the levels of consultant use among competitive open seat candidates is incredibly similar to the levels among vulnerable incumbents. The drop off in consultant use between competitive and noncompetitive open seat candidates is also comparable to like incumbents (except in 1992, where use among noncompetitive open seat candidates fell according to the general pattern). Finally, far fewer challengers use professionals regardless of com-

Table 4.6
Use of Consultants by Competitiveness and Incumbency Status

	Competitive*				Not Competitive*			
	Inc.	Chal.	Open	All	Inc.	Chal.	Open	All
Overall								
Hired at least one consultant	89.4% (235)	55.9% (113)	85.1% (120)	77.2% (468)	67.7% (333)	11.8% (55)	48.5% (47)	41.2% (435)
Did not hire at least one	10.6% (28)	44.1% (89)	14.9% (21)	22.8% (138)	32.3% (159)	88.2% (411)	51.5% (50)	58.8% (620)
All	34.8% (263)	30.2% (202)	59.2% (141)	36.5% (606)	65.2% (492)	69.8% (466)	40.8% (97)	63.5% (1055)
1990								
Hired at least one consultant	86.6% (103)	44.8% (43)	86.8% (33)	70.8% (179)	57.8% (166)	4.5% (11)	55.0% (11)	34.1% (188)
Did not hire at least one	13.4% (16)	55.2% (53)	13.2% (5)	29.2% (74)	42.2% (121)	95.5% (234)	45.0% (9)	65.9% (364)
All	29.3% (119)	28.2% (96)	65.5% (38)	31.4% (253)	70.7% (287)	71.8% (245)	34.5% (20)	68.6% (552)
1992								
Hired at least one consultant	91.7% (132)	66.0% (70)	84.5% (87)	81.9% (289)	81.5% (167)	19.9% (44)	46.8% (36)	49.1% (247)
Did not hire at least one	8.3% (12)	34.0% (36)	15.5% (16)	18.1% (64)	18.5% (38)	80.1% (177)	53.2% (41)	50.9% (256)
All	41.3% (144)	32.4% (106)	57.2% (103)	41.2% (353)	58.7% (205)	67.6% (221)	42.8% (77)	58.8% (503)

Note: Numbers in parentheses are *N*s.
*The totals for these categories include third party candidates in those races where only one of the two major parties had a candidate in the race. There were 19 such candidates in 1990 and 18 in 1992.

petitiveness. Nevertheless, many more competitive challengers hire consultants than do noncompetitive ones. Overall, 55.9 percent of challengers in close races hired an operative, whereas only 11.8 percent of those in noncompetitive races did so (χ^2 = 145.834, *df* = 1, *p* = .000).

Summary

The evidence presented in this chapter represents the first systematic attempt to report the level of consultant use in congressional elections *without using survey data*. Of course, I have yet to address the issue of whether professionalized campaigns are more successful than those run without the assistance of consultants. Nevertheless, I have found a number of important things about consultant use in House elections.

Briefly, the results of this chapter suggest that the use of consultants increased significantly between 1990 and 1992. Furthermore, incumbents, nonincumbent winners, and incumbent losers, Democrats, quality nonincumbents, and candidates in close races are more likely to hire consultants than nonincumbents, nonincumbent losers, and incumbent winners, Republicans, nonincumbent novices, and candidates in noncompetitive races. There were no significant differences between the level of consultant use for men and women.[23]

As for the types of consultants most used, pollsters lead the way, followed closely by media consultants. There were some minor differences in this pattern depending on incumbency status (open seat candidates were more likely to hire media specialists than pollsters in 1990) and party (Democrats, like open seat candidates generally, used media consultants more than pollsters in 1990). Still, pollsters are clearly more relied upon by congressional candidates than are other consultant types.

Again, this summary masks some of the more subtle findings of this chapter. Nonetheless, the results herein are important. Until now, political scientists have had only sketchy estimates of the level of professionalism in congressional elections. The next chapter uses the same data set to begin exploring the question of consultant influence in congressional elections.

· 5 ·

The Influence of Consultants: Incumbents and Challengers

Equipped with a theory explaining how consultants are able to affect candidates' electoral fortunes and with empirical evidence on the level of use of political professionals by congressional candidates, I now turn to an analysis of consultant influence. Our guiding question is whether or not consultants help their clients garner more of the vote than they would otherwise receive without professional assistance. The present chapter deals with incumbents and challengers, whereas the next covers open seat races.

We are likely, of course, to find different consultant effects for incumbents and challengers. Incumbents possess a number of advantages in running for reelection, whereas challengers have few. Indeed, most challengers begin their races so far behind that even if consultants provide a significant boost in their vote shares, they are unlikely to prevail. Nevertheless, it is important to determine whether consultants are able to deliver something tangible for their fees. Thus, while this chapter and the next deal with the impact of consultants on a candidate's percentage of the vote, chapter 7 will deal with the odds of winning (among other things).

Context—The Incumbency Advantage

The consequences of the enormous advantage that incumbents have over their opponents are well known. Only fifteen House incumbents lost in the general elections of 1990, and only twenty-four were defeated in 1992 (Jacobson 1993a, 167).[1] Put another way, 96 percent of incumbents seeking reelection (i.e., those who did not retire) were successful in 1990 and

88.3 percent were successful in 1992, widely considered a tumultuous year for incumbents (Ornstein, Mann, and Malbin 1994, 58).[2] That means, of course, that House challengers had less than a one in ten chance of winning in the early 1990s (for a sophisticated estimate of the incumbency advantage before 1990, see Gelman and King 1990). What accounts for this disparity? To what, in other words, does the "incumbency advantage" owe its existence? This section will review the explanations that have previously been offered to answer this question.

To begin with, David Mayhew (1974a) has argued that "the organization of Congress meets remarkably well the electoral needs of its members" (81). Indeed, "if a group of planners sat down and tried to design a pair of American national assemblies with the goal of serving members' electoral needs year in and year out, they would be hard pressed to improve on what exists" (81–82). What is it about the design of Congress that is so beneficial to members' electoral efforts? Gary Jacobson (1992, 37) notes that the decentralized committee system allows members to become specialists in policy areas that match their constituents' interests. Members are also able to take advantage of a legislative process that allows (in fact, in some ways encourages) pork barreling and "Christmas tree" bills (i.e., those with gifts for numerous interests). Parties also rarely, if ever, enforce loyalty, enabling an individual member to place the district over his/her party. In addition, Jacobson points out that members of Congress have at their disposal professional staffs and well-equipped offices, good salaries, as well as travel and communication allowances (e.g., the "franking privilege") that are of enormous help in running for reelection (38). With regard to staffs in particular, Timothy Cook (1989) has highlighted the importance of the press secretary in congressional offices and has pointed out that this position, "at least as an explicitly designated post, has evolved from a luxury in the early 1970s to a commonplace component of most members' staff" (72). Indeed, these indispensable staffers have made it easier for members of Congress to "make news as they make laws." And let us not forget that the wonderful civic service provided by C-SPAN unintentionally allows congressional representatives to play an "official" role denied, by definition, to those not holding office.[3]

Members' behavior has also been offered as an explanation for their advantage over challengers. To return to Mayhew, members of Congress engage in three specific activities intended to put themselves in good stead with the voters back home (Mayhew 1974a, 49). The first of these is advertising, which Mayhew defines as "any effort to disseminate one's name among constituents in such a fashion as to create a favorable image but in messages having little or no issue content." By advertising, incumbents essentially create high name recognition, or a "brand name," for themselves. They do so by sending letters of congratulations to high school graduates, mailing newsletters to the district, appearing at local events such as Fourth of July parades, and giving nonpolitical speeches at community functions.

Members of Congress also claim credit for having done important things for the district from their seat in Washington. As Mayhew defines it, credit claiming is "acting so as to generate a belief in a relevant political actor (or actors) that one is personally responsible for causing the government, or some unit thereof, to do something that the actor (or actors) considers desirable" (1974a, 52–53). Members can communicate their accomplishments in many ways including newsletters and press conferences held in the district. As incumbents are well aware, announcing the acquisition of federal funds for a district project virtually guarantees positive local news coverage.

The third activity that incumbents engage in for electoral advantage is position taking. Mayhew defines this as "the public enunciation of a judgmental statement on anything likely to be of interest to political actors" (1974a, 61). Unlike the member who is claiming credit for work accomplished, the congressional representative "as position taker is a speaker rather than a doer" (62). "The electoral requirement," continues Mayhew, "is not that he make pleasing things happen but that he make pleasing judgmental statements" (62). Thus, position taking need not be specific but may simply be a general agreement with a broad policy direction. Furthermore, members of Congress are likely to be strategic about how they take positions. Notes Mayhew, "A solid consensus in the constituency calls for ringing declarations. . . . Division or uncertainty in the constituency calls for waffling" (64).

The advantage incumbents possess over their challengers is also the result of the "home styles" they cultivate when visiting their districts. According to Richard Fenno (1978), incumbents have various styles of relating to the "folks back home," but for each "their home style is the most important determinant of their political support" (210). Such styles are made up of three "ingredients," namely, an allocation of personal resources, the presentation of self to others, and an explanation of one's Washington activities (33). The ultimate goal of the congressional representative is to cultivate trust with his/her constituents. This process takes a good bit of effort, however, which explains why members spend so much time in their districts (56). While it appears that home styles successfully keep members of Congress in office, Fenno cautions, "A focus on home style makes it clear that incumbency is not an automatic entitlement to a fixed number of votes or percentage points toward reelection. . . . Incumbency should be seen as a resource to be employed, an opportunity to be exploited; and the power of incumbency is whatever each member makes of the resource and the opportunity" (211).

Incumbents make use of the resources at their disposal by serving their constituency. And helping constituents helps incumbents get re-elected (Fiorina 1977a, 1977b). Morris Fiorina (1989) has shown that between 1960 and 1974, resources devoted by members of Congress to constituency service increased dramatically, whether one looks at the percentage of staff assigned to district offices, the number of such offices open year round, or the percentage of members with more than one office in the district (54). In turn, the percentage of voter evaluations of incumbents based on constituency attentiveness more than doubled between 1958 and 1978 (89). This, according to Fiorina, explains the "vanishing marginals," by which he means those districts with congressional races that were once close (either in the 45 to 54.9 Democratic percentage of the two-party vote range or the 40 to 59.9 range) but are now safe seats (see also Mayhew 1974b, 304). The number of marginals, according to some scholars, was cut in half between 1945 and 1972.[4] This apparent rise in incumbent protection is the result, so the argument goes, of an augmented incumbency advantage brought about by the increased emphasis on constituency service, among other things (Fiorina 1989, 99–101).[5]

Another possible explanation for the incumbency advantage is the ability of incumbents to raise more money, and therefore spend more, than challengers. When 1990 and 1992 figures are combined, median incumbent spending was over six times that of challengers ($414,696 to $66,727) and their receipts were nearly nine times greater ($444,628 to $49,467.50). In 1990, the median incumbent raised nearly seventeen times the amount collected by the median challenger.

Yet while it is true that incumbents possess an enormous monetary advantage over their opponents, that edge does not seem to be of much help to them. The reason is that voters already know members of Congress as well as they are going to know any candidate. Therefore, the money incumbents spend on additional campaigning is ineffective (see Jacobson 1980, 36–38). In fact, the more incumbents spend, the worse they seem to do (Jacobson 1992, 53). This is the result of reactionary spending on the part of members of Congress who are in, or who believe they are in, electoral jeopardy (Jacobson 1980; see also Jacobson 1978 and Ansolabehere and Gerber 1994).

On the other hand, some scholars have found evidence that incumbent spending helps their election prospects (Green and Krasno 1988, 1990; Thomas 1989; Kenny and McBurnett 1992; and Goidel and Gross 1994). Much of the disagreement between these two camps relates to methodological issues surrounding the subject. Nevertheless, all agree that money is important, that incumbents can get more of it and can do so more easily than challengers, and that the relative benefit of campaign spending is greater for the latter than for the former.

Other prominent explanations for why incumbents get reelected at such high rates have to do with characteristics of the challengers rather than the incumbents. As should be obvious from the discussion of money above, challengers are at a spending disadvantage in House campaigns. Regardless of whether incumbent spending is effective, it is undeniable that challenger spending is significantly tied to electoral success (Jacobson 1992). But raising money is an uphill battle for challengers. To begin with, PACs are more willing to give to incumbents, who they know have better than a 90 percent chance of winning (on average), than to a challenger who is likely to lose. Furthermore, because all incumbents "run scared" (Mann 1977; Fenno 1978; Jacobson 1987b; and King 1997), they raise and spend as much early money as they can, creating the perception of incumbent strength and potentially making it even more difficult for challengers to raise funds.[6] Thus, "seed money," which is essential for a challenger's hopes, is hard for them to come by (Sorauf 1992, 80).[7] Challengers are therefore in a position of having to prove their viability to raise campaign funds while needing money to indicate that they are viable candidates. Few challengers find a way out of this quandary.

If any challengers are to break that vicious circle, it will be those who have held past elected office. The advantage these challengers hold over novices is that, depending on the level of the office, they have considerably more resources at their disposal (Herrnson 1995, 64). Having already won an election, they have donor lists for raising money and voter lists for persuasive direct mail and phone contacts. They are also likely to have staff and volunteers who have helped with their campaign efforts in the past. Furthermore, officeholders are strategic about when to run for higher office and are better equipped to announce their candidacies when the time is right: for example, when the economy favors their party, the president is a fellow partisan and is popular, etc. (see Jacobson and Kernell 1983; Robeck 1982; Bond, Covington, and Fleisher 1985; Bianco 1984; and Jacobson 1989).[8]

A final important characteristic of challengers is that most of them are unknown. As indicated earlier, Hinckley (1981) asserts that most voters in House elections have "essentially no choice" because they know only one of the two candidates in the race (51; see also Hinckley 1980; Mann and Wolfinger 1980; Abramowitz 1980; and Ragsdale 1981, 1989). The known quantity is, of course, the incumbent. This gives members of Congress another enormous advantage. As Jacobson (1980) notes, "The more information voters have about a candidate, other things equal, the more likely they are to vote for him" (36–37). Lyn Ragsdale (1981) adds to this school of thought by suggesting that there is an interaction between challenger invisibility and incumbent popularity. She argues that neither "can be seen as solely responsible for incumbent victory. Rather, their influences should be treated concurrently, so as to gauge voters' responses to both candidates in a specific election contest" (214). Thus, we have come full circle. Not only do people not know who is challenging the incumbent in most House races but they like their members of Congress. And incumbents remain popular by taking advantage of those things at their disposal which are designed for incumbent protection.

Expectations

Having established the context of House races involving incumbents, I now turn to analyzing political consultant influence. As I suggested in chapter 2, the general hypothesis of this project is that political consultants have an impact on the electoral performance of congressional candidates. Specifically, candidates who hire political consultants will garner more votes than those who do not. The justification for believing that, in general, candidates with consultants will run more successful races than those without professional assistance should be clear from the theory of deliberate priming. If consultants are experts at deliberate priming, and deliberate priming frames the campaign in the priming candidate's favor, then those candidates who hire consultants should be more successful than those who do not.

One might reasonably ask at this point whether or not all consultants can be treated as equals. Surely consultants differ in terms of talent. That is undoubtedly true, although the differences between consultants are not as big as consultants themselves suggest. After all, their business depends on convincing candidates that they are more skillful than the competing consultants. Nevertheless, while the skill level may vary from consultant to consultant, those differences are not great; on the other hand, the similarities between consultants are considerable (see Medvic 1998 and 2000).

Indeed, as explained in chapter 2, social learning theory would suggest that campaigners determine which techniques and strategies work and which do not by acting in various electoral contexts (Hershey 1984, 39). Because there are features that most campaigns have in common (e.g., two major parties, the media, voters who have similar levels of interest and knowledge), professionals are able to develop models of campaigning that can be applied to future campaigns (60–73). In addition, professional handlers are increasingly employing skills they learned before they were consultants, for example, as party operatives or at campaign "schools" (Arterton 1997; Hamilton 1997; Kolodny and Logan 1998). Thus, individual differences in consultant skill will be less useful in explaining election outcomes than will a measure of consultant use generally. In other words, a candidate's decision about whether or not to hire a consultant is more important for his/her success than is the decision about which specific consultant to hire.

One could also ask whether my general hypothesis holds for all candidates. It seems likely that consultants will have different influences on different types of candidates. Therefore, a more specific expectation is that challengers who hire at least one political consultant will get a higher percentage of the vote than challengers who do not have at least one professional handler. Incumbents, on the other hand, are not expected to benefit from the use of consultants. In fact, incumbents may very well do worse when they hire a consultant because those who are in electoral trouble are more likely to rely on consultant assistance than are safe members of Congress (see tables 4.1, 4.2, and 4.6).

In addition, I will examine the impact of the number of different types of consultants hired. I would hypothesize that the more types of consultants hired by a challenger, the higher the percentage of the vote that candidate will receive; in other words, the more professionalized a campaign, the better it will do. Thus, a fully professionalized campaign, that is, one in which each of the campaign tasks is handled by a professional consultant, should be more successful than a less professionalized one. Again, however, I would not expect this pattern to hold for incumbents.

A maximum of seven consultant types, corresponding to the categories provided by *C&E*, could be hired by candidates. Specifically, media handlers, pollsters, generalists, persuasion mail specialists, fund-raising mail handlers, direct mail specialists (those who do both persuasion and fund-raising mail), and fund-raising event consultants were included in this analysis. While fund-raising consultants (whether event or mail fund-raisers) are not expected to have a direct effect on the vote (see below), they are included at this point because I am attempting to determine whether the level of professionalization has an impact on a campaign's success.

As for the impact of specific consultant types, one might guess that pollsters will add more to the vote shares of challengers than any other consultant type, followed by media and voter contact specialists, and then by generalists.[9] Again, this hypothesis is based on the theory outlined in chapter 3. In examining this hypothesis, only the four consultant types just mentioned were utilized. Two categories not included are fund-raising event handlers and fund-raising mail specialists. According to the theory of deliberate priming, there is no reason to expect a direct impact on the vote by these consultants. Fund-raisers are supposed to help acquire the resources that enable other consultants to effectively prime voters. Otherwise, their work is unrelated to deliberate priming. Consequently, their influence as measured by share of the vote would be indirect at best. The impact of fund-raisers on the amount of money congressional candidates raise will be examined in chapter 7.

It may not be immediately apparent that pollsters would be the most effective consultants in terms of garnering a larger share of the vote, but a brief consideration of the aforementioned theory should reveal the preeminent place of pollsters in the deliberate priming equation. In describing deliberate priming in chapter 3, I dealt with pollsters first. This was not by accident, as they play a crucial role in the ability of a campaign to successfully prime voters. Without pollsters, a campaign would have virtually no idea which issues (whether thought of as policy propositions or as personal characteristics) to emphasize and which to ignore. Pollsters help candidates determine the grounds upon which the campaign will be fought, and without the information they provide, candidates—and, indeed, other consultants—campaign blindly. Furthermore, pollsters are linked directly to voters to the extent that they tap their opinions, attitudes, and preferences through surveys and focus groups.

Media and voter contact specialists should be the next most important consultants because they also provide a direct link between the campaign organization and the voters. Obviously, this link moves in the opposite direction from that of the pollster, who takes information from voters and gives it to the campaign; media and voter contact consultants take a message from the campaign and give it to voters. For example, once a candidate has decided (based on information provided by the pollster) to use crime as an issue with which to prime, these consultants produce the pieces of communication that will activate (or foreground) the schemas of the voters on this issue. The difference in the direction of the linkage between media and voter contact specialists, on the one hand, and pollsters, on the other, accounts for the priority of the latter to the former. Quite simply, the pollster link is more essential for deliberate priming than the media and voter contact link. If candidates did not have media handlers, their messages would still get out, albeit less effectively. They would still get at least some earned (or "free") media coverage and would still talk to thousands of voters through retail ("in person") politics. Pollsters, however, provide the road map for the long haul of the campaign. Without them, candidates would have no reliable means of determining which issues should be emphasized and used for priming.

Finally, generalists should be the least influential type of consultant. Although they are undoubtedly more skilled at theme and message creation than novices, the function performed by generalists can readily be applied by pollsters and/or media specialists. In fact, it often is. This is not to say that generalists will not prove to significantly impact the vote; they may very well be important influences on a congressional candidate's vote because, as professionals, they create potent themes and messages as well as develop winning strategies and tactics. The third hypothesis simply says that generalists will be less influential than the other three consultant types. As with the first two hypotheses, the third applies exclusively to challengers. Since incumbents are not expected to be helped by hiring at least one consultant or by the number of consultants hired, we would not expect specific types of consultants to matter either.

In terms of the variables to be employed herein, the most important are those accounting for the use of consultants in individual campaigns. These include a dichotomous variable for having or not having hired a consultant, a variable measuring the number of different types of consultants hired, and dichotomous variables for each of four consultant types. Other variables to be included are a candidate's campaign expenditures, a dichotomous variable for challenger quality, a measure of district partisanship, and one accounting for midterm versus presidential election years.[10]

The basic equation to be estimated with ordinary least squares regression is as follows:

$IV = a_0 + b_1$ Year $+ b_2$ District Partisanship $+ b_3$ Challenger Quality $+ b_4$ Democratic Expenditures $+ b_5$ Republican Expenditures $+ b_6$ Democratic Consultant $+ b_7$ Republican Consultant $+ e_i$,

where
   IV is the incumbent's percent of the vote;
   a_0 is the intercept (here, the incumbent's share of the vote when neither candidate hires a consultant);
   Year is a dummy variable coded as 0—1990 and 1—1992;
   District Partisanship is the district's percent of the vote for Michael Dukakis in 1988;[11]
   Challenger Quality is a dummy variable coded as 1—held previous elective office, 0—did not hold previous elective office;
   Democratic Expenditures is the base 10 log transformation of the amount of money spent for campaign activities;[12]
   Republican Expenditures is the base 10 log transformation of the amount of money spent for campaign activities;
   Democratic Consultant is a dummy variable coded as 1—Democratic candidate hired a consultant, 0—Democrat did not hire a consultant;

Republican Consultant is a dummy variable coded as 1—Republican candidate hired a consultant, 0—Republican did not hire a consultant;

e_i is the error term.

The district partisanship measure is necessary as a control for the partisan leanings of voters in each district. In addition, the variable for year serves to control for the presidential election of 1992.[13] Furthermore, "quality" challengers, as has been noted, should run more competitive races than those challengers who have not held past elective office. And the more money a challenger spends, the better he/she will do, although the same is not true for incumbents. Finally, candidates who hire consultants should be more successful than those who do not. Again, as has been mentioned, this is not likely to hold for incumbents. Consultants, like money, may be used to a greater degree by incumbents who are vulnerable. Thus, we would not be surprised to see those incumbents who hire consultants perform more poorly than those who do not turn to professionals for help.

Results

One way to lay the groundwork for more sophisticated analyses is to establish simple trends or patterns. In the case of political consultants, we might ask, do the vote percentages of those candidates who hire professional operatives differ significantly from those who do not? To answer this question, we might analyze the difference in the mean percentage of the vote received by the two groups of candidates.

The results of an analysis of variance (ANOVA), using the candidate's share of the vote as the dependent variable, are reported in table 5.1. In order to account for the influence of incumbency and party, those factors were included along with the simple political consultant variable. The logged transformation of spending on campaign activities served as a covariate. As we might guess, those challengers who hire consultants are more successful than those who do not. Both Democratic and Republican challengers received approximately 42 percent of the vote when they hired consultants, but only 34 percent when they did not. On the other hand, as was also expected, incumbents failed to increase their percentage of the vote by hiring consultants. In fact, those who did not hire consultants received roughly 10 percent more of the vote than did those who hired handlers. This pattern mirrors the one for incumbent spending discussed earlier.

When we look at the main effects of incumbency, party, and political consultant use, we see that the first and last of these variables have a sig-

Table 5.1

Percent of the Vote by Incumbency Status, Party, and the Presence of
a Political Consultant: Analysis of Variance

		Political Consultant		Covariate:
		Yes	No	General Spending (Logged)
Challengers:	Democrats	42.24	34.44	547.82***
		(N=74)	(N=133)	
	Republicans	42.22	33.96	
		(N=94)	(N=239)	
Incumbents:	Democrats	64.68	74.21	
		(N=338)	(N=122)	
	Republicans	63.76	75.49	
		(N=230)	(N=65)	
Main effects:	Incumbency status			$F(1, 1295) = 1713.95$***
	Party			$F(1, 1295) = 1.68$
	Political consultant			$F(1, 1295) = 4.48$**
Interaction effects:	Incumbency × Party			$F(1, 1295) = .017$
	Incumbency × Consultant			$F(1, 1295) = 176.87$***
	Party × Consultant			$F(1, 1295) = .920$
	Incumbency × Party × Consultant			$F(1, 1295) = .85$

Note: Entries in top half of table are mean percentages of the vote. This table includes only major party candidates, with the exception of Bernie Sanders (I-VT), who was counted as a Democrat.

***$p < .001$, **$p < .05$.

nificant impact on the variance in percentage of the vote received. When the factors are interacted, only the "incumbency x consultant" effect is significant. This means that there is little difference in the vote variance between the parties with regard to either incumbency or the use of consultants. But there is an obvious difference with respect to the use of consultants by challengers and incumbents. The important finding here, however, is that consultant use, on its own, significantly accounts for at least some of the variance in candidates' share of the vote.

Ultimately, we are interested in knowing how much consultants add to a candidate's share of the vote. To determine this, I now turn to multiple regression analysis. Separate regressions were run for Democratic and Republican incumbents.[14]

The results for the first model are reported in table 5.2.[15] One can see that both versions of the model produce essentially the same findings.

Table 5.2
*Model 1: The Effect of Hiring a Consultant on a
Candidate's Share of the Vote (OLS)*

	Democratic Incumbent			Republican Incumbent		
	b	(Beta)	α	b	(Beta)	α
Year	−.067	(−.004)	.930	2.900	(.186)	**.001**
District Partisanship	.269	(.321)	**.000**	−.061	(−.056)	.316
Challenger Quality	−1.730	(−.078)	**.080**	−1.652	(−.084)	.154
Democratic Spending[a]	−3.673	(−.161)	**.004**	−4.488	(−.397)	**.000**
Republican Spending[b]	−3.610	(−.288)	**.000**	−1.269	(−.044)	.527
Consultant hired by Democrat	1.884	(.083)	**.090**	−3.724	(−.230)	**.004**
Consultant hired by Republican	−2.673	(−.138)	**.008**	−1.006	(−.044)	.441
Constant	85.488			92.148		
R^2	.438			.448		
Adjusted R^2	.426			.429		
N	333			207		

Note: Standardized betas are in parentheses. The constant represents the incumbent's share of the vote when every variable is set to zero. To make reading the table easier, I have bold-faced the alphas (α) that reached a significance level of .100 or less.
[a] Log of the Democrat's general campaign expenditures.
[b] Log of the Republican's general campaign expenditures.

Namely, hiring a political consultant significantly helps challengers run more competitive races.

Turning first to the Democratic incumbent version of the basic model, we see that the more Democratic a district, the better the incumbent Democrat did. For each percentage point increase in the vote for Dukakis, Democratic incumbents received .269 percent more of the vote themselves. On the other hand, when the Republican challenger had held elected office (i.e., was a "quality" challenger), the Democratic incumbent got over 1.5 percent less of the vote. Not surprisingly, the presidential year of 1992 proved no better for Democrats than did 1990.

As for campaign spending, Democratic incumbents did significantly worse the more they spent. This finding is in keeping with some of the past campaign spending literature. Republican challengers, of course, did significantly better as they spent more money.[16] For such candidates, an increase of 1 percent in expenditures leads to an average 3.610 percent decrease in the Democratic incumbent's share of the vote.[17]

Finally, and of most importance for our purposes, Republican challengers are significantly helped by hiring at least one political consultant. They can reduce their Democratic opponent's share of the vote by nearly 2.7 points by simply hiring a professional operative. This is an important finding given the congressional election literature's skepticism about the impact of most nonmoney variables. Democratic incumbents, surprisingly, also add to their vote by employing a consultant. Although the coefficient does not reach the conventional .05 level of significance, it does meet the more lenient .10 level, making it a fairly safe bet that the variable is explaining some of the variance in the vote.

The Republican version of the first model shows much of the same, although there are a few differences. The most glaring difference between the two versions is the significance of the presidential year for Republicans. On average, Republican incumbents ran with nearly three additional percentage points in 1992 versus 1990. This unexpected finding may simply indicate that Republican incumbents fared worse when they were burdened by being the party in control of the White House during the midterm election of 1990. The president's party has lost seats in every midterm election in the twentieth century except 1934 and 1998.

There are two primary explanations for this phenomenon, which has virtually reached the status of a law of congressional elections. The first explanation for this pattern holds that there are, in effect "two electorates." Called the "surge and decline" explanation (see Campbell 1960), this theory holds that two different electorates vote in presidential and midterm election years (see a revised version of the argument in Campbell 1991, 1993). In the presidential elections, habitual partisan voters go to the polls along with nonhabitual, less interested swing voters who essentially give the winning candidate a victory. In the midterm election, however, the less committed voters stay home, putting the party who benefited in the presidential year at a disadvantage.

The other prominent explanation for presidential loss of seats in midterm elections is that these elections serve as a referendum on the president's performance (see Tufte 1975). A negative evaluation, however, is likely to be a stronger impetus to vote than is satisfaction with the president (Kernell 1977). Thus, the president's party is always likely to be in a position to lose seats in the off-years.

Hinckley (1981) warned that both explanations could be incorrect (or are, at least, explaining only part of the story) because worrying about seat changes was, in effect, a mismeasure of congressional voting. As she noted, "The number of seats gained or lost for a party is a highly *relative* measure *depending entirely on the number of seats held before the election"* (124; emphasis in original). Thus, an alternative measure is needed to fully understand the change in House seats from one election to the next (126–29). When using the "normal vote" (i.e., the vote expected without the influence of nationwide short-term effects) or the average number of seat changes over time, Hinckley finds that midterm and presidential year elections are remarkably similar (129).

Nevertheless, my findings suggest that in a year when Bill Clinton won the presidency (1992), Republicans did better in congressional races than when a member of their own party sat in the White House (1990). Beyond a midterm slump for the party "in power," do my results indicate a coattail effect *for the opposition*? I will answer that question momentarily, but I should first note the potential influence of a desire for divided government on the part of the electorate. Could it be that voters are so committed to divided government that they purposefully vote for it? While this posits more strategic calculation than voters seem to engage in, there is evidence that voters split tickets with divided government in mind. Fiorina (1988, 1990, 1992, 1994, 1996a) has argued that voters seek to balance the policy extremes represented by Democrats and Republicans. (For a critique of this "policy-balancing model," see Born 1994a, 1994b, and Petrocik and Doherty 1996.)[18]

Jacobson (1990b) explains the long pattern of divided government in recent American history by suggesting that voters' policy preferences and their partisan and institutional expectations combine to produce divided control of government. People want a balanced budget, strong defense, and low inflation as well as numerous social programs and low unemployment (112). Furthermore, people perceive Republicans as better able to deliver the first set of preferences and Democrats as more likely to provide the latter. Finally, voters expect presidents to "pursue broad national interests" and produce "diffuse collective benefits at the expense of concentrated particular interests." Members of Congress, on the other hand, protect local interests (112). Thus, from 1954 to 1993, when government was divided, it was divided between a Republican president and a Democratic House and, usually, Senate (save 1981 to 1987; Jacobson 1996a, 62).

In 1992, however, voters chose a Democratic president and kept the House and Senate in Democratic hands. Is this evidence that voters wanted unified government? Fiorina says no. "Counting Perot voters," he notes, "presidential-congressional ticket-splitting was at an all-time high in 1992, and even not counting them, ticket-splitting was at a level comparable to that in elections of the 1980s" (Fiorina 1996a, 36). Given that the election of 1994 reinstated, and the 1996 and 1998 elections reinforced, divided government, Fiorina's basic argument that voters seek to balance the policy extremes of the two parties seems to have been confirmed.[19]

In answering the question about presidential coattails in 1992, one is reminded that Democratic incumbents did no better in that year than in the previous election cycle. Could it be that Republican incumbents capitalized on Clinton's victory but Democratic incumbents were unaffected by it? Perhaps the incumbency advantage enjoyed by Democratic members of Congress was strong enough to neutralize the voters' desire for divided government. At the same time, voters in districts with Republican incumbents may have sent a strong message in favor of divided government. At first glance, this difference between districts with Republican and Democratic incumbents seems an implausible occurrence. Yet, as Petrocik and Doherty (1996) found, "Party identification was one of the few things that did matter in 1992—and in a sensible way: Democrats tended to support united government; Republicans preferred division" (105).[20]

By regressing Republican incumbents' vote shares on Clinton's percentage of the vote in each district, we see that Clinton's coattails work in the expected direction (see table 5.3). For each percentage point increase in Clinton's share of the vote in a district, the Republican incumbent lost .37 points. Conversely, a similar simple regression for Democratic incumbents' vote percentages showed that they gained half a point for each percentage point increase in Clinton's district vote. The bottom half of the table reveals that adding district partisanship and spending as control variables eliminates the significant decrease in Republican incumbents' votes while Democratic incumbents continued to gain (significantly) .31 points for each Clinton point. In other words, Republicans were probably unaffected by Clinton's electoral performance in 1992 while Democrats likely benefited from it.[21]

As for other variables in the Republican version of model 1 (see table 5.2 again), the district's partisanship did not significantly affect the Republican's vote, although the direction of the coefficient is in the expected direction (i.e., as the district's vote for Dukakis increased, the Republican member of the House lost votes). Again, the Republicans' incumbency advantage in these districts likely mitigated their constituents' partisanship.

Democratic challengers who had held prior elected office did not significantly reduce the incumbent's share of the vote, although the coefficient was negative as expected. This finding contradicts most earlier work on quality candidates. Yet those studies made no allowance for the presence of consultants. I would argue that previous research was largely measuring campaign professionalism when it included quality as a predictor of vote totals.

As for spending, the Democratic challenger's expenditures significantly reduced the Republican incumbent's total vote. For each 1 percent

Table 5.3
*The Effect of Clinton's Coattails on Democratic and Republican Incumbents'
Vote Shares (Simple Regression and OLS)*

	Democratic Incumbent			Republican Incumbent		
	b	*(Beta)*	*α*	*b*	*(Beta)*	*α*
Clinton's district vote percentage	.504	(.586)	**.000**	−.369	(−.334)	**.000**
Constant	38.299			75.026		
R^2	.344			.111		
Adjusted R^2	.340			.104		
N	193			120		
Clinton's district vote percentage	.308	(.348)	**.002**	−.123	(−.112)	.413
District Partisanship	.052	(.059)	.604	−.047	(−.046)	.739
Democratic Spending[a]	−3.129	(−.121)	**.050**	−7.099	(−.587)	**.000**
Republican Spending[b]	−6.449	(−.452)	**.000**	−.556	(−.017)	.849
Constant	92.933			104.467		
R^2	.565			.432		
Adjusted R^2	.555			.410		
N	178			109		

Note: Standardized betas are in parentheses. The constant represents the incumbent's share of the vote when every variable is set to zero. To make reading the table easier, I have bold-faced the alphas (α) that reached a significance level of .100 or less.
[a] Log of the Democrat's general campaign expenditures.
[b] Log of the Republican's general campaign expenditures.

increase in spending, the Democrat reduced his/her opponent's vote by nearly 4.5 percentage points. Republican spending had a negative impact on the incumbent's vote though not significantly, which is also in keeping with the literature.

The hiring of a consultant by the challenger again reduced the incumbent's share of the vote significantly. When Democrats hired a professional, they reduced the incumbent's vote by 3.7 percentage points. Republican incumbents did worse, though not significantly, when they hired consultants, reflecting the incumbent's urge to seek professional assistance when in electoral trouble.

In all, the two versions of the first model explained roughly 43 percent of the variance in the incumbent's vote. I consider the findings for this model strong evidence that hiring at least one consultant matters, though most clearly for challengers. While Democratic incumbents were also helped by using a professional handler, the latter's impact on challenger success is unequivocal. Challengers do considerably better when they hire professional consultants, all other things being equal.[22]

Turning now to the second model of consultant influence, table 5.4 reports the findings of the effect of the number of consultant types hired on a candidate's share of the vote. The version of the model involving Democratic incumbents is similar in many ways to the previous model. Again, district partisanship, the Republican challenger's quality, and both Democratic and Republican spending were found to be significant influences, in the expected directions, on the Democratic incumbent's share of the vote. Specifically, quality Republican challengers reduced the incumbent's vote total by roughly 1.8 percentage points while a 1 percent increase in Republican spending lowered it by nearly 4 points. Spending by incumbent Democrats also significantly reduced their vote by over 3 points per 1 percent increase in expenditures. Finally, for 1 percentage point increase in the district's support for Dukakis, the Democratic incumbent's vote increased by over .25 point.

The variable of interest here, the number of consultant types hired, was significant for the Republican challengers but not for Democratic incumbents. For each consultant the Republican hired to conduct an additional campaign function, the Democratic incumbent's share of the vote was reduced by 1.2 percentage points. In practice this means that a fully professionalized Republican challenge (i.e., one hiring consultants to perform seven campaign activities) would, on average, trim the Democrat's vote by just under 8.5 points.

Looking at the Republican version of the model shown in table 5.4, one sees that the same variables that were influential in the first model are again significant. Republicans benefited from the presidential election year of 1992 and were not significantly harmed by the district's partisanship (although the direction of the coefficient is negative). The Democratic challenger's spending did reduce the Republican incumbent's vote at a rate of 4.3 points per 1 percent increase in spending.

In addition, this version of model 2 reveals that Democratic challengers are more successful the more consultant types they hire. In fact, for each consultant type employed by the Democrat, the Republican incumbent loses slightly more than 1.7 percentage points. For a fully professionalized campaign, that amounts to a 12-point difference in the final vote.

Neither party's incumbents were helped by hiring more consultant types, just as Republican incumbents were not helped by hiring consultants in the first place. Incumbents, it appears, do not benefit in any general way from simply hiring political consultants. On the other hand,

Table 5.4
*Model 2: The Effect of the Number of Consultant Types Hired
on a Candidate's Share of the Vote (OLS)*

	Democratic Incumbent			Republican Incumbent		
	b	(Beta)	α	b	(Beta)	α
Year	−.267	(−.015)	.726	2.906	(.187)	**.001**
District Partisanship	.270	(.322)	**.000**	−.055	(−.050)	.363
Challenger Quality	−1.795	(−.081)	**.072**	−1.828	(−.093)	.107
Democratic Spending[a]	−3.070	(−.135)	**.022**	−4.283	(−.379)	**.000**
Republican Spending[b]	−3.774	(−.301)	**.000**	−.943	(−.033)	.638
No. of types of consultants hired by Democrat[c]	.230	(.035)	.505	−1.735	(−.261)	**.000**
No. of types of consultants hired by Republican[c]	−1.193	(−.119)	**.019**	−.431	(−.067)	.268
Constant	83.938			89.069		
R^2	.428			.465		
Adjusted R^2	.416			.446		
N	333			207		

Note: Standardized betas are in parentheses. The constant represents the incumbent's share of the vote when every variable is set to zero. To make reading the table easier, I have bold-faced the alphas (α) that reached a significance level of .100 or less.
[a] Log of the Democrat's general campaign expenditures.
[b] Log of the Republican's general campaign expenditures.
[c] Measured from 0 to 7.

challengers, needing all the help they can get, are more successful when they purchase the assistance of a political consultant and when they hire additional consultants.

What happens when we look at specific consultant types? It has already been established that both the mere presence of consultants and the number of different types of consultants matter, but only systematically for challengers. What effect do pollsters, media handlers, voter contact specialists, and generalists have? Do pollsters matter most, as my theory would suggest? Or does another type of consultant appear to be more useful to candidates? And, finally, do different types of consultants matter to different types of candidates? Just because consultants do not

Table 5.5

*Model 3: The Effect of Different Consultant Types on a
Candidate's Share of the Vote (OLS)*

	Democratic Incumbent			Republican Incumbent		
	b	*(Beta)*	*α*	*b*	*(Beta)*	*α*
Year	−.280	(−.016)	.720	3.340	(.214)	**.000**
District Partisanship	.281	(.336)	**.000**	−.043	(−.039)	.486
Challenger Quality	−1.816	(−.082)	**.074**	−1.613	(−.082)	.162
Democratic Spending[a]	−3.186	(−.140)	**.023**	−4.420	(−.391)	**.000**
Republican Spending[b]	−3.707	(−.296)	**.000**	−.903	(−.031)	.663
Consultant types (Democrat):						
Media specialist	.944	(.053)	.305	−.812	(−.041)	.550
Pollster	−.036	(−.002)	.969	−3.314	(−.187)	**.014**
Voter contact[c]	.138	(.007)	.880	.279	(.010)	.866
Generalist	−.525	(−.017)	.702	−2.042	(−.068)	.215
Consultant types (Republican):						
Media specialist	−1.346	(−.056)	.249	−1.118	(−.071)	.221
Pollster	−2.636	(−.109)	**.028**	−1.223	(−.076)	.226
Voter contact[c]	1.709	(.038)	.396	.945	(.051)	.360
Generalist	−.278	(−.008)	.857	−1.382	(−.076)	.169
Constant	83.648			89.133		
R^2	.433			.475		
Adjusted R^2	.410			.439		
N	333			207		

Note: Standardized betas are in parentheses. The constant represents the incumbent's share of the vote when every variable is set to zero. To make reading the table easier, I have bold-faced the alphas (α) that reached a significance level of .100 or less.

[a] Log of the Democrat's general campaign expenditures.

[b] Log of the Republican's general campaign expenditures.

[c] This category was created by combining persuasion mail and direct mail specialists.

generally help incumbents garner more of the vote does not mean that each specific type of consultant is useless to them.

Table 5.5 provides answers to these questions. Again, the first version of this model is for Democratic incumbents, the second for Republicans. Each of the nonconsultant variables in model 3 produced results identical to the other two models.

As for specific consultant types, model 3 reveals that no single campaign specialist significantly increased a Democratic incumbent's share of the vote. The closest were media handlers, the coefficient for whom, while not significant, was positive. The coefficients for the other consultant types did not approach significance for Democratic incumbents, and two were negative. For Republican challengers, pollsters were the only type of consultants who had a significant impact on the vote. When a pollster was hired for such candidates, the Democratic incumbent received, on average, over two and a half points less than if a pollster had not been used.

Similar results hold for the Republican incumbent version of model 3. No consultant type had a significant influence on the incumbent's share of the vote. On the other hand, Democratic challengers, like their Republican counterparts, are helped by pollsters, although they gain more from hiring these consultants than did Republicans. Republican incumbents lose well over three percentage points when Democratic challengers hire pollsters.

The finding that pollsters are more influential than other types of consultants is in keeping with the theory of deliberate priming. As I noted above, pollsters provide the essential component for any campaign—information. It is upon the information pollsters gather that a deliberate priming strategy is crafted. Without such information, candidates are forced to rely upon their own anecdotal "reading" of district concerns or upon their own policy interests (regardless of whether or not those interests relate to constituency concerns). Using a "sense of the district" is something incumbents, given their experience, can do more reliably than challengers. Thus, it should be no surprise that pollsters matter only for challengers.

Summary

The results of this chapter are among the first pieces of evidence that consultants have an impact on congressional election outcomes (but see Medvic and Lenart 1997; Dabelko and Herrnson 1997; Medvic 1998, 2000; Herrnson 2000). In three separate regression models, I have shown that hiring a consultant increases a challenger's share of the vote; that the more consultant types a challenger employs, the worse their incumbent opponents do; and that challengers' pollsters significantly influence elections to the advantage of their clients. These conclusions hold independent of candidate spending levels, making them particularly noteworthy. It remains to be seen whether similar results will be found for open seat elections. At this point, however, we can proceed with confidence, having established a considerable amount of evidence for consultant influence. In addition, the theory of deliberate priming survived this first attempt to falsify it. The following chapter will put it to the test once more.

.6.

The Influence of Consultants: Open Seat Races

The most obvious difference between those races that involve incumbents and those that do not is also the most important characteristic of open seat races: In open seat races there are no incumbents. As a result, open seat races are widely viewed, by parties and potential candidates, as valuable opportunities to win a seat in Congress. Without an incumbent to be dealt with, open seats are considered level playing fields. It is true that many districts have partisan advantages that are routinely passed on to the favored party's open seat candidates and are therefore less competitive than other seats. But, in general, the absence of an incumbent presents unequaled opportunities for partisan and personal advancement.

This chapter examines such races and the influence of consultants in them. In many respects, the analysis to be conducted here is like that of the last chapter. Yet that one distinguishing factor—the lack of an incumbent—makes these races sufficiently different to warrant their own inquiry.

There has been relatively little written on open seat races (Gaddie 1995a, 203). This is especially true when compared with the literature on races involving challengers and incumbents. Nevertheless, a few characteristics about open seat candidates are known.

To begin with, about a third of all voters can recall from memory the name of the open seat candidates in their districts (Jacobson 1992, 118; Herrnson 1995, 156). This represents more recall than exists for challengers but less than for incumbents (Jacobson 1992, 98). In terms of recognizing candidates' names from a list, more voters could identify the name of open seat candidates than challengers but, again, less than incumbents (118). Indeed, throughout the 1980s, nearly 80 percent of voters could recognize the names of the open seat candidates in their districts, whereas only 54 percent could recognize challengers' names (118; but see Hinckley 1981, 24). Thus, open seat candidates are fairly well known and do not face the challenger's disadvantage of being invisible.

In addition, candidates for open seats face more difficult primary competition than do challengers or incumbents (Jacobson 1992, 97; Schantz 1980; Banks and Kiewiet 1989). Because the odds of winning the general election are better, more qualified candidates seek their parties' nominations when there is no incumbent running in the fall.[1] But several candidates have the same thing in mind, so each party's nomination is more hotly contested than usual.

When we look at the number of quality challengers and open seat candidates, we see that quality politicians do, indeed, wait to run until incumbents are not seeking reelection.[2] Just as Jacobson and Kernell (1983, 32) and others have found, the data for 1990 and 1992 show that open seat candidates are of higher quality than those facing incumbents. In 1990, 67.2 percent of open seat candidates had previously held elected office whereas only 12.4 percent of challengers had. In 1992, the numbers are 55.7 and 22 percent, respectively. Overall, nearly 60 percent of open seat candidates and just over 17 percent of challengers can be considered quality candidates.

Beyond the difference in the number of quality open seat candidates and quality challengers, my data reveal that the number of such open seat candidates dropped between 1990 and 1992, although the decline was not significant (χ^2 = 2.40, df = 1, p = .121). In fact, the overall decrease on this score was the result of a drastic reduction in the number of quality Republican open seat candidates between 1990 and 1992, from 78.6 percent to 46.5 percent; that decrease was statistically significant (χ^2 = 8.75, df = 1, p = .003).[3] One explanation for this pattern may lie in the strategic behavior of potential congressional candidates. Jacobson and Kernell (1983, 66–71) argue that the political and economic circumstances in the spring of an election year influence the decisions of individuals considering a bid for office in that year. Specifically, the president's average popularity between March and May and the real income level in the spring help potential candidates decide whether the time is right for their candidacy.[4] From January to July 1992, George Bush's popularity averaged 40 percent in the Gallup poll and never climbed above 42 after early February (Gallup 1993, 131, 142).[5] Furthermore, economic conditions were perceived to be unfavorable. By late April 1992, 73 percent of registered voters disapproved of Bush's handling of the economy, 48 percent thought economic conditions were "poor" (12 percent said "good" or "excellent"), and 45 percent believed those conditions were getting worse, down from the 70 percent who thought so in early February (75). As a result of such sentiment, qualified Republican politicians, being strategic, stayed out of the fray.

Candidates running for open seats also spend more money, on average, than challengers and almost as much as, if not more than, incumbents (Herrnson 1995, 129). When median spending figures by candidate type are examined, we find that open seat candidates spent more than incumbents in their bids for congressional seats during the 1990 election cycle ($481,330 to $350,845.50). In fact, when comparing mean spending, open seat candidates spent more than four times what challengers spent ($537,561.43 to $130,802.76) and over $100,000 more than incumbents (who spent $402,014.33).

In 1992, however, incumbents outspent open seat candidates (with median spending at $510,073 and $366,846, respectively) as challengers continued to spend the least ($83,913). Although spending increased for both incumbents and challengers between 1990 and 1992, it decreased for open seat candidates. This is probably the result of the decline in the number of quality candidates in open seat races.

In 1990 and 1992 combined, open seat spending is on par with that of incumbents. While the latter have a higher mean expenditure level ($485,603.58 to $449,955.13), open seat candidates have a slightly higher median value ($421,472 to $414,696). Challenger spending lags far behind both of the other candidate types. Because money matters, we can assume that open seat races are competitive events. When spending figures are coupled with the numbers of qualified candidates in these races, we have even more reason to believe that they are hard fought contests.[6]

Another characteristic of open seat candidates is the professionalization of their campaign organizations. The results of Paul Herrnson's (1995) extensive survey of congressional candidates, campaign managers, and staffers provides evidence suggesting that open seat campaigns are similar to incumbent campaigns in their use of professional campaign assistance. Of the nine campaign activities for which Herrnson has data, a higher percentage of open seat candidates than incumbents use consultants (as defined by the respondents) in three of them. Those three activities are campaign management, press relations, and get-out-the-vote drives (GOTV). For issue and opposition research, an equal number of incumbents and open seat candidates hired consultants for assistance. For fund-raising, accounting/FEC reporting, polling, media, and legal advice, incumbents relied on professionals more than did open seat candidates, but never by more than twelve percentage points (66–68). Usually, the two candidate types used consultants to nearly the same extent. For example, 76 percent of incumbents hired media handlers while 71 percent of those seeking open seats used professional help with advertising.

In terms of the level of professionalization, Herrnson (1995) finds that incumbents use consultants or paid staff for an average of 6.9 campaign activities while open seat candidates use them for 5.8 and challengers for 4 of the 9 activities (68). Thus, one can conclude from Herrnson's data that open seat candidates have campaign organizations that are much more professional than challengers but only somewhat less professional than incumbents.

The numbers I presented in chapter 4 measured professional political consultant use under a different operationalization of "consultant." Table 4.1 revealed that in 1990 a higher percentage of open seat candidates hired at least one consultant than either incumbents or challengers. And, on average, those running for open seats hired consultants to handle more of the possible seven campaign functions than did incumbents (with means of 1.7 and 1.3, respectively). In 1992 the numbers reversed as incumbents became more likely to simply hire professional help and used more consultant types than did open seat candidates (see table 4.2). A quick calculation determines that overall (that is, in 1990 and 1992 combined) 75.2 percent of incumbents hired at least one consultant, whereas 70.1 percent of open seat candidates did so (and only 25.1 percent of challengers did). The conclusion to be drawn from this is similar to the one based on Herrnson's data: Open seat campaigns are considerably more professionalized than challengers' but less so, if only slightly, than incumbents'.

Finally, we should review those factors that have been found to influence open seat elections. Not surprisingly, campaign spending has a significant impact on open seat candidates' prospects for victory (Jacobson 1980 and Gaddie 1995a). Jacobson (1980) offers clear evidence that, unlike races in which an incumbent is present, both candidates in an open seat race benefit by spending more money (47). Yet he also found that spending was relatively more beneficial for Republican open seat candidates (46–47). This is in keeping with his hypothesis that "campaign spending is more important for candidates disadvantaged for any reason" (48). The disadvantage that Republicans faced in the early and mid-1970s (the time period of Jacobson's original work—specifically, party identification that favored Democrats) was considerable (48). Nevertheless, money means votes, and more money means more votes, for both candidates in an open seat race.

Other relevant factors for open seat success are candidate experience (Gaddie 1995a), district partisanship (Jacobson 1980, 47), and a presidential coattail effect (Mondak 1993; Flemming 1995; and Gaddie 1995a). The last factor—presidential coattails—is a controversial one. Depending on whether they use individual-level, district-level aggregate, or national-level aggregate data, scholars differ on the nature of the coattail effect (Mondak and McCurley 1994, 152). Using individual-level data, Jacobson

(1976, 1992) found a significant coattail effect (see also Mondak 1990; Mondak and McCurley 1994); Calvert and Ferejohn (1983), however, see this effect waning. District-level analyses also find a coattail effect at work in House races (Born 1984; Ferejohn and Fiorina 1985; Mondak 1993), although this does not necessarily mean that coattails affect outcomes (Edwards 1979, 1980; Burnham 1975). Finally, after examining national-level aggregate data, Ferejohn and Calvert (1984) argued that coattails have been eroding throughout the century (but see Campbell 1986 and 1991).

We are left with a confused picture of the effect of presidential coattails on congressional elections. In summary, we might say that presidential candidates do influence individuals' voting decisions for House candidates but that the influence is not great enough to affect the outcomes of races. Nevertheless, as in chapter 5, I will not include a measure of presidential coattails in the models for open seat races. Instead, I will simply control for the presidential election year. I now turn to some expectations regarding consultant influence in open seat elections.

Expectations

The expectations for open seat elections are similar to those in chapter 5. Again, the general hypothesis is that open seat candidates who hire at least one political consultant will get a higher percentage of the vote than will open seat candidates who do not have at least one professional handler. This hypothesis does not account for potential differences between the parties. Instead, it holds that all open seat candidates, whether Democratic or Republican, will benefit from the use of consultants. Yet, as Jacobson (1980) has correctly noted, certain campaign variables, like money, are more important for candidates who start a campaign with a disadvantage (48). This explains why campaign spending is more influential for challengers than for incumbents and more influential for Republican open seat candidates than for Democrats (46–48). We might assume that the same pattern would hold for the political consultant variables. In other words, open seat candidates of a party that is disadvantaged would benefit more from consultants than would those who are not, even if candidates of both parties are significantly helped by professional operatives.

Before 1994, Republicans appear to have been at a disadvantage in open seat races. Connelly and Pitney (1994) argued that "interests, institutions, individuals, and ideas" appeared to be conspiring to make congressional Republicans a "permanent minority" (143). Indeed, as they noted in a later piece, at least one of those elements had always worked against Republican House candidates (Pitney and Connelly 1996, 48). It was not until 1994 that most of those factors worked in the GOP's favor.

An insightful structural argument for why Republicans found it difficult to win House seats has been proffered by James Campbell (1996). According to Campbell, the Republicans' disadvantage in House races was
based on the single-member-district electoral system and the Democrats'
ability to win "very-low-turnout districts—the cheap seats" (10). Indeed,
even in the 1994 elections, "Democrats carried a large majority of the
cheap seats . . . and, as in past years, because of this more Democrats sat
in the House than would have under a neutral electoral system" (xix).

Another explanation for the previous Republican disadvantage was
the party differential in lower-level offices (Jacobson 1996b). Gaddie
(1995a) examined the question of "why, despite high turnover in Congress, popular Republican presidents, and the growth of GOP identifiers
in the South (Stanley 1991), the Republican party made no substantial
gains in open seat elections" (204). He found that both Republican and
Democratic candidates benefited from prior political experience and that
both significantly increased their respective shares of the vote by spending more money (207–8). Given that, at least until 1994, Democrats were
better able to field quality candidates, that in the 1980s they began to
help their open seat candidates compete financially, and that these factors have a significant influence on open seat outcomes, the previous Republican disadvantage is clear (210–11). As Gaddie concluded, "Despite
advantages from redistricting in the South, the Republican party still
faces a major impediment in fielding candidates. . . . The nature of the
Democratic advantage is a reflection of the residual strength of the Democratic party in down-ticket elections. Given the opportunity to cast
ballots in the absence of incumbents, voters chose the more politically
experienced, better funded candidates, who are largely Democrats"
(211).[7] Thus, if there are differences to be found among parties with regard to consultant influence, we would expect Republicans to benefit
more from professional assistance than Democrats.

The second hypothesis to be tested in this chapter also resembles one
from chapter 5 and deals with the number of consultant types hired: The
greater the number of types of consultants hired by an open seat candidate, the higher the percentage of the vote that candidate will receive.
Again, if party differences are to be found, Republicans should benefit
more from hiring additional consultant types than should Democrats.

Finally, my expectation from chapter 5 about the most influential
consultant types is posited here as well. For open seat candidates, pollsters should be the most influential consultants, followed by media and
voter contact specialists and then by generalists. There should be no
party differences as to which types of consultants are more influential for
a given party. Within specific consultant types, however, Republicans
may gain more from their use than will Democrats. In other words, poll-

sters should be the most influential type of consultant for both Republicans and Democrats, but Republicans may benefit more from their use than Democrats.

Results

The basic equation that was followed in chapter 5 will also be employed for the analyses here, with the addition of candidate quality measures for both candidates in the race. Table 6.1 indicates the results of an analysis of variance for a candidate's share of the vote. In this analysis, incumbency has been replaced by candidate quality, while party and the consultant variable remain in place. The report of the mean shares of the vote at the top of the table reveals a striking result. Whereas Democratic open seat candidates marginally increased their vote when they hired a consultant (from just under 53 percent to nearly 55 percent), their Republican counterparts were able to raise their share of the vote by more than 16 percentage points by using a professional operative (from 35.56 percent without one to 51.76 with a consultant). This may be preliminary evidence that the Republican disadvantage in House races will, indeed,

Table 6.1

Percent of the Vote for Open Seat Candidates by Quality, Party, and the Presence of a Political Consultant (Analysis of Variance)

		Political Consultant		Covariate:
		Yes	*No*	*General Spending (Logged)*
	Democrats	54.97	52.95	63.42***
		(*N*=99)	(*N*=19)	
	Republicans	51.76	35.56	
		(*N*=68)	(*N*=39)	
Main effects:	Quality			$F(1, 225) = 17.52$***
	Party			$F(1, 225) = 17.23$***
	Political Consultant			$F(1, 225) = 2.83$+
Interaction effects:	Quality × Party			$F(1, 225) = 3.97$*
	Quality × Consultant			$F(1, 225) = .202$
	Party × Consultant			$F(1, 225) = 10.34$***
	Quality × Party × Consultant			$F(1, 225) = .367$

Note: Entries in top half of table are mean percentages of the vote. This table includes only major party candidates, with the exception of Bernie Sanders (I-VT), who was counted as a Democrat.

+ $p < .10$, * $p < .05$, ** $p < .01$, *** $p < .001$.

mean that consultants have more of an impact in Republican campaigns than in Democratic ones.

Each of the main effects, namely, Quality, Party, and Political Consultant, produce significant differences in a candidate's vote total, although the consultant variable was significant only at the .10 level. Still, Democrats, candidates who held past elected office, and candidates with consultants were more successful than Republicans, candidates without elective experience, and candidates without professional help.[8] The finding for party is clearly due to the poor showing of Republicans who did not hire consultants. Their mean share of the vote was low enough to decrease the overall Republican mean to a point where it differed significantly from the overall Democratic mean. As for the consultant variable, the difference between the mean vote for Republicans with and without handlers, combined with the modest difference for Democrats who hired consultants and those who did not, was enough to produce a significant effect. The Republican influence on this effect may, however, be hiding an insignificant difference for Democrats.

With regard to interaction effects, the Quality x Party and the Party x Consultant two-way interactions were significant. Indeed, the significance of the latter interaction indicates that Democratic use of consultants may not have been significant on its own, while Republican use certainly was. There is also, apparently, some difference between the advantage Democrats derived from being quality candidates and that received by Republicans. In all likelihood, Republicans were helped more by having held previous elected office than were Democrats.

Many of the speculations drawn from the analysis of variance can be verified by multiple regression analysis. Table 6.2 reports the results from my simplest model. The dependent variable is the Republican open seat candidate's share of the vote. District partisanship had a highly significant influence on the vote. For each percentage point increase in the district's vote for Dukakis, Republicans lost .46 percent of a point. Thus, in districts where Dukakis got 50 percent of the vote, the Republican open seat candidate lost 24 points (with everything else held constant). On the other hand, I did not find a significant influence for the presidential election year.

In addition, candidates did not significantly benefit from having held past elected office. This finding is somewhat surprising given that prior research has revealed this factor to be of importance. Yet, in at least one case (Gaddie 1995a), district partisanship was not used as a control factor. In another (Jacobson 1990b), candidate spending was not included in the regression model. The results herein suggest that, when all the relevant variables are controlled for, we can be skeptical about the influence of candidate quality in open seat races.

Table 6.2
Model 4: Effect of Hiring a Consultant on a Candidate's Share of the Vote (OLS)

	Republican Open Seat Candidate		
	b	*(Beta)*	*α*
Year	.123	(.005)	.934
District Partisanship	−.461	(−.441)	**.000**
Democratic Quality	−1.496	(−.065)	.238
Republican Quality	.424	(.019)	.743
Democratic Spending[a]	−6.678	(−.205)	**.003**
Republican Spending[b]	6.422	(.318)	**.000**
Consultant hired by Democrat	−.386	(−.012)	.861
Consultant hired by Republican	4.927	(.211)	**.004**
Constant	66.015		
R^2	.756		
Adjusted R^2	.735		
N	103		

Note: Standardized betas are in parentheses. The constant represents the Republican open seat candidate's share of the vote when every variable is set to zero. To make reading the table easier, I have boldfaced the alphas ($α$) that reached a significance level of .100 or less.
[a] Log of the Democrat's general campaign expenditures.
[b] Log of the Republican's general campaign expenditures.

Spending by candidates of both parties does have a significant impact on their shares of the vote. In fact, spending helps the two parties' candidates nearly equally. Democrats gain 6.68 percent of the vote for each 1 percent increase in spending while Republicans increase their vote by 6.42 percent with a similar increase in spending.

Finally, and most important, only Republican open seat candidates are helped by hiring professional assistance. They gained nearly 5 percent of the vote by simply employing at least one political consultant. Democrats, on the other hand, did not benefit by using professional handlers. This is in keeping with Jacobson's assumption that candidates of parties that are disadvantaged will benefit more from certain factors than will those from parties not facing such disadvantages. If we believe Gaddie (1995a), the Republicans were at a disadvantage in open seat races from 1982 to 1992. Thus, they were more likely to gain from consultant use in 1990 and 1992 (the time period covered by my data) than were Democrats.

In all, almost 75 percent of the variance in the Republicans' share of the vote is explained by this model. More important, the results provide additional evidence that hiring a political consultant can significantly add to a candidate's share of the vote. This makes theoretical sense given what I have argued consultants actually do for candidates. But the findings are beginning to suggest that only certain types of candidates benefit from consultant use. Just as challengers, but not incumbents, gained votes when they hired consultants, only Republican open seat candidates seem to enjoy the fruits of consultant labor. This indicates that candidates at some sort of electoral disadvantage will benefit more from consultant use than will those not so disadvantaged.

Table 6.3 shows the results of the regression analysis for a second model of consultant influence in open seat races. Again, district partisanship is a significant influence on an open seat candidate's share of the vote. In this model, however, Democratic quality appears to matter. Democrats gained more than two percentage points when they had held prior elected office. Spending, of course, is still highly significant, although in this model Republican candidates gained a full point more than Democrats for each 1 percent increase in spending.

As for consultant influence, Democrats were again not helped by professional assistance; they did not significantly add to their vote total with each additional consultant type hired. Republicans, on the other hand, gained roughly a point at the polls for each handler they hired. A fully professionalized Republican open seat campaign would have run seven and a half points better than one without any professional help. Again, the entire model explained nearly three-quarters of the variance in a Republican open seat candidate's share of the vote.

The final model, the results of which are in table 6.4, examines the impact of specific consultant types on a candidate's vote total. Significant variables were district partisanship, prior elective experience for Democrats, and spending for candidates of both parties. The consultant variables, however, produced unexpected results. To begin with, pollsters were not helpful to either party's candidates. Yet the presence of voter contact specialists cost Democrats 2.7 percent of the vote. Indeed, this is a puzzling finding. Republican partisans might be tempted to argue that when Democrats effectively disseminated their message, which voter contact consultants helped them do, voters were less likely to vote for them.

An alternative explanation is that Democrats who used voter contact specialists faced turnout problems in their districts. In fact, voter contact consultants are often used to get out the vote. Thus, Democratic campaigns confronted with the potential for low turnout among their supporters may have relied on voter contact professionals to handle the

Table 6.3
*Model 5: Effect of the Number of Consultant Types Hired on a
Candidate's Share of the Vote (OLS)*

	Republican Open Seat Candidate		
	b	*(Beta)*	α
Year	−.239	(−.009)	.873
District Partisanship	−.451	(−.431)	**.000**
Democratic Quality	−2.341	(−.102)	**.062**
Republican Quality	.455	(.020)	.731
Democratic Spending[a]	−6.466	(−.198)	**.004**
Republican Spending[b]	7.633	(.378)	**.000**
No. of types of consultants hired by Democrat[c]	.152	(.017)	.790
No. of types of consultants hired by Republican[c]	1.084	(.143)	**.031**
Constant	59.538		
R^2	.747		
Adjusted R^2	.726		
N	103		

Note: Standardized betas are in parentheses. The constant represents the Republican open seat candidate's share of the vote when every variable is set to zero. To make reading the table easier, I have boldfaced the alphas (α) that reached a significance level of .100 or less.
[a] Log of the Democrat's general campaign expenditures.
[b] Log of the Republican's general campaign expenditures.
[c] Measured from 0 to 7.

situation. Consultant use for voter contact would therefore indicate turnout trouble. Unfortunately, it is virtually impossible to determine whether these consultants assisted in GOTV efforts, because my data source simply reported the use of persuasion and direct mail consultants by candidates (which I, in turn, combined to create the voter contact category).

Republicans, on the other hand, were helped by media specialists. By hiring professional media handlers, Republican open seat candidates gained 4.7 percent of the vote. The standardized beta of .192 for this variable makes it the fourth most influential factor in the model (behind Republican spending, district partisanship, and Democratic spending). These results for specific consultant types were not predicted by the

Table 6.4
Model 6: Effect of Different Consultant Types on a
Candidate's Share of the Vote (OLS)

	Republican Open Seat Candidate		
	b	(Beta)	α
Year	−.483	(−.018)	.740
District Partisanship	−.421	(−.403)	**.000**
Democratic Quality	−2.449	(−.106)	**.043**
Republican Quality	.417	(.018)	.746
Democratic Spending[a]	−7.650	(−.234)	**.001**
Republican Spending[b]	8.233	(.408)	**.000**
Consultant types (Democrat):			
Media specialist	−.107	(−.004)	.944
Pollster	.689	(.029)	.614
Voter contact[c]	2.698	(.114)	**.047**
Generalist	−2.511	(−.082)	.117
Consultant types (Republican):			
Media specialist	4.652	(.192)	**.001**
Pollster	.057	(.003)	.967
Voter contact[c]	−1.467	(−.048)	.388
Generalist	1.952	(.075)	.190
Constant	61.034		
R^2	.784		
Adjusted R^2	.750		
N	103		

Note: Standardized betas are in parentheses. The constant represents the Republican open seat candidate's share of the vote when every variable is set to zero. To make reading the table easier, I have boldfaced the alphas (α) that reached a significance level of .100 or less.
[a] Log of the Democrat's general campaign expenditures.
[b] Log of the Republican's general campaign expenditures.
[c] This category was created by combining persuasion mail and direct mail specialists.

theory of deliberate priming. This is cause for questioning whether the theory can hypothesize about the influence of the various consultant functions. Perhaps the theory only posits an influence for professionals in general as well as a cumulative consultant effect. General strategic planning, voter contact, message dissemination, and polling are all part of deliberate priming. To arrange the component parts in a hierarchy of influence is to disturb the complex interconnections at work in such a strategy. Thus, the findings for the third model in this chapter make it clear that no one consultant type can be singled out, a priori, as the most effective. Deliberate priming requires all consultant functions in roughly equal measure, or at least it allows for different functions to be more important at various stages in the campaign or in different campaign contexts.

Summary

This chapter revealed a number of important things about open seat elections. For one thing, district partisanship has a major impact on candidates' vote shares. In addition, the quality of the candidates was less significant than other studies have found it to be. In fact, in my most basic model, candidate quality was not significant at all. Models measuring consultant use in more detail revealed some influence of holding prior office, but only for Democrats. Not surprisingly, spending was a significant influence for both Democrats and Republicans.

Consultants were not found to have the universal influence that was assumed at the beginning of the chapter. Democrats were not helped by simple consultant use or by hiring additional consultant types. Republicans did significantly benefit from both varieties of consultant use. As for specific consultant types, Republicans were significantly helped by media handlers, whereas Democrats were hurt by hiring voter contact specialists. This effect is something of a mystery but may be the result of district circumstances (e.g., low turnout among Democratic supporters) of which hiring this type of consultant is simply an indication. The significance of media consultants for Republicans, however, is not in keeping with the expectation put forward earlier in this book.

These findings bring the influence of political consultants in House races into sharp focus. Political consultants do not help all nonincumbents. Instead, as research by Jacobson made clear for campaign spending, consultants help candidates who are in some way disadvantaged in their quest for office. Thus, as chapter 5 found, challengers have more to be gained by hiring consultants than do incumbents; and Republicans, hindered in a number of ways in open seat contests for 1990 and 1992, had more to gain than did Democrats. The latter result would be subject to revision as the electoral environment changes, which it seems to have done in 1994.

The next chapter will examine miscellaneous effects of consultants in House races. The goal is to determine whether or not consultants influence campaigns and elections in ways not measured by shares of the vote. As such, I will examine candidate success (defined as simply winning), fund-raising, campaign efficiency, and voter turnout.

· 7 ·

Other Types of Consultant Influence: Winning, Fund-Raising, Efficiency, and Turnout

The previous two chapters have examined the influence of professional political consultants on candidates' shares of the vote. I have found that candidates who are disadvantaged in some way, whether as challengers or as certain open seat candidates, benefit more from the use of consultants than candidates not faced with such disadvantages. Nevertheless, the evidence that consultants influence election results is considerable, if qualified.

In this chapter, I explore other potential influences of campaign operatives: While a candidate's share of the vote is an important measure of electoral performance, winning is the bottom line of serious bids for office; money's effect on elections is so great, especially for nonincumbents, that a candidate's ability to raise it may be the most important aspect of his/her campaign; given the aforementioned influence of money, spending it efficiently may be as essential as raising it in the first place; finally, voter turnout impacts election outcomes, and its level has serious implications for democracy. This chapter will examine whether or not consultants help candidates win, raise money, and spend campaign funds efficiently, as well as the extent to which consultants influence turnout levels. The intention is to explore each area briefly, but rigorously, in the hope that these initial findings will serve as a foundation for future research.

Winning and Losing

Few, if any, studies have specifically examined the factors affecting a candidate's chances of winning. Instead, political scientists simply assume that those things which add to a candidate's share of the vote also increase his/her chances of winning. Yet some variables may not significantly increase the probability that a candidate will win, even if they did significantly add to that candidate's vote total. Thus, we should also determine the extent to which given variables increase the odds that a candidate will win.

In analyzing the effect certain factors have on the probability of winning, I will use the same variables that made up the models of consultant influence on a candidate's share of the vote. The only difference is that the criterion (i.e., dependent) variable will be the dichotomous measure, Won/Lost.

To determine the impact that our independent variables have on the dichotomous dependent variable, it is necessary to use dichotomous logistic regression (DLR). DLR enables researchers to determine predicted EVENT probabilities and predicted ODDS (Lottes, Adler, and DeMaris 1996). The EVENT probabilities are simply the probabilities that the event (in this case, winning) will occur for each variable. Predicted ODDS are the change in the odds of the event occurring at each level of a given independent variable, all things being equal.

With regard to winning and losing, I expect that nonincumbent candidates who hire professional political consultants will have a significantly higher probability of winning than will those who do not hire such consultants. Again, we would assume that incumbents are so likely to win that hiring a consultant would not increase their chances of success. Yet nonincumbents should significantly increase the odds that they not only will gain more of the vote but will win the election when they hire a consultant.

An alternative hypothesis, dealing with open seat candidates, recognizes that candidates who start a campaign with some disadvantage will increase their odds of winning by hiring consultants whereas advantaged candidates will not (see the discussion in the previous chapter). Thus, for open seat candidates, Republicans should have a greater probability of winning when they hire consultants than should Democrats.

Table 7.1 displays the results from the logistic regression analyses of those races involving incumbents. The equation for Democratic challengers produced a significant result only for the Democratic spending variable. Both consulting variables were insignificant. Nevertheless, we can calculate the probability that the Democratic challenger will win, even if we cannot be confident that the results are not due to chance. To do so, we set the independent variables to hypothetical values and determine the predicted probability of winning when hiring a consultant. I have chosen to set the year to 0 (1990), district partisanship to 39.06 (the mean vote for Dukakis in the districts under analysis), challenger quality to 1 (held past elected office), Democratic spending to 4.6818 and

Table 7.1
Effect of Consultants on Challengers' Chances of Winning (DLR)

	Democratic Challenger			Republican Challenger		
	b	Exp(b)	α	b	Exp(b)	α
Year	−1.039	.354	.142	.580	1.785	.342
District Partisanship	.079	1.083	.136	−.054	.947	**.083**
Challenger Quality	.007	1.007	.994	−.084	.920	.881
Democratic Spending[a]	3.628	37.644	**.021**	.579	1.785	.660
Republican Spending[b]	−.354	.702	.881	3.500	33.099	**.001**
Democratic Consultant	8.112	3333.396	.802	−1.664	.189	**.048**
Republican Consultant[b]	7.261	1423.193	.915	.163	1.177	.809
Constant	−37.211			−20.977		
MODEL χ^2	51.936			45.761		
R^2 PSEUDO[c]	.201			.121		
−2 log likelihood$_{INITIAL}$	107.626			145.715		
R^2CAN[d]	.588			.398		
% correctly predicted	92.75			93.99		
N	207			333		

Note: To make reading the table easier, I have boldfaced the alphas (α) that reached a significance level of .100 or less.
[a] Log of the Democrat's general campaign expenditures.
[b] Log of the Republican's general campaign expenditures.
[c] R^2 PSEUDO = MODEL chi-square / $(N$ + MODEL chi-square$)$.
[d] Lottes, Adler, and DeMaris (1996) point out that R^2PSEUDO in DLR "tend(s) to be lower than analogous R^2s in OLS" (296). For that reason, Hagle and Mitchell (1992) suggest using an adjusted R^2PSEUDO. The corrected version, R^2CAN, is described by Lottes, Alder, and DeMaris (1996) in the following way: R^2CAN = R^2PSEUDO / $(-2$ log likelihood $_{INITIAL}/N$ + $[-2$ log likelihood$_{INITIAL}])$.

Republican spending to 5.4714 (the mean logs of Democratic and Republican general campaign expenditures), and the consultant variable to 1 for the Democrat (but 0 for the Republican incumbent). The predicted probability that the Democrat would win when hiring a consultant is .0000174.[1] When neither candidate hires a consultant, that probability drops to 5.2263–09. Obviously, the chances of a Democratic challenger winning are not good, whether they hire a consultant or not.

For Republican challengers, the prospects are not much better. Here, district partisanship and challenger (i.e., Republican) spending are significant, although the former has a negative effect on the challenger's chances of winning (as expected since here district partisanship is a measure of Democratic strength) and is only significant at the .10 level. Surprisingly, the "Democratic Consultant" variable is also significant. Thus, when the Democratic incumbent hired a consultant, the Republican challenger's chances of winning significantly declined.[2] As I did for Democrats, I determined the probability that Republican challengers will win when they hire consultants. Setting the year to 0 (1990), district partisanship to 50.37 (the mean vote for Dukakis in the districts under analysis), challenger quality to 1 (held past elected office), Democratic spending to 5.4401 and Republican spending to 4.7487 (the mean logs of Democratic and Republican general campaign expenditures), and the consultant variable to 1 for the Republican (but 0 for the Democratic incumbent) yields a predicted probability of Republican victory of .1471266. When neither candidate hires a consultant, the probability is only slightly lower at .1278261; but if only the Democratic incumbent has professional assistance, it drops to .0316359.

What explains the significant use of consultants by Democratic incumbents? The early 1990s can be seen, in retrospect, as the beginning of the end of Democratic control of the House. Alan Abramowitz (1995) suggests that party identification among the electorate shifted immediately following the 1980s. "Between 1990 and 1994," says Abramowitz, "there was a surge in Republican identification and a corresponding decline in Democratic identification" (887). In addition, "There was a substantial increase in conservative ideological identification between 1990 and 1994. Meanwhile, the Democratic party was perceived as increasingly liberal" (887). The result was a softening of support for Democrats, including incumbents. Yet by hiring consultants, according to my analysis, Democratic incumbents were able to protect themselves against possible defeat.

This explanation, however, seems to contradict the discussion in chapter 6 about the Republican Party's disadvantage in congressional elections before 1994. Yet the electoral environment should influence incumbents and nonincumbents differently, regardless of party, based at least in part on the resources they have at their disposal. Thus, it is perfectly reasonable to suggest that Democratic incumbents were losing the edge they had enjoyed over their opponents (for reasons Abramowitz identified) while Republican nonincumbents continued to face the disadvantages arrayed against them (for reasons Jacobson and Gaddie pointed out). Nevertheless, my findings suggest that consultants influenced both types of candidates, albeit in different ways—Democratic incumbents significantly bolstered the overall odds that they would win while Republican challengers gained more of the vote than they otherwise would have.

The results for challengers (of both parties) also seem to contradict the findings in the previous two chapters. There, I argued that challengers could add significantly to their shares of the vote by using consultants. But here, consultants do not make a dent in the probability that a challenger will win. To understand such disparate findings, one has to realize that most challengers begin their election bids so far behind the incumbent that gaining ground in terms of percentage points seems almost inevitable. But many start from so far behind that even a gain of 20 percentage points does not make them competitive candidates. Thus, the marginal boost in vote share that consultants can give challengers does not show up when the dependent variable becomes the chances of winning or losing.

The DLR results for open seat candidates can be found in table 7.2. The model uses the Republican open seat candidate's chances of winning as the dependent variable. Once again, district partisanship and both spending measures are significant. As for the consultant variables, I found that only the Republican candidate significantly increased his/her chances of winning by hiring a consultant. Indeed, Republicans who hired consultants increased their odds (Exp[b]) of winning by a factor of nearly 8.5 over those who did not. Furthermore, the probability of a Republican win increases from .0267458 when only the Democratic candidate hires a consultant to .7242676 when only the Republican does.[3]

To summarize the results for consultant impact on winning and losing, I find that professional consultants did not significantly increase challengers' chances of winning. Instead, according to the logistic regression results from this chapter, challengers can best help themselves by spending as much money as possible (and by running in districts that favor their party). The question of whether consultants can help candidates spend that money more wisely will be dealt with later in this chapter.

Democratic incumbents were helped by hiring consultants perhaps because they found themselves at some disadvantage in the 1990 and 1992 elections. With partisanship and ideology in the electorate moving in non-Democratic directions, Democratic incumbents may have delayed the seemingly inevitable loss of control of the House of Representatives by using professional campaign operatives.

As with consultant influence on vote share, only Republican open seat candidates significantly increased their chances of winning by hiring professional handlers. This is likely the result of the disadvantage faced by Republicans in open seat races before 1994. Of course, spending significantly increases the probability of winning for open seat candidates of both parties, as does district partisanship.

This section highlighted the difference between adding points to a candidate's vote total and winning an election. Even professional political consultants, with all the supposed magic they have at their disposal,

Table 7.2
Effect of Consultants on Open Seat Candidates' Chances of Winning (DLR)

	Republican Open Seat Candidate		
	b	*Exp(b)*	*α*
Year	.927	2.527	.176
District Partisanship	−.099	.905	**.020**
Democratic Quality	−.633	.531	.277
Republican Quality	.190	1.209	.764
Democratic Spending[a]	−2.432	.088	**.060**
Republican Spending[b]	2.227	9.270	**.055**
Democratic Consultant	−2.429	.088	.153
Republican Consultant[b]	2.131	8.423	**.025**
Constant	5.450		
MODEL χ^2	63.050		
R^2 PSEUDO[c]	.380		
−2 log likelihood$_{INITIAL}$	139.263		
R^2CAN[d]	.661		
% correctly predicted	78.64		
N	103		

Note: To make reading the table easier, I have highlighted the alphas (α) that reached a significance level of .100 or less.
[a] Log of the Democrat's general campaign expenditures.
[b] Log of the Republican's general campaign expenditures.
[c] R^2 PSEUDO = MODEL chi-square / (N + MODEL chi-square).
[d] Lottes, Adler, and DeMaris (1996) point out that R^2PSEUDO in DLR "tend(s) to be lower than analogous R^2s in OLS" (296). For that reason, Hagle and Mitchell (1992) suggest using an adjusted R^2PSEUDO. The corrected version, R^2CAN, is described by Lottes, Alder, and DeMaris (1996) in the following way: R^2CAN = R^2PSEUDO / (−2 log likelihood $_{INITIAL}$ / N + (−2 log likelihood $_{INITIAL}$)).

cannot help challengers overcome virtually predetermined electoral outcomes. But Republican, or more precisely disadvantaged, open seat candidates can increase the chances that they will win if they hire a consultant. That fact is of utmost importance in understanding the nature of political consulting in congressional elections.

Fund-raising

It has been widely established that nonincumbents need vast amounts of campaign cash if they are to mount serious bids for office. As a result, one of the most important tasks facing nonincumbents is fund-raising.

Many observers have noted that challengers have an easier time raising money when it appears that they have a decent chance of winning.[4] Few actually win, of course, but the perception that one is a competitive candidate makes a considerable difference. One of the best ways to appear to be a serious contender is to assemble a professional campaign team. Paul Herrnson (1995) notes that House challengers with professional campaigns (consultants and/or paid staff) are able to raise about four times as much party money as those with less professionalized efforts (143). Party money, in turn, makes candidates more attractive to donors because it signals, especially when given early in the cycle, the party's willingness to support the candidate throughout the campaign.

But professionals help in other ways as well. To begin with, the mere presence of a political consultant sends a message to potential contributors similar to the one sent by parties when they give assistance to candidates. This is especially true when the consultant has something of a reputation. Furthermore, consultants have the technical expertise to raise more money than amateur fund-raisers. Most consultants (whether fund-raising specialists or not) know how to put together PAC "kits" containing information intended not only to acquaint PACs with candidates but to convince them that the candidate is a good investment (see Sabato 1984, 113; Luntz 1988, 179–80). If candidates have a pollster on board and some relatively favorable early poll numbers, they are equipped with still more weapons to fight the fund-raising battle.

All of this means that the mere presence of a consultant should help candidates raise more money than they would without professional help. In addition, fund-raising consultants, whether event or mail specialists, should be particularly effective in bringing in funds for their clients. I will test both possibilities in this section.

With regard to the first proposition, Paul Herrnson (1992) examined the impact of using political consultants to attract party, PAC, and individual campaign contributions. Arguing that "[o]ne aspect of elections that affects fund-raising success that is under a candidate's control is the quality of his or her campaign organization,"[5] Herrnson used two-stage least square estimation (TSLS) to determine whether assembling a professional campaign helped candidates raise more money than if they relied on amateurs (859, 861). Using a survey of 385 candidates and their campaign managers from 1984, he found that professionalism helped nonincumbent candidates raise money from PACs and parties but not from individuals (863–66). Individuals, it seems, are not likely to be aware of the composition of a nonincumbent's (or, for that matter, any candidate's) campaign organization. PACs and parties, on the other hand, are quite aware of the caliber of any campaign team a candidate puts together.

The analyses in this section follow, in part, Herrnson's lead. My first expectation is that the more professional consultants a nonincumbent candidate hires, the more money that candidate should raise. By examining this claim, I intend to test the basic argument that a professional organization will attract more contributors than will an amateur effort. It will be examined in a number of ways, each of which will be explained below.

Another expectation to be examined herein puts fund-raising event and mail specialists to the test. If these consultants are effective, nonincumbent candidates who hire fund-raising consultants should raise significantly more money than those who do not hire fund-raisers. These consultants escaped scrutiny in chapters 5 and 6, but it is now time to see if they deliver what they are hired to deliver—namely, campaign funds.

Like Herrnson (1992), I used TSLS to analyze the influence of consultants on fund-raising in order to account for "reciprocal causality between the independent and dependent variables" (861n. 4).[6] Herrnson (1992) explored the impact of campaign professionalism on PAC, party, and individual contributions. I am more interested in determining how professionalism influences fund-raising generally, so I used total campaign receipts (measured in thousands) as the dependent variable. As did Herrnson, I used an index to measure campaign professionalism. The index ranges from 0 (no consultants employed) to 7 (consultants hired to provide seven services). An index can better approximate the real world influences on contributors than can a dichotomous measure of hiring or not hiring a consultant.[7] According to my expectations, professionalism should be positively related to fund-raising. I also used a measure of campaign competitiveness, although my variable differs slightly from Herrnson's.[8] In my model, competitiveness is measured as the absolute value of the Democrat's vote percentage minus the Republican's (i.e., the vote margin). Here, the expected relationship is negative (the lower the vote margin, the more money raised). Finally, Herrnson accounted for the partisanship of the candidate in his model. I did not do so, because I ran separate regressions for both parties' candidates. Thus, while Herrnson had three independent variables, I have only two.

The instrumental variables I used differ for each candidate type and will be discussed separately for each TSLS procedure. For incumbents, the instrumental variables were "district partisanship" (the district's vote for Dukakis in 1988), "last Democratic vote" (the district's vote for the Democratic candidate in the last congressional election), "challenger quality" (1 if he/she held prior office, 0 if he/she did not), "challenger's net receipts" (total receipts for the challenger, in thousands), "challenger hired a consultant" (1 if he/she did hire a consultant, 0 if he/she did not), and "coordinated expenditures on behalf of incumbent." Each of these variables is likely to influence the vote margin and/or the level of a candidate's campaign professionalism.

Table 7.3 reports the findings for all candidate types, including incumbents. Recall that I expect the level of professionalization to influence fund-raising only for nonincumbents. Yet, as one can see from this table, Democratic incumbents raise significantly more money for each additional consultant they bring on board. Indeed, they raise over $384,000 per consultant, on average. The competitiveness of the race, however, did not influence Democratic fund-raising. And, unlike their counterparts, Republican incumbents were not helped by professionals just as competitiveness did not seem to affect their fund-raising ability. The party difference is somewhat puzzling, but it may be explained by the Republicans' well-known ability to assist their candidates financially. Essentially, this means that Republican contributors, whether PACs, the party, or individuals, give equally to their incumbents regardless of how close the race or how professionalized the campaign. This is a reasonable conclusion for incumbents, who raise enormous amounts of money under any circumstances. That said, Democratic incumbents were still able to significantly increase the amount of money they raised when they elevated the level of professionalization in their campaigns.

For challengers, the instrumental variables I employed were "district partisanship," "last Democratic vote," and "challenger quality," as well as "challenger's PAC receipts" (total receipts from PACs), "challenger's party receipts" (total receipts from the party), and "incumbent hired a consultant" (1 if the incumbent hired a consultant, 0 if he/she did not). Again, these variables were used to estimate values for competitiveness and the level of professionalization.

The results for the challenger's TSLS are also shown in table 7.3. Here, both Democrats and Republicans benefited from an increased level of professionalization. As Democratic challengers' campaigns became more professional, they raised more money. In fact, for each additional consultant hired, they gained over $96,000. Republicans, on the other hand, gained over $325,000 per consultant hired.

Democratic challengers were also significantly helped by close races. For each point increase in the vote margin, Democrats lost $8,840. The vote margin did not have a significant impact on Republican fund-raising success. Again, the explanation most likely lies in the Republicans' superior ability to raise money. Notwithstanding the level of professionalization of their campaigns, all Republican challengers, those competitive and not so competitive, raised roughly equal amounts of money.

Table 7.3
*Effect of a Candidate's Campaign Professionalization Level on
Campaign Receipts (TSLS)*

	Democratic Candidate			Republican Candidate		
	b	(Beta)	α	b	(Beta)	α
Incumbents[a]						
Vote Margin	6.32	(.339)	.384	–7.65	(–.397)	.177
Professionalization	384.41	(1.550)	**.019**	89.65	(.427)	.281
Constant	–356.08			554.06		
Adj. R^2	.083			.153		
N	366			213		
Challengers[b]						
Vote Margin	–8.84	(–.617)	**.083**	.07	(.005)	.975
Professionalization	96.84	(.616)	**.024**	325.51	(1.332)	**.000**
Constant	287.60			8.93		
Adj. R^2	.546			.249		
N	181			300		
Open Seats[c]						
Vote Margin	–2.29	(–.094)	.588	–11.57	(–.272)	.191
Professionalization	254.26	(.918)	**.005**	25.07	(.059)	.810
Constant	10.90			631.72		
Adj. R^2	.094			.021		
N	80			80		

Note: Standardized betas are in parentheses. To make reading the table easier, I have bold-faced the alphas (α) that reached a significance level of .100 or less.

[a] The instruments used in this model were district partisanship, last Democratic vote, challenger quality, challenger's net receipts, challenger hired a consultant, and coordinated expenditures on behalf of incumbent.

[b] The instruments used in this model were district partisanship, last Democratic vote, challenger quality, challenger's PAC receipts, challenger's party receipts, and incumbent hired a consultant.

[c] The instruments used in this model were district partisanship, last Democratic vote, Democrat's quality, Republican's quality, Democrat's PAC receipts, Republican's PAC receipts, Democrat's party receipts, Republican's party receipts, opponent's total receipts, and opponent hired a consultant.

The model for open seat candidates adds a number of instruments. Along with "district partisanship" and "last Democratic vote" are "Democrat's quality," "Republican's quality," "Democrat's PAC receipts," "Republican's PAC receipts," "Democrat's party receipts," "Republican's party receipts," "opponent's total receipts," and "opponent hired a consultant."

With regard to open seat candidates (see table 7.3), only Democrats seem to benefit from increased levels of professionalization. With each additional political operative employed, Democrats were able to add over $254,000 to their campaign coffers. Neither party's candidates were able to increase their fund-raising by running close races.

It would be hard to compare these findings to those of Herrnson (1992), since he looked at the impact of professionalism on party, PAC, and individual contributions separately. Yet his basic conclusion that "campaign professionalism influences the resource allocations of political parties, PACs, and individuals, and increases the campaign receipts of congressional candidates" (866) was given qualified support in my analysis. The level of professionalization in a campaign influenced fund-raising for Democratic incumbents and open seat candidates and for challengers of both parties. This is more clear evidence of the positive impact of consultants on challengers' campaigns. My expectations, however, were not entirely confirmed. The findings for Democratic incumbents and Republican open seat candidates mean that professionalization does not solely influence nonincumbent fund-raising nor does it help all nonincumbents. Further research on this topic is needed to determine whether these findings are anomalies or evidence of some underlying pattern of fund-raising success.

It remains to be seen if fund-raising consultants, specifically, help candidates raise more money. Again, I expect that only nonincumbents will benefit from the use of fund-raising event and/or mail handlers. The instruments for the TSLS procedures for each of the three versions of the model are the same as those used to test the influence of the level of professionalization. Vote margin is again used to measure the competitiveness of the race; the level of professionalization index has been replaced by dichotomous variables for the use of fund-raising event consultants and fund-raising mail specialists.

Table 7.4 reports the effect of fund-raisers on candidates' campaign receipts, including incumbents. Whereas Democratic incumbents were helped by increasing the level of professionalization in their campaigns, they do not appear to benefit from hiring fund-raising consultants. Fund-raising event specialists were nearly significant at the lenient .10 level, but fund-raising mail consultants clearly had no influence on the amount of money raised. Republicans also did not benefit from hiring fund-raising consultants. They did, however, raise more money when they were in close races (a finding that differs from the level of professionalization model).

The results for challengers can also be found in table 7.4. As with the

Table 7.4
Effect of Fund-raising Specialists on a Candidate's
Campaign Receipts (TSLS)

	Democratic Candidate			Republican Candidate		
	b	(Beta)	α	b	(Beta)	α
Incumbents[a]						
Vote Margin	−5.08	(−.273)	.210	−13.45	(−.698)	**.000**
Fund-raising event consultant	1206.30	(1.773)	.129	−10.42	(−.019)	.978
Fund-raising mail consultant	−510.02	(−.327)	.742	593.96	(.486)	.632
Constant	258.11			837.01		
Adj. R^2	.043			.110		
N	366			213		
Challengers[b]						
Vote Margin	−17.96	(−1.253)	**.037**	−6.01	(−.447)	**.002**
Fund-raising event consultant	87.00	(.153)	.813	914.02	(.942)	**.001**
Fund-raising mail consultant	na	na	na	612.78	(.162)	.572
Constant	567.58			278.33		
Adj. R^2	.349			.172		
N	181			300		
Open Seats[c]						
Vote Margin	−4.87	(−.199)	.370	−14.51	(−.342)	**.097**
Fund-raising event consultant	875.51	(1.208)	**.020**	−170.10	(−.108)	.756
Fund-raising mail consultant	na	na	na	na	na	na
Constant	278.78			748.48		
Adj. R^2	.079			.019		
N	80			80		

Note: Standardized betas are in parentheses. To make reading the table easier, I have bold-faced the alphas (α) that reached a significance level of .100 or less.

[a] The instruments used in this model were district partisanship, last Democratic vote, challenger quality, challenger's net receipts, challenger hired a consultant, and coordinated expenditures on behalf of incumbent.

[b] The instruments used in this model were district partisanship, last Democratic vote, challenger quality, challenger's PAC receipts, challenger's party receipts, and incumbent hired a consultant.

[c] The instruments used in this model were district partisanship, last Democratic vote, Democrat's quality, Republican's quality, Democrat's PAC receipts, Republican's PAC receipts, Democrat's party receipts, Republican's party receipts, opponent's total receipts, and opponent hired a consultant.

previous model, Democratic challengers raised more money when they were in close races. Fund-raising event consultants did not, however, significantly help them increase campaign funds.[9] Republican fund-raising benefited from close races as well as from fund-raising event consultants. When Republican challengers hired professionals to handle their fund-raisers, they garnered, on average, over $900,000 more than if they had not employed them (all other things being equal). Of course, they also lost $6,000 for every additional point in the vote margin. Fund-raising mail consultants did not significantly add to Republican campaign receipts.

The final version of this fund-raising model is for open seat candidates (see table 7.4). As in the previous model, open seat Democrats were not helped by the closeness of the race. They did, however, significantly increase their campaign coffers when they hired a fund-raising event consultant.[10] In fact, they gained over $875,000 when doing so. Republican open seat candidates did not gain from hiring fund-raising specialists. They did, on the other hand, benefit from close races (although the vote margin variable was just barely significant at the .10 level).

Specific fund-raising consultants did not produce unequivocal results for their clients. My expectations about fund-raising consultants were confirmed to the extent that only nonincumbents raised significantly more money when using fund-raising (event) handlers. As was the case for the level of professionalization, however, not all nonincumbents benefited from such services. In fact, only Republican challengers and Democratic open seat candidates were able to raise more in campaign funds by using fund-raising professionals. Clearly, this area of consultant influence requires further research to determine whether these patterns would hold up over time and, if so, what explains them.

Efficiency

In chapter 2 I noted an argument about resource allocation that was put forward by Dan Nimmo (1970) in *The Political Persuaders*. He begins by pointing out the high cost of a professionally managed campaign (37–38). After citing some figures (c. 1968), Nimmo asserts, "Such fees appear exorbitant, but they may be a relatively small price to pay if they assure that the candidate's total resources will be allocated wisely" (38). More directly, he maintains that rational resource allocation is the *primary* task of the political consultant and adds, "A serious candidate desires to maximize his electoral strength through efficient expenditures of each resource. Through careful planning and attention to detail, the professional campaigners structure and control the campaign to the advantage of their client" (41). While other scholars have suggested such an influence, none have done so as clearly as Nimmo (see, e.g., Pitchell 1958, 279).

This section puts Nimmo's assertion to the test. Do professional political consultants make campaigns more efficient? Or are they inefficient, wasting more money than they save? From this point forward, I will operationalize campaign "efficiency" as a candidate's cost per vote ratio (total campaign expenditures/total votes received).[11] Hence, "cost per vote" will be the dependent variable in this section. Following Nimmo, I hypothesize that candidates who hire at least one professional political consultant will have a lower cost per vote ratio than will those candidates who do not hire a professional consultant. This expectation holds for both parties and all types of candidates (i.e., incumbents, challengers, and open seat candidates).

To put the "cost per vote" measure in some context, the median cost per vote, in dollars, for incumbents (in 1990 and 1992 combined) was 3.83, while it was 1.04 and 3.88 for challengers and open seat candidates, respectively. In all three cases, the mean cost per vote was significantly higher (according to t-tests) for those candidates who hired political consultants than it was for those without professional assistance. That fact runs counter to my expectations; that is, I assumed that consultant-run campaigns would be more efficient, in cost per vote terms, than would amateur campaigns. Of course, t-tests do not control for the amount of money spent by a candidate or the voting age population in a district, factors I will include in the regression analyses below.[12]

Also worth mentioning are the maximum cost per vote figures. Among incumbents, Robert Dornan (R-CA 46) spent $1,581,503 to get 55,659 votes in his 1992 reelection bid, making his cost per vote $28.41. William Koeppel's (R-NY 17) challenge of Ted Weiss in New York in 1990 cost $28.35 per vote ($431,513 for 15,219 votes). Finally, the highest cost per vote total for open seat candidates, as well as among all candidates in my data set, is Michael Huffington's (R-CA 22) $41.41 per vote in 1992. He spent a staggering $5,435,177 to get 131,242 votes. While these figures suggest campaign inefficiency, it should be noted that Dornan and Huffington won their races, and it is certainly not clear whether they could have done so with lower cost per vote ratios.[13]

I ran OLS regressions on the cost per vote using the voting age population and the general spending of both candidates as controls and the dichotomous variable for whether or not a candidate hired a political consultant as the predictor variable of interest.[14] The opponent's general spending is included to serve as an indicator of the total spending effort in the election. Simply using a combined measure of total spending by both candidates would have obscured the effort of the candidate whose cost per vote is under examination.

Table 7.5
Effect of Political Consultants on the Campaign Efficiency of Incumbents (OLS)

	Democratic Incumbent			Republican Incumbent		
	b	(Beta)	α	b	(Beta)	α
Voting Age Population	−5.25E–06	(−.064)	**.060**	1.75E-06	(.036)	.367
Democratic Spending	8.02E-06	(.742)	**.000**	2.41E-06	(.151)	**.002**
Republican Spending	9.73E-07	(.057)	.145	8.84E-06	(.740)	**.000**
Political Consultant	.580	(.065)	**.070**	−.181	(−.023)	.572
Constant	3.28			.137		
R²	.626			.689		
Adjusted R²	.622			.683		
N	334			208		

Note: The dependant variable is the candidate's cost per vote ratio (total campaign expenditures/total votes received). Standardized betas are in parentheses. To make reading the table easier, I have boldfaced the alphas (α) that reached a significance level of .100 or less.

In table 7.5, I report the findings for the regression analysis of the effect of consultants on incumbents' campaign efficiency. If Nimmo is correct, hiring a political consultant should significantly decrease a candidate's cost per vote. In fact, political consultants had no effect on Republican incumbents' efficiency and significantly increased Democrats' cost per vote. In other words, Democratic incumbents ran more *inefficient* races when they used consultants. It cost them 58 cents more, per voter, than it would have if they had not hired campaign handlers.

Among the other independent variables, the voting age population had a significant negative effect on Democratic incumbents' cost per vote. Democratic spending significantly raised the cost per vote for both parties' incumbents, while Republican spending affected only the efficiency of Republicans. The models explained 62 and 68 percent, respectively, of the variance in incumbents' cost per vote.

The results for challengers can be found in table 7.6. Here, professional consultants significantly added to the costs per vote of both Democrats and Republicans (but only at the .10 level). Democratic challengers spent, on average, 24 cents per vote more when they hired a consultant than when they did not. Consultants raised the cost per vote of Republicans by nearly 44 cents.

Spending for both parties' candidates proved to be a significant influence on challengers' cost per vote in both models. Voting age population had, once again, an effect on only Democrats' cost per vote. Finally, the

Table 7.6
Effect of Political Consultants on the Campaign Efficiency of Challengers (OLS)

	Democratic Challenger			Republican Challenger		
	b	(Beta)	α	b	(Beta)	α
Voting Age Population	−1.39E-06	(−.039)	.088	−2.80E-06	(−.041)	.230
Democratic Spending	1.04E-05	(.886)	**.000**	−7.32E-07	(−.081)	**.038**
Republican Spending	4.69E-07	(.053)	**.047**	1.13E-05	(.788)	**.000**
Political Consultant	.231	(.056)	**.072**	.439	(.070)	**.100**
Constant	.731			1.94		
R^2	.901			.624		
Adjusted R^2	.899			.620		
N	208			333		

Note: The dependant variable is the candidate's cost per vote ratio (total campaign expenditures/total votes received). Standardized betas are in parentheses. To make reading the table easier, I have boldfaced the alphas (α) that reached a significance level of .100 or less.

explained variance for the Republican model was similar to the models for incumbents at 62 percent. The Democratic model, however, explained nearly 90 percent of the variance in the cost per vote.

The last analysis of this section is reported in table 7.7. Political consultants had no significant effect on open seat candidates' cost per vote. The spending variables performed as they did in the incumbent model; Democratic spending significantly raised Democratic open seat candidates' cost per vote, while spending by candidates of both parties influenced Republican efficiency. Finally, the voting age population had an impact on Republicans' cost per vote but not Democrats'.

There may have been good reason to be skeptical of Nimmo's suggestion that professionally run campaigns are more efficient than amateur efforts even before the above analyses. Although it is possible that professional campaign handlers would allocate resources more rationally, and therefore more efficiently, than those without experience, the opposite assumption was equally reasonable. Indeed, my analyses suggest that consultants significantly *increase* the amount challengers, and some incumbents, spend per vote.

An alternative claim—that consultants drive up the costs of campaigns—was given limited support in this section. Perhaps consultants convince their clients to use cutting-edge, high-tech (and, consequently, expensive) techniques for reaching voters. Yet the pool of

CHAPTER 7

Table 7.7
*Effect of Political Consultants on the Campaign Efficiency of
Open Seat Candidates (OLS)*

	Democratic Open Seat			Republican Open Seat		
	b	*(Beta)*	*α*	*b*	*(Beta)*	*α*
Voting Age Population	–8.40E-06	(–.086)	.161	–1.46E-05	(–.129)	**.001**
Democratic Spending	1.28E-05	(.852)	**.000**	1.82E-06	(.104)	**.011**
Republican Spending	5.78E-07	(.079)	.186	7.71E-06	(.906)	**.000**
Political Consultant	–.931	(–.079)	.222	.020	(.002)	.960
Constant	3.40			6.76		
R^2	.669			.862		
Adjusted R^2	.656			.856		
N	103			103		

Note: The dependant variable is the candidate's cost per vote ratio (total campaign expenditures/total votes received). Standardized betas are in parentheses. To make reading the table easier, I have boldfaced the alphas (α) that reached a significance level of .100 or less.

potential voters in any one district is fairly static.[15] Therefore, if costs increase and the number of voters stays the same, the cost per vote will increase.[16]

I believe the cost per vote ratio is a good measure of campaign efficiency, although some may disagree. Until a better measure is created, the cost per vote allows us to analyze the impact of consultants on an aspect of campaign spending that can reasonably be considered efficiency. This section provides fairly solid support for the argument that consultants drive up the costs of elections and against the suggestion that professional political consultants provide efficient resource allocation.

Turnout

The final effect to be tested in this chapter is consultants' impact on voter turnout. I discussed turnout at length in the section on the "mobilization" function of campaigns in chapter 2. Here, I shall reiterate some important points.

Robert Jackson (1996b) notes that there are two categories of influences on voter turnout. One is the characteristics of the electorate and district in which an election is taking place. Examples of such sociodemographic factors would be the education and income levels of those living in the district, the population density in the district, and the size of the district's minority population (429–30). The other category is made up of campaign-specific characteristics, or campaign environment factors. Examples would be the total expenditures in the race, the presence and closeness of races at the top of the ballot (e.g., races for Senate or governor), and the competitiveness of the race in question (429–30).

In this study, I am interested only in factors from the campaign environment and will use only campaign-specific variables in determining whether or not consultants have an impact on turnout. As I noted in chapter 2, Jackson (1996b) suggests that campaign spending is the primary influence on turnout levels among campaign-specific factors (432).[17] Additional work has confirmed the effect of other campaign variables, such as the closeness of the race, party competition, and the presence of a Senate race, on turnout in House races (Silberman and Durden 1975; Dawson and Zinser 1976; Caldeira, Patterson and Markko 1985; Gilliam 1985; Crain, Leavens, and Abbot 1987; and Cox and Munger 1989).

The purpose of this section is to determine what impact political consultants have on the level of voter turnout in an election. The argument that they may have a negative effect is based on a number of claims. One is that consultants often purposely attempt to keep turnout low. This is thought to be typically done with negative advertising (Sabato 1981, 16; Ansolabehere and Iyengar 1995). The strategy is to lower the favorability of an opponent's supporters to such an extent that they will stay home on election day (if not vote for the attacking candidate). Recently "push polling" and other high-tech stealth tactics for smearing an opponent have been added to the consultant's arsenal. Push polls appear to be surveys of voters that tap their positions on major issues. But the wording of the polls is biased and, therefore, they are not scientific surveys intended to gather data but strategic instruments used to plant certain negative information about an opponent (Sabato and Simpson 1996, 245).

Consultants differentiate between negative advocacy calls (or what I have been calling "push polls"), which are not polls at all and are placed to tens of thousands of voters, and surveys that are asked of scientifically chosen random samples of voters and may contain legitimate "push questions" which help a candidate test elements of his/her message (Faucheux 1996; Bolger and McInturff 1996). An example of a valid "push question" (assuming it is truthful) would be, "If you knew that Candidate X opposes a balanced budget amendment, how would that affect your vote?" Thus, according to Ron Faucheux (1996), publisher and editor of *Campaigns and Elections*, "there is no such thing as a 'push poll'" because push polls are not polls at all and surveys gather information, not push it (5). Nevertheless, the media have used the concept of "push polling" to describe a practice that is seen as questionable by many voters. The result is that the device commonly known as a "push poll" adds to the general negativity of campaigns and, therefore (so the argument goes), to lower levels of turnout.

Of course, not all professionally run campaigns use push polls and/or negative advertising. Still, consultants have been charged with making campaigns homogeneous, ambiguous, and symbolic as well as with focusing on antiparticipatory aspects of campaigns, for example, advertising and fund-raising (see Petracca 1989). As such, consultants may be contributing to a shift "from direct personal involvement to spectatorship" (Mancini and Swanson 1996, 16; see also Edelman 1988; Bennett 1992; Zarefsky 1992; Gurevitch and Kavoori 1992; Hart 1994, 1996).

It is, therefore, a fairly common assertion that the use of political consultants in campaigns leads to, among other negative things, a decrease in turnout.[18] Where consultants are present, so the argument goes, campaigns are nasty, brutish, and long; as a result, voters are bored, or offended, to such an extent that they refuse to vote. As O'Shaughnessy (1990a) summarized the effect, "The growth of consultants is clearly related to a decline in public political involvement and an increased voter apathy" (13). Based on arguments like this, my expectations are that (a) those races in which at least one consultant is present will have significantly lower turnout than those where no consultants are used and (b) those races in which media consultants are present will have significantly lower turnout than those where no media consultants are used.

The dependent variable, turnout, is measured as the total votes cast in a district divided by the total voting age population. To control for other effects, I will use factors that have been found in previous research to influence turnout. Those factors are the absolute values of the vote margins in gubernatorial and/or senatorial races;[19] presidential or non-presidential election year (0 for 1990, 1 for 1992);[20] the base 10 log transformation of the total general spending of the two major party candidates in the House race; and the vote margin in the House race. The latter is a measure of the closeness of the race and is computed as the absolute value of the raw vote for the Democrat minus the raw vote for the Republican, divided by the total votes cast.[21] Each of the controls is expected to have a positive effect on turnout, except for the vote margin variables (for which the higher the value, the less competitive the race and, consequently, the lower the turnout).

The results of two OLS regression models of consultant influence on turnout can be found in table 7.8. The first model examines the simple presence of at least one consultant in an incumbent versus challenger race. The margins in both senatorial and gubernatorial races had a significant negative impact on turnout in House races. In other words, as the

Table 7.8
Effect of Political Consultants on Turnout (OLS)

	Incumbent v. Challenger			Open Seat		
	b	(Beta)	α	b	(Beta)	α
Senate margin	−4.03E-04	(−.092)	**.003**	6.87E-05	(.014)	.867
Governor margin	−5.86E-04	(−.103)	**.005**	−.002	(−.241)	**.024**
Closeness[a]	−.006	(−.007)	.827	−.007	(−.372)	**.000**
Presidential Year	.177	(.733)	**.000**	.147	(.526)	**.000**
Total Spending[b]	.030	(.087)	**.019**	.134	(.293)	**.002**
At least one consultant	.014	(.039)	.238	−.083	(−.164)	**.071**
Constant	.228			−.261		
R^2	.550			.381		
Adjusted R^2	.545			.343		
N	542			103		

Note: The dependant variable is the turnout level in a district (total votes cast/total voting age population). Standardized betas are in parentheses. To make reading the table easier, I have boldfaced the alphas (α) that reached a significance level of .100 or less.
[a] Closeness was measured as the absolute value of the Democrat's raw vote total minus the Republican's raw vote total divided by the total votes cast. See appendix C for more on closeness and turnout.
[b] Log of the combined expenditures of both candidates.

margin in those two top-of-the-ballot races widened, fewer people went to the polls. The variable with the largest effect was "Presidential Year." Turnout in House races was significantly greater in the presidential election year of 1992 than it was in the previous midterm election, as we would expect. In fact, the average level of turnout in House districts rose by nearly 18 points between 1990 and 1992. Total spending also had a significant positive effect on turnout. The more money spent by both candidates in a race, the higher the level of voting. Surprisingly, the closeness of the House race itself did not have an impact on turnout; while the coefficient is negative, as expected, it does not even approach significance. This presents less of a puzzle than we may at first realize, and I explain it in more detail in appendix C. As for consultant influence, this model finds no significant influence on turnout.

The second half of table 7.8 shows the results of the same model for open seat races. There are a few differences in the two types of races. In contests for open seats, the margin in a Senate race does not influence turnout. Yet close gubernatorial races continue to boost turnout in House elections. There is no theoretical reason to expect this outcome, so the cause must lie in the idiosyncrasies of the specific Senate races in 1990 and 1992. Adding additional years to the data set would address this possibility.

The presidential election year was again a highly significant positive influence on turnout. Total spending added significantly to voting levels as well. And, unlike in incumbent races, the closeness of open seat races had a significant negative impact on turnout. This means that the closer the race, the higher the percentage of voting age population that went to the polls. This is as we would expect. Finally, the presence of at least one consultant in a race did significantly decrease turnout. Unfortunately, only nine races for open seats did not involve at least one consultant. While this undoubtedly threatens the reliability of the findings, it suggests that further research, with additional data, may very well uncover an important pattern in turnout among voters in open seat House elections.[22]

I also ran regressions to determine if the use of media consultants affected turnout. After all, if mud-drenched negative ads decrease turnout, perhaps the presence of the men and women who produce such ads would have equally negative effects. Of course, it is not the presence of media consultants in and of themselves that would reduce turnout but what they do to the campaigns for which they work. In other words, media consultants may encourage a more negative atmosphere (in terms of campaign practices) than would otherwise exist. Therefore, the presence of media consultants acts as a proxy for negative campaigning. Frankly, there is little evidence to suggest that media consultants invite more negativity than other types of consultants. Still, popular commentary on negative campaigning often blames media consultants more than other consultant types for such activity (see Barnicle 1994). Thus, the following analysis is mostly a test of conventional wisdom.

The "media consultants" variable in this model is an ordinal one with 0 representing no media consultants in a race, 1 representing only one in the race (of either party), and 2 representing the use of media consultants by both candidates. I also used the nonconsultant variables found in the first set of models in this section. Table 7.9 reports the results for both incumbent and open seat races. The nonconsultant variables all functioned as they did previously. As for the media consultant variable, it was insignificant in both versions of this model. Thus, while the commercials they produce may cause turnout to decrease (again, see Ansolabehere and Iyengar 1995), the simple presence of media consultants does not appear to cause turnout to drop.

Table 7.9
Effect of Media Consultants on Turnout in House Races (OLS)

	Incumbent v. Challenger			Open Seat		
	b	(Beta)	α	b	(Beta)	α
Senate margin	−4.05E-04	(−.093)	**.003**	2.29E-04	(.047)	.578
Governor margin	−5.87	(−.103)	**.005**	−.002	(−.235)	**.028**
Closeness[a]	−.003	(−.004)	.915	−.007	(−.376)	**.000**
Presidential Year	.177	(.735)	**.000**	.151	(.540)	**.000**
Total Spending[b]	.030	(.087)	**.023**	.083	(.181)	**.048**
Total no. of media consultants[c]	.006	(.034)	.331	.021	(.120)	.178
Constant	.234			−.070		
R^2	.549			.372		
Adjusted R^2	.544			.333		
N	542			103		

Note: The dependent variable is the turnout level in a district (total votes cast/total voting age population). Standardized betas are in parentheses. To make reading the table easier, I have boldfaced the alphas (α) that reached a significance level of .100 or less.

[a] Closeness was measured as the absolute value of the Democrat's raw vote total minus the Republican's raw vote total divided by the total votes cast. See appendix C for more on closeness and turnout.

[b] Log of the combined expenditures of both candidates.

[c] The number of media consultants was computed by adding the media consultant variable for Democrats and Reublicans. This produced an ordinal variable with values of 0 (neither hired a media consultant), 1 (either the Democrat or Republican, but not both, hired a media consultant), and 2 (both candidates hired a media consultant).

Summary

I have attempted to investigate a broad range of potential consultant effects in this chapter. Although some of the hypotheses may have been based on flimsy theoretical grounds, originating, as a few of them did, in conventional wisdom, I wanted to cover as much of the possible range of consultant influences as I could.[23] Consequently, the analyses in this chapter are preliminary. I hope that does not mean, however, that they are less than rigorous.

In focusing on winning, fund-raising, efficiency, and turnout, I uncovered a few important consultant influences. With regard to the first, I found that, when employed by Democratic incumbents, consultants significantly decreased the chances that a Republican challenger would win.

This might be explained by the situation in which Democratic incumbents found themselves in 1990 and 1992. Some have argued (see Abramowitz 1995) that the Republican takeover of the House in 1994 was only a matter of time given the changes in party identification and ideology that began to appear between 1990 and 1994.[24] If this is the case and my findings are correct, Democratic political consultants may have saved some incumbents from what would otherwise have been upsets at the hands of Republican challengers in 1990 and 1992.

On the other hand, consultants significantly increased the likelihood that Republican open seat candidates would win. Just as money is more important to those at some disadvantage in an election, so too are consultants. There is some evidence that Republicans vying for open seats faced certain hurdles that remained in place even as the aforementioned shifts that should have advantaged them were occurring (see Gaddie 1995a). Thus, their use of consultants significantly increased their chances of winning in the first two elections of the 1990s.

As for fund-raising, I found that consultants significantly helped Democratic incumbents raise more money. Challengers of both parties and Democratic open seat candidates also pulled in many more contributions when they hired a consultant than when they did not. The lack of consultant influence for Republican open seat candidates appears to fly in the face of the earlier argument that Republicans were disadvantaged. Yet the argument was that Republicans were disadvantaged in largely nonfinancial ways (e.g., the quality of their candidacies). If there was one area in which Republicans were not disadvantaged, it was in campaign finance (Herrnson 1995, 147). Fund-raising specialists, I should note, did not significantly increase the campaign funds of candidates who hired them.

Campaign efficiency, defined as a candidate's cost per vote, was also affected by consultants. Democratic incumbents and both parties' challengers spent more per vote when they used consultants than when they did not. While some may argue that cost-per-vote is a poor measure of efficiency, these findings suggest that, at the very least, consultants often contribute to the rising costs of campaigns.

Finally, the use of consultants generally and media consultants specifically had little effect on turnout. Only in open seat races did the mere presence of consultants significantly decrease turnout. Of course, serious caution should be taken when interpreting these findings because only nine open seat races used no consultants whatsoever. Besides that single finding for turnout, it appears that consultants do not adversely affect participation in elections, at least not in any general sense.

That does not mean that consultants are good for the system or that they are not negative influences in other ways. Those possibilities are discussed in the final chapter. After a review of the findings herein, I will address the normative aspects of political consulting.

.8.

Conclusion

This study approached the subject of political consultants from both theoretical and empirical perspectives and thus could be read as consisting of two distinct parts. In the first part, I attempted to address concerns over the lack of a theoretical explanation for what consultants do. In the second, I tried to ascertain whether consultants actually influence the course of congressional elections. At first glance, the two parts may seem to be working toward separate goals. But my aim in addressing consultants from two perspectives was to answer two of the most basic questions about political professionals: What do they do, and how successful are they? From my point of view, these questions ought to be answered before less fundamental questions are asked.

On the other hand, I am not entirely willing to treat the two parts of this book as completely unrelated. While my empirical examination is not a direct test of the theory established herein, it is premised on an assumption that professional campaigns are different than amateur efforts. If one explores the possibility that consultants help candidates, the implicit argument is that they do something for those candidates that nonprofessionals do not. To test for influence without addressing what that something is leaves one open to the charge of methodologically putting the cart before the horse (i.e., of being atheoretical).

One final concern that is often voiced about consultants is the impact they have on democratic processes. After a brief review of the book's findings, I will offer a normative discussion of the implications of those findings and of the political consulting industry in general.

Summary of Findings

In chapter 2 I dealt with various barriers to the study of political consultants—as well as how I might overcome them, particularly with regard to data—and operationalized "political consultants." I also discussed the "proto-theory of consultant influence." To grossly oversimplify the proto-theory's conclusion, consultants influence elections because they are experts at political communication. There is little explanation given for what exactly consultants do or how it affects voters.

Thus, chapter 3 developed a theory of consultant influence called "deliberate priming." It combines insights from voting behavior (schema theory) and communication scholarship (semiotics) to suggest that consultants manipulate signs in order to prime voters. By producing campaign messages that focus on issues that are to their client's advantage (which is determined by polling), consultants can alter the criteria voters use to evaluate candidates. When voters actually use those issues, consultants' clients benefit greatly. The choice of signs as well as issues is crucial to this process.

Chapter 4 began the empirical part of the study. There I reported the level of consultant use by congressional candidates at length. For example, 45.6 percent of all House candidates hired a political consultant in 1990, and 62.6 percent did so in 1992. This vast upsurge in consultant use may be attributed to the uncertainty of the first election cycle after redistricting. In addition, I found that pollsters were the consultant type most used by congressional candidates. Finally, Democrats used consultants to a greater extent than Republicans did in both 1990 and 1992, and there was no difference in consultant use by male and female candidates.

The influence of consultants on candidates' shares of the vote is the subject of chapters 5 and 6. The analyses in chapter 5 produced clear evidence of a consultant effect for House challengers. Challengers were able to reduce the incumbents' share of the vote by between 2.8 and 3.6 percentage points when they hired at least one consultant. Furthermore, the use of additional consultants significantly added to the challenger's vote total. Finally, pollsters were the only consultant type to significantly help challengers reduce the incumbents' share of the vote.

In chapter 6, I attempted to determine the impact of consultants on open seat candidates' vote percentages. The results showed that Republican open seat candidates added significantly to their vote totals when they hired consultants while Democrats did not. Furthermore, Republicans gained votes with each additional consultant brought on board and Democrats did not. As for consultant types, Republicans ran more successful campaigns when they hired media consultants, while Democrats ran better with generalists. The explanation for these results lies in the fact that Republican nonincumbents faced a variety of electoral disadvantages before 1994.

Finally, chapter 7 addressed four other potential consultant influences: on candidates' chances of winning, on their fund-raising efforts, on campaign efficiency, and on turnout. With regard to the first of these, consultants significantly increased the chances that a Democratic incumbent would win.[1] This, I proposed, was due to the fact that Democrats began facing shifting tides of partisanship and ideology within the electorate in the early 1990s.

As for an effect on fund-raising, I found that a professionalized campaign helped Democratic incumbents and open seat candidates, and both parties' challengers, raise more money. Fund-raising specialists, on the other hand, had limited impact on the total campaign receipts of their clients. I also found that consultants significantly added, not reduced as some had suggested, the cost per vote of Democratic incumbents and both parties' challengers. They had no effect on the efficiency of open seat campaigns. Finally, consultants appeared not to decrease turnout in House elections. In only one model, when at least one consultant was used by either candidate in an open seat race, did consultants significantly reduce the level of participation by voters.

The results from the empirical part of this study offer some clear evidence of consultant influence in House elections (e.g., in challengers' campaigns). Other findings contained herein were not so clear and will require further research to tease out the patterns of influence (e.g., for consultant types in open seat races). Still other results dispelled myths and/or fears about consultant activity (e.g., that consultants depress turnout). One consequence of the findings taken as a whole is that a middle ground has been struck between those who hype consultants as campaign magicians and those who doubt that consultants have any discernible impact at all. In fact, consultants can help certain candidates in certain circumstances, but only at the margins. For those candidates in tough election battles, that marginal advantage may make the difference between winning and losing. Unfortunately, only a handful of congressional races are competitive in any given cycle, so the number of candidates who could even potentially benefit from the use of consultants is small.

While the results of this project may contribute something to our understanding of the consulting phenomenon (as does, I hope, the theory of deliberate priming), a normative evaluation of consultants remains in order. I conclude, therefore, with a brief discussion of the impact of consultants on democracy in the United States.

What Have Consultants Wrought?

Criticisms of campaigning, in general, have existed for at least 150 years in the United States. As Gil Troy (1996) has suggested, "Since the first truly popular presidential campaign in 1840, Americans have found campaigns too lengthy, too costly, too nasty, and too silly" (4). They have also looked suspiciously upon those who work "behind the scenes" in campaigns. Yet today, because a consultant hiring is often a newsworthy event, we know more about those running campaigns than we did in the days of the old "smoke-filled room." That does not prevent critics, however, from pinning most of the blame for the state of American politics on consultants.

Former *Boston Globe* columnist Mike Barnicle (1994) offers a particularly vivid condemnation:

> There is no lower form of life than these political consultants who make substantial sums preparing TV commercials that lower the public dialogue to food-chain level as they try to get us to respond to our darkest and most selfish emotions. . . . Politics has never been more despicable. It has been robbed of joy, life, spontaneity, fun, wit and original thought by a larcenous joint venture of consultants and candidates who use the media . . . to persuade us that nothing is any good and everyone is lousy so we might as well vote against something or someone rather than for an issue or an individual. (21)

Barnicle goes on to call consultants "greedy morons who employ the airwaves to lie, deceive, twist, maim and loot reality." His (tongue-in-cheek?) prescription is to ban consultants from working on campaigns. Aside from the practical difficulties of such a solution, it is based on unsubstantiated claims of consultant attempts to manipulate voters.[2]

From the perspective of the empirical theory I developed in chapter 3, consultants are less manipulative than descriptions like Barnicle's make them out to be. If the theory of deliberate priming approximates reality, consultants merely attempt to capitalize on those issues voters already think are important and on which their candidates have an advantage over the opponent. They rarely try to plant new issues in the minds of voters, and they never try to change the positions voters have already formed on issues. If voters think the environment and crime are the two most important issues in an election, it is a good bet that the Democrat will push environmental buttons while the Republican will talk about crime. That may be unsettling to those who wish candidates would do more leading than following. But it should give pause to those who think consultants "brainwash" voters.

This is not to say that candidates, sometimes at their consultants' urging, do not engage in negative campaigning. And this may often seem petty or even distasteful, as when opponents' past indiscretions are used against them. But voters are very good (in that, as V. O. Key said, they are not fools) at ignoring those things they find irrelevant and embracing those they deem important. When a given subject is not on the minds of the voters, it will only be placed there if voters are willing to consider it.

Before addressing specific criticisms leveled at consultants, I want to comment on two contradictory claims often made about campaign handlers in general: (1) that consultants make candidates too reliant on polls, which means that candidates' positions are subject to change with the whims of the electorate; and (2) that consultants manipulate the opinions of the voters, fashioning public opinion to meet the needs of the candidate. Consultants cannot, simultaneously and completely, do both. I maintain that consultants do combine elements of each approach but that the ramifications for democracy are not necessarily destructive.

Candidates do, indeed, rely on polls. The extent to which they do so, however, is often overstated. Few candidates will change a position on abortion, for example, to form a better fit with their constituency. The vote on the balanced budget amendment in 1995 is a good indication of this point. Many members of Congress voted against the measure even though they were up for reelection and majority opinion seemed to favor the amendment.[3] Yet there appears to me to be nothing inherently wrong, and there is arguably even something comforting, with candidates or elected officials taking positions that match their constituencies' on issues that the representatives either have no prior position on or do not feel strongly about.

On the other hand, candidates do attempt to discuss those issues that are most beneficial to their campaigns. They cannot talk about every issue under the sun. Therefore, they pick those on which they have an advantage in an election. Voters may rank the reform of welfare as their fifth most important issue, but if a candidate is at a disadvantage on the top four and advantaged by the fifth, he/she will emphasize welfare reform in the campaign. This is simply a matter of "putting one's best foot forward," not manipulation.

As Jacobs and Shapiro (1994) noted, a theory like deliberate priming is "consistent with a conception of liberal democracy in which political leaders both respond to and direct public opinion" (537). Indeed, the old debate between the delegate and trustee form of representation has been settled—all politicians are a mixture of the two, leading (i.e., being trustees) when they have strong opinions and/or their constituents have no position and following (i.e., being delegates) when they have no opinion and/or their constituents have a very strong opinion (see Ragsdale 1985). Thus, if deliberate priming is valid as a theory of consultant influence, neither the charge that consultants are too poll-oriented nor the charge that consultants manipulate voters is justified.

In and of itself, the manipulation indictment rests on two assumptions: (1) that there is a standard form of campaign behavior and (2) that there is a pure form of the voter's internal deliberation.[4] Both, it seems to me, are false.

The first holds either that candidates have fallen away from a previously high standard of campaigning due, in part, to consultant influence, or that candidates have never held to a very high standard and consultants make that fact no better. Those clinging to an ideal of the "golden age of campaigning" ought to be disabused of such a notion. Again, Gil Troy's (1996) marvelous study of presidential campaigning should do the trick. As he says, that golden age "never in fact existed. In 1988, the Kennedy-Nixon debates of 1960 were remembered fondly. In 1960, however, many Americans had found the debates disappointing, especially when judged against the mythic standard of the Lincoln-Douglas debates of a century before. That clash, however, had taken place during the 1858 *state legislature* campaign in Illinois; during his 1860 *presidential* campaign, Abraham Lincoln refused to say anything about any issues" (4).

But simply because the ideal campaign has never existed is no reason not to apply some standard to contemporary campaigns. The problem, as Troy asks, is "[w]hat . . . would constitute a 'good' campaign" (ix). Stanley Kelley Jr. (1960) devoted much effort to answering that question. Having assumed that "the discussion found in campaigns tends to impair the judgment of the electorate and to upset the formulation of coherent public policies" (2), Kelley set out to establish those elements of a campaign that would "help voters make rational voting decisions" (3). This assumption, that the primary purpose of campaigns is their "informing function," is hardly realistic. Candidates cannot be expected to campaign in ways that differ from how we all act in "everyday life." As Erving Goffman (1959) argued in *The Presentation of Self in Everyday Life,* "when an individual appears in the presence of others, there will usually be some reason for him to mobilize his activity so that it will convey an impression to others which it is in his interests to convey" (4). Thus a candidate, like each of us, is merely a "*performer,* a harried fabricator of impressions involved in the all-too-human task of staging a performance" (252).

Kelley, it seems, recognizes this social phenomenon. Because a campaign is an adversarial situation, "Each party to the proceeding can be expected to distort; to put its case in the best possible light and its opponent's in the worst" (Kelley 1960, 14). And still Kelley seeks to fashion campaigns after the rules of debate (17–22). This means that candidates must have equal access to the same audiences and equal abilities to disseminate their arguments to those audiences. To the extent that these two requirements "are not naturally present in the campaign situation, campaign discussion cannot be expected to assume a debate-like form" (21).

The rest of Kelley's book, then, is devoted to determining how to acquire the means for realizing the goal of an informed electorate.[5] His suggestions include reforming section 315 of the Federal Communications Act so that it applies only to major party candidates;[6] state subsidies for voters' pamphlets; extension of the franking privilege to all candidates; penalties for "false statements and last minute attacks"; "anti-smear legislation"; a more active media role in evaluating campaign communication and discouraging "the more flagrant distortions in campaign discussion";[7] and "citizen group action" against "undesirable practices" (Kelley 1960, 155–57).

Even if these measures could practically be enacted, it is not clear that they would raise the level of campaign activity in any noticeable way. Free television time, for example, might give major party candidates equal access to voters. Yet it says nothing about the substance of the statements that will be made during that time. Candidates would still be free to campaign with "emotionalism, sentimentality, distortion, and a poverty of ideas" (Kelley 1960, 17). Indeed, none of the above measures could prevent candidates from making such appeals. Furthermore, "false statements" and "smears" are notoriously hard to define. The complexity of any potential standard for campaign behavior is overwhelming to contemplate.

At root, the problem with establishing a standard form of campaign behavior is that, in a democracy, no one standard is likely to be agreed upon. Beyond this practical consideration, I find myself, with Troy (1996, ix), having difficulty determining what such a standard would look like *in theory*. Kelley addressed, by his own admission, only a fraction of the factors affecting campaign rationality (Kelley 1960, 147). I remain unconvinced that we can discover all such factors, let alone arrive at one ideal form of the campaign. Thus, to hold contemporary campaigns, and the consultants that run them, to a standard that does not exist, and perhaps cannot exist, is to waste reform efforts on an insoluble (because indefinable) problem.

That there is no standard of campaign behavior is not to say that "anything goes." Certainly, all types of illegal activity are condemned in the electoral arena. Campaign supporters would not, for example, be free to physically intimidate voters, because physical threats and battery are illegal per se. Furthermore, there are limits placed on what a candidate can do and say that result, largely, from the tastes of the media and the citizenry. The boundaries that constrain campaign behavior constitute no discernible criterion but rather a set of aesthetic intuitions.[8] Condemnation occurs when a given campaign activity offends a sufficient number of citizens (or members of the media). Voters are unlikely to be able to express a standard that is applied to electoral conduct; like pornography, we cannot define "bad" campaign behavior, but we know it when we see it.

The calculus of the aesthetic judgments that citizens pass on these matters consists of more than a preference for the pleasing over the offensive. Among those things that people consider when evaluating campaign activity are the professed values of their society and political culture. For example, because racism has become taboo in the United States, overt appeals to racial prejudice are met with disapprobation. The problem, of course, is arriving at a consensus on what constitutes "overt" racism. Thus, infamous political commercials like the 1988 Willie Horton ad or the 1990 Jesse Helms "White Hands" spot were roundly condemned by many as over the line but were considered by others to be within acceptable boundaries (see Jamieson 1992 and Mendelberg 1997).[9] The point, however, is that when campaign behavior challenges the fundamental values of enough people, candidates will be taken to task.[10]

We are now squarely within the realm of what Claudia Mills (1995) calls internal, or subjective, choice situations (97). These consist of those purely cognitive, or rational, considerations that are part of the decision-making process. Here, persuasion is used by one party to influence the choice that a second party makes. Those who find manipulation in campaigns assume, as noted above, that internal deliberation can be pure. To remain pure, one's internal deliberation can be affected by nothing short of Mills's "persuasive ideal," which is "influence that appeals only to the best reasons, broadly understood, for forming beliefs and desires, and so leading a person to a targeted conclusion" (100).

Mills's first step in explaining what is entailed by this ideal is to weaken it. Noting that advocates should not be morally required to offer *all the best* reasons for their positions (because they are allowed to put their position in an advantageous light and the best reasons are not always the most persuasive) nor *all the relevant* reasons (because it is "unreasonably time-consuming" to demand "complete comprehensiveness"), Mills argues that advocates are only obliged to provide *good* reasons (101–2). She then addresses the question of "what counts as a good or bad reason." Logical fallacies are bad reasons. Yet much more is needed if we are to have a guideline for detecting campaign manipulation (107).

Rather than undertake the impossible task of establishing a standard of good reason, however, Mills gives "a range of possibly problematic campaign strategies" (108). Some of these potentially problematic tactics turn out to be perfectly acceptable. Tailoring a message to one's audience, for example, is fine because "no politician can address every issue on every occasion, and it seems only appropriate to address a particular group on issues presumed of uppermost priority to it" (108). Other campaign practices depend upon the relevance of the statements made as part of those strategies. So the use of empty symbolism and appeals to emotion are acceptable if they are "centered on some particular real issue," whereas mudslinging, or character assassination, is tolerated as long as the issue (say, an opponent's extramarital affair) "does indeed provide a good and relevant reason for the electorate to vote against a candidate" (108–9). Fear-mongering is deemed "manipulative when the fear played upon is greatly exaggerated" (110). Of course, who is to judge when exaggeration has taken place? Besides, as Mills recognizes, "all of us have to push some button or other, appeal to some rational or emotional lever, to get others to do anything" (110).

Ultimately, Mills deems as unequivocally manipulative only racist appeals (and other forms of "hate-mongering") and lying. Of course, as mentioned above, racist appeals are rarely made today in such an overt way as to be seen by everyone as, indeed, racist.

Lying may even be more difficult to detect. Disagreement is at the heart of politics (Crick 1972). As Kenneth Minogue has argued (1996), political disagreement may arise from three quarters. In the first, the nature of the world is at issue. Since we have imperfect knowledge of that world, we disagree on "objective" reality. Second, our "subjective" perspectives, our "values and interests," often cloud our perceptions, causing disagreement based on our different "ways of looking at the world." But Minogue sees a third problem, "a split in human perception which is logically immune to resolution" (217). For him, many political problems take the form of the famous duck/rabbit perceptual puzzle. Viewed one way, the image is a duck; another perspective, however, transforms the image into a rabbit. The switch can occur even though nothing changes in the "objective facts" or in our "subjective positions." How does the perceptual shift take place? The answer lies in the process of perception itself. "We respond to *signs*," says Minogue, "and we respond to them as a continuous flow of experience" (222). Signs, in turn, are necessarily indeterminate. "It is as futile to try to ground signs in some ultimate and unambiguous reality as it is to ask the question: what lies behind a smile? Merely ganglia, of course, but for us a smile is a *sign* that a 'Person' (which is also a composition of signs) is 'pleased' or 'amused'" (223).

Minogue offers as a political example Margaret Thatcher's attempt to levy a "community charge" on all adults in Britain. Those opposed to the fee labeled it a "poll tax," which suggested that people were being taxed "for the mere fact of being human beings (or 'polls,' heads)" (224). In this country, we might take the example of abortion rights. Opponents call themselves "pro-life" and those on the other side of the issue "pro-abortion," whereas abortion rights advocates call themselves "pro-choice" and their opposites "anti-choice." Both refer to the same issue positions with different names. This perceptual paradox leads Minogue to answer the question of why "politicians so often say the opposite of what they clearly mean," by concluding that "we can, in one sense, validly see things differently, and even in contradictory ways" (226). Thus, "lying" in politics is not as clear as Mills wishes us to believe.

I hope this protracted discussion of manipulation sufficiently reveals the complexity of the issue. It is just too simplistic to claim that candidates and the consultants who "work the strings" are manipulative. Of course, such a charge sounds plausible. Consultants cannot be up to any good, say the critics, since they are interested only in winning elections for their clients. Yet, like the U.S. judicial system, American politics is adversarial. Contrary to popular belief, such a system has advantages over its alternatives (see Crick 1972). It naturally follows that consultants, like lawyers, should be committed only to being the best advocates they can be for their clients.

There are, however, more specific claims made against consultants than that they manipulate voters. While some of the accusations take the form of empty invectives like "consultants are merchandising candidates" or "consultants are nothing but sloganeers," others are more substantive. I now turn to an examination of the more serious claims made against professional campaign handlers.

Perhaps the most common assertion about consultants is that they have increased the negativism in politics (see Clark 1996).[11] As Sabato (1981) maintains, consultants' "marks have been detected on some of the more shameful modern acts of political deception" (322). Yet as he recognizes, negativity has been a permanent part of campaigning for nearly two centuries in the United States. Consultants were not the first to conceive of dirty politics.

A more serious claim is that consultants make negative appeals a standard part of elections. They institutionalize such behavior by taking such tactics with them to every campaign they handle. In other words, consultants make negative campaigning easy. But is it really the consultants who have done this, or is it technology? (See Delli Carpini 1996 for a good review and assessment of information technology and its use in campaigns.) The Internet, fax machines, and satellite dishes make instant and widespread dissemination of attacks feasible.[12] The ease with which a candidate can attack, and respond, leads to a cycle of charges and countercharges that appears to be never-ending. Whereas it used to take a week to make an accusation and get a reply, the process can now take place twice over in the passage of a day. While consultants may operate the machinery that makes this possible, they did not invent it.

Other critics lament what they see as poll-driven politics. The complaint is that "consultants make candidates 'too responsive to public opinion'" (Larry Sabato quoted in Clark 1996, 869). As Rosenbloom (1973) put it, "Leaders should lead" (163). In addressing this concern above, I maintained that campaigns, properly understood, provide a blend of leadership and responsiveness.

A related criticism of consultants, however, is that the reliance on polls and focus groups "militates against any careful, broad-based discussion of public concerns during an election campaign" (Levine 1994, 3). Levine explains it this way: "After they [consultants] have identified a divisive 'wedge issue' on which their candidate happens to agree with the majority, they often want to *prevent* any shift in public opinion. Thus they are adept at using rhetorical formulas that discourage reflection and discussion, that freeze public opinion in place, and that polarize and inflame voters" (3). Throughout this study I have discussed campaigns' unwillingness and inability to "convert" voters to positions other than those they originally held. The mythical campaign that seeks to educate voters, leading them in a quest for the "truth," has never existed. Furthermore, campaigns handled by consultants are no more likely to seize one or two issues on which they have an advantage than are those run by party leaders (see, for example, Budge and Farlie 1983).

Still another related allegation is that consultants, not candidates, set campaign agendas (Levine 1994, 2). Consultants, according to O'Shaughnessy (1990a), "have evolved from technicians to the choosers of issues" (12). And Petracca (1989) complains, "The use of consultants shifts the control of a campaign's agenda from the candidate to the consultant. This threatens the primary assumption of what elections mean as instruments of political choice, namely, that they represent the selection of elites by the mass electorate based on the authenticity of a candidate's stand on the issues" (13). Leaving aside what it would mean for candidates to take "authentic" stands on issues, let alone how voters would be able to determine what is and is not a sincere policy position, why is it any more threatening to democracy to have professional handlers set the agenda, in consultation with candidates, than it was for party elites to do it? Kelley's (1956) question about "what it means for our system of government to have political discussion increasingly monopolized by members of a restricted skill group" (38) could be posed to party leaders as easily as to consultants.

On the face of it, critics are saying that candidates should set the agenda. But if they are to do so independent of the public, then the same threat to democratic deliberation supposedly posed by consultants and party leaders applies to candidates as well. If, on the other hand, they are to follow the public's lead, we must revisit the criticism about an overreliance on polls. The fact of the matter is that most options for agenda-setting limit political choice in one way or another. Ideally, the public would set the agenda for candidates to address (see Schumpeter [1942] 1975 for an argument to the contrary). There are, of course, any number of obstacles to having the citizenry do so (although the theory of deliberate priming may offer a way out). It is this point, then, that raises a more serious issue for democratic governance.

Critics also decry consultants' use of symbols in campaigns, claiming that they rely on emotion rather than rational thought and produce ambiguity rather than clear choice. Sabato (1981) blames this, along with "the trivialization of politics," on direct mail consultants (329). Petracca (1989) claims that, as with negative campaigning, consultants increase (rather than introduce) symbolic activity in campaigns because "they make this standard practice and . . . it becomes institutionalized in the organization and running of the campaign" (13). I do not see, however, any evidence to suggest that campaigns are more symbolic (or negative) today than at other times in American history.

Another concern about consultants is that they have reduced the level of participation among citizens (Rosenbloom 1973, 160). This critique takes two forms. On the one hand, Levine (1994) and Petracca (1989) are concerned about the reduction in the numbers of volunteers who work on campaigns. Consultants emphasize activities, like fundraising, advertising, and polling, that do not require grass-roots assistance (Petracca 1989, 13). Admittedly, an active citizenry contributes to the health of a democracy, and there is evidence that the number of people volunteering for parties and/or candidates has decreased in recent years, as have all types of participation (see Rosenstone and Hansen 1993, 56–70). I am aware of no empirical evidence, however, that points to consultants and their activities as the culprit. Furthermore, I have yet to see a campaign where volunteers had nothing to do because all of the work that needed to be done required professional assistance. If volunteers are staying home, it has more to do with a general decline in civic engagement than in professionalized campaigning (on civic disengagement see Putnam 2000 and Skocpol and Fiorina 1999).

Others, like O'Shaughnessy (1990a, 13), blame consultants for a decrease in voter turnout. I dealt with this issue at some length in chapter 7. The results of my analyses suggest that consultants do not, in and of themselves, reduce turnout. It may well be that the products of consultant activities (e.g., advertisements) lead to lower levels of participation at the polls. Indeed, there is some experimental evidence to suggest this (see Ansolabehere and Iyengar 1995). Furthermore, consultants may have added to a cumulative effect that has reduced political participation in the system. If so, they are only a part of that effect, along with television, the "personalization of politics," the "detachment of parties from citizens," "autonomous structures of communication," and other elements of the modern campaign (Mancini and Swanson 1996, 14–17). The increased costs of campaigns are often attributed to consultants as well. Sabato (1981) claims that "political professionals have surely added to the spiral of campaign costs, not merely by charging exorbitant fees . . . but also by making enormously expensive technologies standard items in modern campaigns" (312–13). Evidence can be found in this study that gives qualified support to Sabato's claim. While more research is needed before we can paint a complete picture of consultant influence on campaign spending, I found that the presence of a consultant significantly increased the cost per vote of challengers (and Democratic incumbents). Open seat campaigns, however, were unaffected by the use of professional handlers.

The primary cause of the rise in spending is the cost of the technology employed in today's campaigns. Still, consultants, as Sabato rightly claims, are also to blame. Consultants apply expensive technology to the process while charging outrageous fees. As noted in the introduction to this study, nearly half of all campaign spending is filtered through consultants for production costs, media time, and other fees for services rendered (Fritz and Morris 1992, 45; Morris and Gamache 1994, 83). Given their paramount position with regard to campaign finance, some type of reform of the consulting industry would be in order. For example, consultants could be required to register with the Federal Election Commission and to report earnings from political work to the FEC. Election laws in West Virginia and San Francisco provide models for such reform.[13]

Sabato (1981, 1989) raises yet another complaint about the effects of consultant activity. "Consultants have also helped to homogenize American politics because the standard techniques that are used in media advertising, polling and so forth are taken to very different states and used in similar ways" (Sabato 1989, 16; see also Sabato 1981, 311–12; Clark 1996; Rosenbloom 1973, 167). But consultants deny using similar tactics in different states. Republican media consultants Winston Lord and Erik Potholm ("Lessons Learned" 1997) have argued, "One size definitely does not fit all. What works in Maine doesn't necessarily work in California, Louisiana, or Kansas" (18). Sabato (1981) would counter that "it is the medium of the message that is now standardized, that helps to shape the way politicians and people outside politics conceive of a campaign and what they expect from it" (312). The widespread use of certain techniques, however, does not mean that campaigns look and sound the same throughout the nation or that candidates in different regions are using identical messages.[14]

It is probably clear by now that I am skeptical of many of the charges made against consultants. One such charge, however, is warranted in my opinion. Gillian Peele (1982) writes that "the role of political consultants poses serious questions of accountability and control" (355). Indeed, accountability plays a central role in virtually all models of democracy, and elections are the primary medium through which public officials are held accountable to the citizenry (Held 1987). Yet consultants appear to escape accountability. They are responsible to their clients, who in turn must answer to the people, but such indirect accountability is weak at best. In fact, recent examples of consultant malfeasance prove that voters are unwilling (or, in some ways, unable) to hold candidates accountable for what their handlers do.[15] As a result, consultants are given a free hand to push the envelope of ethical campaign behavior.

Not only are political professionals unaccountable to the electorate, they may serve to restrict candidates' accountability as well. When consultants are caught stepping over the line, candidates are in the convenient position of being able to say, "I had no knowledge of my consultant's activities in this matter." It becomes very difficult for voters to assign blame in such situations because campaign chains of command are foreign to most citizens. Unfortunately, short of punishing candidates at the polls, there is no real answer for the lack of consultant accountability.

The list of consultant sins goes on, including their "vested interest in polarising politics" (O'Shaughnessy 1990, 11), their maintenance of the status quo by preferring to work for incumbents rather than challengers (Sabato 1981, 312), and their propensity to lengthen the campaign season (313). Again, I am doubtful that consultants are the prime suspects on many of these charges. Before I am made an apologist for the industry, however, I should point out that consultants have not fixed, nor are they in the process of fixing, the problems with our electoral system. In fact, consultants have actively sought to capitalize on the disorders that exist (e.g., the weakening party system, the pervasiveness of television, a corrupt campaign finance system, etc.). The arrival of political consultants on the political scene did not improve the system and may have even solidified its deficiencies. On the other hand, I think it unlikely that they have made it measurably worse.

Instead, I would maintain that consultants serve as intermediaries in a complex of media/cultural/political practices that often seem to have a life of their own. Political professionals have, more often than not, taken adaptations within this network and devised ways for candidates to deal with them. Thus, in place of permanent parties, consultants establish temporary organizations (Rosenbloom 1973, 160). Amidst the pomp of commercial media, campaign handlers produce pithy "spots" (Nimmo 1996, 40). And confronted with the paradoxical situation in which "a *flood* of information leaves a residue of *missing* information" (44), consultants appeal to the heuristic shortcuts that voters use in making decisions (Popkin 1994). Still, campaign operatives are often blamed for things that are largely out of their control.

Viewed as a whole, then, the impact of political consulting leaves us with many chicken-and-egg type questions. Did consultants weaken political parties, or did they merely fill a void left by parties that were damaged by other means? Do consultants simply respond to a "media logic" that developed independently, or is media coverage of campaigns shaped by consultant activity? Have political professionals created a cynical public by their "manipulative" ways, or do they just conform to cynicism that exists as a result of modernization and its attendant alienation? Definitive answers are nearly impossible to come by given the intricate interconnectedness of electoral systems and the larger social conditions within which they exist. As Swanson and Mancini (1996b) write, "In a democracy's electoral practices are found the influence and imprint of much that makes a culture as it is. Thus, electoral campaigns speak beyond themselves, and it is for this reason that significant changes in a democracy's electoral processes may reflect and portend related transformations in some of the institutions and relationships that shape nations" (247). The study of political consultants in terms of both their electoral impact and their role in modern democracy is, therefore, a subject that deserves a great deal more inquiry. I have attempted to provide some answers, however tenuous, and I can only hope that this project is something of a springboard into further exploration.

Coding Decisions for Questionable Cases

The following cases presented difficult coding decisions. For each, an explanation of the final decision is included.

In 1990, Dan Glickman (D-KS, 4) used ads that had been produced by Squire/Eskew for his 1988 campaign (Fritz and Morris 1992, 272). This was coded as having had professional help (i.e., a media consultant) in 1990.

In 1990, Jim Slattery (D-KS, 2) used Penn and Schoen to poll for a potential, but ultimately abandoned, gubernatorial race. I counted it as having used a pollster for his congressional race because they gave him information necessary to his run for Congress (not the least of which was that he should not run for governor). A similar decision was applied to Bill Richardson's (D-NM, 3) use of Peter D. Hart in 1990 for exploratory polls regarding a possible gubernatorial bid (Fritz and Morris 1992, 270, 375).

William Clinger's (R-PA, 23) $500 retainer in 1990 for the Wirthlin Group did not count as having had a pollster because it was not clear that he ever used their services (Fritz and Morris 1992, 476).

Jack Brooks (D-TX, 9) had one firm, Campaign Strategies, for both general consulting and persuasion mail in 1990. That was coded as having hired a consultant in each category. The same was done for Carlos Moorhead's (R-CA, 22) 1990 use of George Young for media and persuasion mail and Dick Chrysler's (R-MI, 8) use of Marketing Resource Group for polling and persuasion mail in 1992 (Fritz and Morris 1992, 503, 161; Morris and Gamache 1994, 345).

In 1992, Big Sky Consulting was counted as a pollster for Bob Filner (D-CA, 50), Luis Gutierrez (D-IL, 4), and Bob Carr (D-MI, 8), even though they did opposition research for these candidates (Morris and Gamache 1994, 212, 269, and 345). In fact, Big Sky Consulting was the only opposition firm in either year to qualify. Because, like polling, such research provides candidates with information upon which they can set strategy, polling was the most logical category in which to code such firms. Carr, I should note, also hired pollsters Greenberg-Lake and therefore would have been coded as having hired a pollster anyway.

Some work, done by consultants on behalf of a candidate, was paid for by the parties or an interest group. For example, in 1992 Michael Andrews (D-TX, 25) used political spots produced by Fenn and King that were paid for by the American Medical Association (Morris and Gamache 1994, 537). This did not count as having had a consultant in my data set.

Variable Descriptions and Data Sources

Variable	Abbreviation	Description
State	[State]	State codes correspond to a state's place in alphabetical order (e.g., Alabama is 01 and Wyoming is 50)
District	[Dis]	District codes correspond to actual district number
Year	[Year]	Last two digits in year
Midterm or Presidential Election Year	[Yearyear]	0 = 1990 (midterm); 1 = 1992 (presidential)
Party Identification[a]	[Party]	0 = Republican; 1 = Democrat; 2 = third party
Incumbency Status[a]	[Incumb]	0 = challenger; 1 = incumbent; 2 = open seat candidate
Hired a Professional Consultant[b]	[Procamp]	0 = did not hire a professional; 1 = hired a professional
Percentage of the Vote[c]	[Pervote]	Candidate's share of the total vote (in percentage points)
Candidate's Sex[d]	[Sex]	0 = male; 1 = female
Hired a Fund-raising Mail Consultant[b]	[Fdrmail]	0 = did not hire; 1 = did hire
Hired a Persuasion Mail Consultant[b]	[Permail]	0 = did not hire; 1 = did hire
Hired a Pollster[b]	[Polling]	0 = did not hire; 1 = did hire
Hired a Media Consultant[b]	[Media]	0 = did not hire; 1 = did hire
Hired a Fund-raising Consultant[b]	[Fndrsng]	0 = did not hire; 1 = did hire
Hired a Generalist[b]	[General]	0 = did not hire; 1 = did hire
Hired a Direct Mail Consultant[b]	[Dirmail]	0 = did not hire; 1 = did hire

Variable	Abbreviation	Description
Candidate Won or Lost	[Wonlost]	0 = lost; 1 = won
Candidate Quality[c]	[Quality]	0 = did not hold past elected office; 1 = held past elected office
District Vote for Dukakis[c]	[Dukavote]	District vote for Dukakis in 1988
Presidential Coattails[c]	[Prescoat]	0 = 1990; district vote for Clinton in 1992
Previous District Vote for Democrat[c]	[Lstdvot]	Percentage of the vote for the Democratic candidate for Congress in previous general election
Senate Race[c]	[Senrace]	0 = no Senate race in state; 1 = Senate race in state
Senate Margin[c]	[Senmarg]	Absolute value of the margin of victory in a Senate race (68 = no race)
Gubernatorial Race[c]	[Govrace]	0 = no gubernatorial race; 1 = gubernatorial race
Gubernatorial Margin[c]	[Govmarg]	Absolute value of the margin of victory in a race for governor (53 = no race for incumbent held House seats; 49 = no race for open House seat races)
Congressional Quarterly Election Preview[e]	[CQ]	0 = no clear favorite; 1/–1 = Leans D/R; 2/–2 = D/R Favored; 3/–3 = Safe D/R
Expenditures[c]	[Money]	Amount spent in dollars
Receipts[f]	[Receipts]	Amount raised in dollars
Spending on Overhead[g]	[Overhead]	Amount spent on campaign overhead in dollars
Spending on Fund-raising[g]	[Fundraze]	Amount spent on fundraising in dollars
Spending on Polling[g]	[Pollcash]	Amount spent on polling in dollars
Spending on Advertising[g]	[Advert]	Amount spent on advertising in dollars
Spending on Other Activities[g]	[Campact]	Amount spent on other campaign activities in dollars

Variable	Abbreviation	Description
Spending on Gifts and Entertainment[g]	[Giftsent]	Amount spent on gifts and entertainment in dollars
Donations to Other Campaigns[g]	[Donation]	Amount given to other campaigns in dollars
Unitemized Spending[g]	[Unitemiz]	Unitemized spending in dollars
Spending on Fund-raising Mail[g]	[Fdmlcsh]	Amount spent on fund-raising mail in dollars
Spending on Persuasion Mail[g]	[Prmlcash]	Amount spent on persuasion mail in dollars
Party Contributions[f]	[Partycon]	Party contributions to the campaign in dollars
Party Expenditures[f]	[Partyexp]	Party expenditures on behalf of the campaign in dollars
PAC Contributions[f]	[PACcon]	PAC contributions to the campaign in dollars
PAC Expenditures For[f]	[PACfor]	PAC expenditures on behalf of the campaign in dollars
PAC Expenditures Against[f]	[PACagain]	PAC expenditures against the campaign in dollars
Independent Expenditures For[f]	[Indepfor]	Independent expenditures on behalf of the campaign in dollars
Independent Expenditures Against[f]	[Indagain]	Independent expenditures against the campaign in dollars
Nonparty Communication Spending For[f]	[Commfor]	Nonparty communication spending on behalf of the campaign in dollars
Nonparty Communication Spending Against[f]	[Commagan]	Nonparty communication spending against the campaign in dollars
Candidate's Total Votes[c]	[Votes]	Total votes cast for a candidate
Voting Age Population[c]	[Votepop]	Voting age population in the district

Variable	Abbreviation	Description
Total Votes Cast[a]	[Votecast]	Total number of votes cast in the district

Sources:
[a] *Congressional Quarterly Almanac* (1990 and 1992)
[b] *Campaigns and Elections* (Beiler 1991 and Brown and Kruse 1993)
[c] *Almanac of American Politics* (1992 and 1994)
[d] Data provided by Paul Herrnson
[e] *Congressional Quarterly Weekly Report* (October 13, 1990, and October 24, 1992)
[f] *FEC Reports on Financial Activity, Final Report* (1989–90 and 1991–92)
[g] *Handbook of Campaign Spending* (1990 and 1992)

A Note on Alternative Measures of Closeness and Its Theoretical Impact on Turnout

Theoretically, the closer a race, the higher the turnout will be for that election. As Gary Cox (1988) points out, there are two distinct ways in which a close race will stimulate an increase in voting levels: one focuses on the voters' behavior and the other on the activities of elites (i.e., the campaigners). Some rational choice scholars have hypothesized and tested the postulate that a citizen decides to vote depending on "how close he thinks the election will be," among other things (Downs 1957, 274; see also Riker and Ordeshook 1968; Barzel and Silberberg 1973; and Silberman and Durden 1975). But this requires voters to know how close a race is and to think that their one vote might affect the outcome.

Ferejohn and Fiorina (1974, 528) offer a twist on Downs's rational voter. They suggest that rather than estimate, and attempt to maximize, the utility received from voting, voters seek to minimize their maximum regret. Such regret would be realized by (a) not voting and (b) seeing their preferred candidate lose by one vote. Or, as Ferejohn and Fiorina (1974, 535) put it, "If asked why he voted, a minimax regret decision maker might reply, 'My God, what if I didn't vote and my preferred candidate lost by one vote?'" Using the "minimax regret" assumption, then, the authors attempted to preserve the rationality of the decision to vote.[1] Of more relevance to our present purpose is the empirical finding of Ferejohn and Fiorina (1975) that the perceived closeness of a race is far less crucial to the decision to vote than is minimax regret. Thus, even within rational choice scholarship, the extent to which election closeness acts as a motivational force is uncertain.

The other perspective on turnout comes from those arguing that concerted effort on behalf of political elites draws people to the polls. In chapter 2, I cited many of the studies that find elite activity stimulating turnout. That activity is theoretically related to closeness because, as the argument goes, elites respond to close races by stepping up their get-out-the-vote efforts (see Key 1949).[2] In this way, closeness affects turnout even if it does not enter into a voter's decision-making process (Aldrich 1993, 268). Such increased effort is usually measured by total campaign spending. This may not be the only, or even the best, way to determine the level of mobilization efforts on the part of campaigns. Yet it continues to be used, most likely because it is the most available measure of campaign effort we have.

The difficulty in studying closeness and turnout is devising a way to measure an electoral margin. The most common operationalization is the percentage margin of victory (see Caldeira and Patterson 1982; Patterson and Caldeira 1983; Caldeira, Patterson, and Markko 1985; and Gray 1976, who uses the percentage vote margin subtracted from 100). Cox (1988), however, suggests that this measure has conceptual and methodological problems. Instead, he suggests using the raw vote margin of victory.[3] Those following this lead are Jackson (1996b) and, with some small variation on Cox's measure, Gilliam (1985—the difference in Democratic and Republican votes divided by the total two-party vote in absolute value), Barzel and Silberberg (1973), and Silberman and Durden (1975), both of whom use the ratio of votes for the winner to that of the total vote, and Cox and Munger (1989—raw votes for the winner minus those for the loser divided by the total votes cast).

One will recall that I measured closeness as the absolute value of the Democrat's raw vote total minus the Republican's raw vote total divided by the total votes cast. This is obviously adapted from Cox (1988), although it is most like Gilliam's (1985) variation. One may also remember that closeness was not a significant influence on turnout in my models for races involving incumbents. In fact, I used a variety of closeness measures, and none produced significant negative results for such races.

Before discussing those alternative measures, I want to speculate as to why I was unable to find the pattern most often found among students of turnout. To begin with, it may certainly be the case, as Ferejohn and Fiorina (1975) suggest, that closeness is not a significant motivational force for going to the polls. Furthermore, Cox and Munger (1989) maintain that with proper measures of elite activity, closeness would no longer produce significant results (229n. 17). And yet, virtually all of the alternative measures of closeness I used were positive, and some were significantly so. I would argue that this is an instance in political science research when social phenomena simply do not correspond with our theoretical assumptions. The races between incumbents and challengers in the congressional elections of 1990 and 1992 produced turnout levels that were higher when the margins of victory were higher. Table C.1 lists the mean turnout levels by seven ordinal groupings of raw vote margins. One can see that, with the exception of the two lowest categories of vote margins, the larger the victory, the higher the turnout. A one-way ANOVA confirms that the differences between categories is significant. Thus, for some inexplicable reason, turnout did not operate in 1990 and 1992 as it has been shown to do time and again.

One immediate response to such a situation is to argue, as Cox has, that the margin variable must be squared in order to control for the mathematical certainty that turnout will increase with the largest margins of victory. As he notes, "Simply regressing T [turnout] on m [raw

Table C.1
*Turnout Levels by Ordinal Groupings of Raw Vote Margins in
Incumbent Races (Analysis of Variance)*

Raw Vote Margins	Mean Turnout Level	N
0–25,000	.426	143
25,001–50,000	.407	200
50,001–75,000	.451	140
75,001–100,000	.510	100
100,001–125,000	.568	35
125,001–150,000	.572	12
150,001 and above	.587	4
Total	.450	634

Main effect of Vote Margin: $F_{(6, 627)} = 19.22^{***}$

$^{***} p < .001.$

Table C.2
*Models 1 and 2: Additional Models for Turnout in Incumbent House Races
Using Various Measures of Closeness (OLS)*

	Model #1			Model #2		
	b	(Beta)	α	b	(Beta)	α
Senate margin	–4.03E-04	(–.092)	**.003**	–4.07E-04	(–.093)	**.002**
Governor margin	–5.86E-04	(–.103)	**.005**	–5.82E-04	(–.102)	**.006**
Margin[a]	–.006	(–.007)	.827	.055	(.068)	.467
Margin^2				–.102	(–.078)	.390
Presidential Year	.177	(.733)	**.000**	.176	(.732)	**.000**
Total Spending	.030	(.087)	**.019**	.031	(.092)	**.014**
At least one consultant	.014	(.039)	.238	.013	(.036)	.275
Constant	.228			.213		
R^2	.550			.550		
Adjusted R^2	.545			.545		
N	542			542		

Note: The dependent variable is the turnout level in a district (total votes cast/total voting age population). Standardized betas are in parentheses. To make reading the table easier, I have boldfaced the alphas (α) that reached a significance level of .100 or less.
[a] "Margin" is the measure of closeness as the absolute value of the Democrat's raw vote total minus the Republican's divided by the total number of votes cast.

Table C.3
*Models 3 and 4: Additional Models for Turnout in Incumbent House Races
Using Various Measures of Closeness (OLS)*

	Model #3			Model #4		
	b	(Beta)	α	b	(Beta)	α
Senate margin	–4.04E-04	(–.093)	**.002**	–3.98E-04	(–.091)	**.002**
Governor margin	–4.71E-04	(–.083)	**.019**	–4.87E-04	(–.085)	**.016**
Raw Difference[a]	8.22E-07	(.223)	**.000**	5.28E-07	(.143)	.112
Raw Difference^2				2.30E-12	(.083)	.343
Presidential Year	.153	(.636)	**.000**	.153	(.637)	**.000**
Total Spending	.063	(.184)	**.000**	.061	(.179)	**.000**
At least one consultant	.010	(.027)	.388	.011	(.029)	.358
Constant	.012			.026		
R^2	.587			.588		
Adjusted R^2	.582			.582		
N	542			542		

Note: The dependent variable is the turnout level in a district (total votes cast/total voting age population). Standardized betas are in parentheses. To make reading the table easier, I have boldfaced the alphas (α) that reached a significance level of .100 or less.
[a] "Raw Difference" is the measure of closeness as the absolute value of the Democrat's raw vote total minus the Republican's.

vote margin] (plus any other variables of interest) does not make sense" (Cox 1988, 773). In the analysis I did for chapter 7, however, I did not square the closeness variable (following Gilliam 1985). Therefore, I reanalyzed the incumbent/challenger turnout model (found in table 7.8) to see if squaring the margin would make it significant (the original model is shown in table C.2 as model #1). As model #2 in table C.2 shows, squaring the margin did not produce a significant coefficient, and it reversed the signs for both closeness variables.[4]

Next, I used a raw difference measure of closeness that simply takes the absolute value of the Democrat's raw vote total minus the Republican's raw vote total. In model #3 of table C.3, the raw difference produces a significantly higher turnout as the margin increases. In model #4, both the raw difference variable and its square are insignificant and positive.

Finally, the measure that divides the absolute value of the raw vote margin by the total voting age population produced a significantly positive coefficient in model #5 of table C.4. The square of that measure in

Table C.4
*Models 5 and 6: Additional Models for Turnout in Incumbent House Races
Using Various Measures of Closeness (OLS)*

	Model #5			Model #6		
	b	(Beta)	α	b	(Beta)	α
Senate margin	–3.89E-04	(–.089)	**.002**	–3.83E-04	(–.088)	**.003**
Governor margin	–4.65E-04	(–.082)	**.019**	–4.79E-04	(–.084)	**.016**
Margin/Vote Pop.[a]	.393	(.251)	**.000**	.243	(.155)	**.087**
Margin/Vote Pop.^{2}				.503	(.100)	.257
Presidential Year	.151	(.625)	**.000**	.151	(.626)	**.000**
Total Spending	.068	(.199)	**.000**	.066	(.194)	**.000**
At least one consultant	.010	(.028)	.376	.011	(.030)	.334
Constant	–.022			–.005		
R^2	.596			.597		
Adjusted R^2	.592			.592		
N	542			542		

Note: The dependent variable is the turnout level in a district (total votes cast/total voting age population). Standardized betas are in parentheses. To make reading the table easier, I have boldfaced the alphas (α) that reached a significance level of .100 or less.
[a] "Margin/Vote Pop." is the measure of closeness as the absolute value of the Democrat's raw vote total minus the Republican's divided by the total voting age population.

model #6 did not change the significance or the sign of the unsquared variable but was insignificant (and positive) itself.

To reiterate, turnout seems to have increased in incumbent races in 1990 and 1992 as the margin of victory in those races increased. While this runs contrary to our expectations about turnout, we can only deal with the hand that the data dealt us. Try as I might to make that data conform, it would not. As a result, I remain skeptical that close races bring voters to the polls.

Potential Methodological Problems in Chapter 5

Multicollinearity, or a linear relationship between two or more independent variables (Kennedy 1992, 44), may be present in the three models of consultant influence in chapter 5 (as well as those in chapter 6). When two variables are collinear, it means that they are highly correlated with one another (Lewis-Beck 1992, 58; Corlett 1990, 158). In other words, collinear variables "provide very similar information, and it is difficult to separate out the effects of the individual variables" (Norusis 1994, 267). With regard to this analysis, one might suspect that campaign expenditures and the presence of a political consultant are collinear. Since consultants cost money, we might assume that the more a candidate spends, the more likely they are to hire a consultant. If this is true to a great extent, then there is a linear relationship between these two variables; in other words, they are collinear (Corlett 1990, 158). Hiring a consultant would simply serve as an indication that a candidate has a lot of money, something already accounted for with the expenditure variable.

The primary consequence of multicollinearity is that a hypothesis is accepted as valid when, in reality, it is not (i.e., Type I error; Corlett 1990, 158).[1] In order to test for such a condition, a number of things can be done. One option is to regress independent variables on one another and look for an R^2 approaching 1.0 (Lewis-Beck 1990, 60). Typically, anything at or above .90 is considered dangerous (DiLeonardi and Curtis 1992, 127). Another approach is to run the regression model and use either the tolerance measure or the variance inflation factor (VIF) to determine whether two variables are collinear (Norusis 1994, 267). Low tolerance or high VIF indicate collinearity (Norusis 1994, 268).

I ran each of these tests in order to determine whether campaign expenditures and consultant use were highly intercorrelated. Regressing expenditures on consultant use produced adjusted R^2s of .147 for Democratic incumbents and .345 for Republican challengers. For Democratic challengers and Republican incumbents, the results were adjusted R^2s of .483 and .080, respectively. As for tolerance and VIF, the complete model for those races involving Democratic incumbents produced tolerance levels of .733, .656, .560, and .536 for Democratic use of consultants, Republican use of consultants, Democratic spending, and Republican spending, respectively. VIFs for the same variables were 1.365, 1.524, 1.785, and 1.865. Results were similar for races involving Republican incumbents.[2] These findings clearly indicate that no collinearity exists between campaign expenditures and consultant use. The findings of these models and those in chapter 6 are therefore free of any bias resulting from multicollinearity.[3]

One other potential threat to the accuracy of my results is autocorrelation. This problem is a violation of the OLS assumption that error terms are uncorrelated. There are a number of causes of autocorrelation including misspecification of the model (Kennedy 1992, 119). Because no model of human behavior will ever include all and only those independent variables which are relevant in explaining the phenomenon in question, autocorrelation will always be present to some extent.

The risk of autocorrelation in my models comes from another source. I grouped data from 1990 and 1992 together, which means that some incumbents are included in my data set twice. Some may argue that including the same candidate in a data set more than once means that any such cases are not independent of each other. However, the regression analyses in chapter 5 are of *races*, not candidates. Thus, each case is fundamentally distinct. Yet it is true that the incumbent can be, and often is, the same for two races, thereby violating the assumption of complete independence.

To test for the possibility of autocorrelation, one can refer to the Durbin-Watson statistic for a regression model (Kennedy 1992, 121–23). A DW result of 2.0 indicates no autocorrelation (121). For the most basic model in chapter 5 (table 5.2) the DW results are 1.70 for the Democratic incumbent version and 1.79 for the Republican. This suggests the potential for autocorrelation. I ran separate regression analyses for 1990 and 1992 to determine whether this alteration would overcome the autocorrelation problem.[4] The DW statistics for the two versions were 1.77 and 2.02, respectively. While the 1992 version seems free of autocorrelation, the 1990 version performed no better than the versions found in model 1 of chapter 5. That result, I believe, suggests that the level of autocorrelation found in chapter 5 is due to a failure to include in the model all the relevant variables that influence a candidate's share of the vote. In other words, the problem lies in model specification.[5] I included, however, all of the variables that have been shown to have an impact on success in congressional elections. Until data and theoretical justification become available for variables not presently included in congressional election models, I will be content to rely on the model specification in chapter 5.

Notes

Chapter 1

1. As Fritz and Morris (1992) note, it is impossible to know exactly how much individual consultants earn because most consultants work in private firms that do not publish financial statements (45).

2. I am not the first to suggest that members of a campaign staff are resources. Leuthold (1968) had broadened the concept of a resource such that the candidate, her/his party, issues, nonpolitical groups (e.g., unions, businesses, etc.), money, and people were all included (2). According to this reasoning, having a consultant is like having any other resource, its value being determined by the use to which it is put and its effectiveness in that usage. Interestingly, Leuthold implies that there is mixed evidence for the worth of "professional campaign workers" (87–89).

3. The paradigms of campaigning that consultants develop are not rigidly applied. Indeed, innovation does occur (Hershey 1984, 60–66). Furthermore, while models in the strict sense of the term are not likely to be consciously recognized by consultants themselves, "implicit" models can be fashioned (see Boiney and Paletz 1991).

Chapter 2

1. This is especially true with regard to incumbents, for whom increased expenditures do not seem to produce more votes (Jacobson 1978, 1980, 1990a; Ansolabehere and Gerber 1994). The relatively complex dynamic of campaign spending will be discussed in chapter 5, as will the incumbency advantage.

2. In fact, one of the criticisms of the campaign spending literature, as Stephen Ansolabehere and Alan Gerber (1994, 1107) have pointed out, is that not all of a candidate's total expenditures are directly related to campaigning. See Ansolabehere and Gerber (1994) for an improved specification of the campaign spending model.

3. Actually, the C&E list does not account for all consultant activity because some consultants subcontract to other firms. Thus, the FEC reports will record payment from a candidate to, say, a general consulting firm. If that firm in turn hired a pollster for its client (and included the cost in its own bill to the client), the second transaction would not be picked up by the FEC. In other words, because only direct payment to a consultant resulted in that consultant's inclusion on C&E's scorecard, those doing subcontracted work for a candidate will not show up in this data set. It is difficult to estimate the extent to which subcontracting occurs, but there is little reason to believe that it is so widespread as to jeopardize the validity of the data set to be used in this study. Furthermore, C&E's follow-up calls may well have caught much of this undisclosed activity.

4. Dan Nimmo (1970, 40–41) suggests that "consultant personnel" are made up of "campaign consultants" and "technical specialists." The former "provide specialized advice for a fixed fee" and include issue experts who can assist in the development of position papers. Technical specialists, on the other hand, offer specific services like "canvassing precincts, designing and distributing direct mail, or preparing television

documentaries." The distinction between these two types of "consultant personnel" no longer seems to serve any valid purpose, and I will not separate the two. Nimmo's notion of consultant personnel and my definition of political consultants, then, are functionally equivalent.

Incidentally, consultants can be distinguished from other campaign operatives in that they are rarely present at a campaign on a day-to-day basis. Because they are involved in multiple races, consultants are constantly on the go, often being physically present at any campaign for only a couple of hours every few weeks. Given the technological advancement of contemporary campaigning, consultants are increasingly able to perform their trade without ever having met their client-candidates.

5. These services include, but are not limited to, media production and placement, direct mail development and production, polling and survey research, opposition research, public speaking and/or communication training, fund-raising (event, phone, and mail), telephone voter contact, press/public relations, computer services, Internet site design, software vending, voter and fund-raising list vending, news clipping and television monitoring, financial reporting, promotional products (e.g., buttons and yard signs), and legal services (Hess 1999, 249–309).

6. As Sabato (1981) points out, professional consultants differ from other paid staffers in that the former are part of a "small and elite corps of interstate political consultants who usually work on many campaigns simultaneously and have served hundreds of campaigns in their careers" (8). This definition is virtually synonymous with the operational definition of consultants that will be discussed below.

7. The American Association of Political Consultants (AAPC) formed in 1969 and established its code of professional ethics in 1975 (Sabato 1981, 45, 306). The code was updated in 1994 and approved by a unanimous vote of the membership. The code can be found at <www.theaapc.org/ethics.html>.

8. There are, however, a growing number of professional campaign "schools" that offer degrees in campaign management/consulting (see Schneier 1987; Hamilton 1997; Arterton 1997). By one count ("Inside Politics," 1996, 21–22), there are roughly forty-nine programs available to train political consultants. Of these, seven are linked to universities (for a list, see "Buyer's Guide," 1997, 55). Credentials from such programs, however, are not required to enter the field.

9. The information on consultant activity in statewide and congressional races came from C&E's "Consultant Scorecards" for 1990 and 1992 (Beiler 1991; Brown and Kruse 1993). Fritz and Morris (1992) and Morris and Gamache (1994) provided the *Handbook of Campaign Spending* data, and AAPC membership lists were found in Hess (1989, 1992).

10. Campaigns can also be waged on behalf of or in opposition to initiative and referenda measures. In fact, political consultants are often employed to assist the issue campaigns of interest groups (see Magleby and Patterson 1998a and 1998b). For instance, one consultant who specializes in ballot access petitions estimates that over 60 percent of signature gathering efforts to get initiatives on ballots are handled by professional consultants (Norquist, Woodward, and Arnold 1994, 35).

11. Keep in mind that in this section I am discussing the role of campaigns in elections, not the role of elections in the American political system (for the latter, see Pomper 1968). Thus, I will not specifically address the role of elections as democratic institutions, which hold incumbents accountable for their behavior in office, or as republican institutions, which serve as devices for selecting representatives in government (Schlozman and Verba 1987, 3; see also Burnham 1987). Of course, campaigns and elections are so closely tied to one another that it is often hard to distinguish them.

The legitimation function of campaigns and elections is a case in point (see discussion below).

12. Some have argued that legitimation occurs in instrumental as well as symbolic ways in campaigns. According to this line of reasoning, campaigns help determine the makeup of political leadership and are sites of "programmatic endorsement" where candidates make campaign promises and voters select those they prefer (Gronbeck 1978, 270). Such an argument presumes the potential for an electoral mandate. (On the various interpretations of the concept "mandate" and the perceptions of its existence after the 1984 presidential election, see Hershey 1994.) Mandates, however, have been challenged by a number of scholars (see Pomper 1968, 246–52; Dahl 1990).

13. In fairness to Downs and the "Columbia studies" (i.e., Lazarsfeld, Berelson, and Gaudet [1944] 1968; Berelson, Lazarsfeld, and McPhee 1954), the use of information shortcuts is not a new finding. The Columbia school, for example, emphasized the importance of political predispositions (religion, social status, and place of residence) and opinion leaders, both of which are shortcuts to information for the average voter. Similarly, Campbell et al.'s (1960) conclusion from *The American Voter* was that, in the absence of information about candidates and issues, voters rely on party identification to make decisions. While Campbell et al. would not agree, others, following Downs if not also the Columbia school, would consider the reliance on party identification as an information shortcut to be natural, acceptable, and, in its own way, entirely rational. This is especially true for those advocating the "responsible party" model of government in which party positions are clearly distinguishable and a party's candidates reflect those positions (see Schattschneider 1942; Committee on Political Parties 1950; Ranney 1962).

14. Candidates and their campaigns may also attempt to persuade "the media that one is a viable enough candidate to deserve attention" (Trent and Friedenberg 1995, 25). This aspect of persuasion takes place during the "surfacing" stage of an election (217–28; Trent 1978).

15. To be precise, social scientists began to have doubts about the potential of the classical democratic ideal in the 1920s. For a detailed treatment of this problem, see Purcell (1973), esp. chaps. 6 and 7.

16. This is not to say that the social influences school did not model *any* communication effects. Indeed, work on the two-step flow of communication model grew out of Lazarsfeld, Berelson, and Gaudet's ([1944] 1968) pioneering study. They had noted, after all, that "ideas often flow *from* radio and print *to* the opinion leaders and *from* them to the less active sections of the population" (151; emphasis in original). See also Katz and Lazarsfeld 1955; Lenart 1994.

17. Over the years there have been quite a few studies showing that campaign specific factors have an impact on election outcomes (see Ezra and Nelson 1995, 224–31; Holbrook 1994 and 1996). Often, such studies approach campaigns and elections from the perspective of candidate characteristics and not the voters' behavior. I have already mentioned the work on the incumbency advantage; other research in this vein focuses on "strategic politicians" (Jacobson and Kernell 1983; Bianco 1984; Born 1986; Jacobson 1989), "quality" candidates (Jacobson 1989; Abramowitz 1988; Krasno and Green 1988; Squire 1989, 1992; Maisel 1992), and money (see Squire 1995, 900–903, for a review of the literature on campaign spending in congressional elections; for a very thorough review of legislative election literature generally, see Ragsdale 1994).

18. Signs will be discussed in more detail below. For now, the reader unfamiliar with the technical meaning of the concept "sign" should treat it as a node of communication or, more crudely and less accurately, a message.

19. The campaign's message, or theme, should not be confused with its strategy,

which is the answer to the question "How will we (the campaign) win?" (Faucheux 1994, 47). Nor should strategy be confused with tactics, which are "devices (campaign appearances, dress, style of contact, dramaturgy) used to reinforce and reiterate the campaign theme" (Baer 1995, 51).

20. To illustrate the point, much of Bob Dole's trouble in the 1996 presidential election stemmed from his perceived lack of message or theme. One could argue that this was the result of the Dole campaign's emphasis on "three umbrella themes: 'reining in the federal government, reconnecting the government to our values, promoting American leadership abroad,'" rather than just one defining theme (Thomas 1996, 59). Conversely, Dole's apparent violation of the single-theme rule could be blamed on "his unwillingness to stay on message" (59, 63). Either way, the Dole campaign strayed from this piece of received opinion about campaign communications.

21. Bradshaw (1995, 44–45) provides a wonderful example of this using Barbara Boxer's 1992 Senate campaign.

22. Although Luntz (1988, 199–200) may be correct in suggesting that innovations in electioneering start at the state and congressional level and work their way up to presidential campaigns, they are generally not widespread at lower levels until their use is well enough established from above to reduce their costs below.

23. Gilliam (1985) lends support to both studies; he finds campaign spending and candidate competition to significantly increase turnout. Incidentally, Cox and Munger (1989) also found that the "closeness" of a race significantly influenced the level of turnout (the closer the race, the higher the turnout).

24. Many of the mobilization studies test the ability of party/campaign activity to influence vote preferences (Katz and Eldersveld 1961; Cutright 1963; Wolfinger 1963; Kramer 1970–71; Crotty 1971; Price and Lupfer 1973; Huckfeldt and Sprague 1992). The results are mixed, at best, with most of the evidence suggesting that canvassing has no significant influence on the vote. In the words of one study, mobilization efforts "need not waste much time talking about the glories of a particular candidate when the chief goal is to increase turnout in a favorable area" (Adams and Smith 1980, 394). Of course, as the authors point out, calls to largely undecided areas may produce some positive results. At present, however, it has not been shown that such a strategy would be effective.

25. Obviously, campaigns contact more than just activists, but they rely on such people to carry out indirect mobilization.

26. The reports referred to concern Ed Rollins's claim that the campaign of Republican Christine Todd Whitman, for which Rollins was chief consultant, spent $500,000 as "walking-around" or "street" money to keep voter turnout low in largely black areas (Berke 1993b). The assumption was that black voters are more likely to vote Democratic, and therefore would have cast votes for Whitman's opponent, Jim Florio. The Whitman campaign denied Rollins's claim (Gray 1993), but the original allegations caused considerable discussion (see Connolly et al. 1993).

27. Such a strategy may actually work. According to Ansolabehere and Iyengar (1995), positive advertising can bring voters back. "On average, positive advertising increased each of the participatory attitudes by approximately the same amount that negative advertising depressed them" (105).

It should also be noted that turnout levels are often irrelevant to election outcomes as a practical matter. In other words, in many districts, it is simply not clear which candidate would benefit from higher turnout levels and in those cases campaigns are likely to ignore the issue.

28. The list of journalistic accounts of political consulting is too long to list here in full, but it includes McGinniss (1969), Bloom (1973), Chagall (1981), and Blumenthal

(1982). For practitioner writing on the subject, see Baus and Ross (1968), Hiebert et al. (1971), Napolitan (1972), Shadegg (1972), Schwartz (1973), Gold (1977), Moore and Fraser (1977), Roper (1978), Greenfield (1980), Moore (1981, 1986), Beaudry and Schaeffer (1986), Armstrong (1988), Runkel (1989), Schwartzman (1989), Matalin and Carville (1994), and Morris (1997). Note that virtually all of the journalist/practitioner work focuses on presidential campaigning. This will be true for much of the scholarly work as well (see, e.g., Kelley 1956; McCubbins 1992; Newman 1994).

29. The consumer analogy (i.e., voter *qua* consumer) will appear throughout the literature on political consultants (see Newman 1994, who, while noting the differences between marketing and politics, continuously treats the two synonymously). While it is beyond the scope of this book to address the consequences of this analogy, the reader should be aware of its use and the fact that it dates to at least the 1950s (recall Adlai Stevenson's 1956 comment about merchandising candidates "like breakfast cereal" and George Ball's criticism of "hucksterism" in politics two years earlier). For a discussion, and experimental study, of the differences between political and commercial advertising, see Thorson, Christ, and Caywood (1991) as well as Bryant (1995, 88), who specifies eight differences between the two "disciplines."

30. Pitchell (1958) does distinguish between three types of people who make up the "political public relations industry" (280). The largest group consisted of professional campaign management firms, followed by the advertising and public relations people and a third group of miscellaneous professionals like lawyers, journalists, academics, and union leaders (282).

31. Nevertheless, Hershey (1974) notes, "The two styles of campaigning cannot be seen clearly in the attitudes and behavior of either the candidates or the managers" of the campaigns she studied (55). On uncertainty, see Downs 1957; Kingdon 1966; Hershey 1974; Kayden 1978; Ferejohn and Noll 1978.

32. It might be argued that nonprofessional campaigns can be as incremental as professionally handled ones. That point is well taken. I would simply maintain that nonprofessionally run campaigns, which are usually directed by the candidate him/ herself or a close associate, are more likely than professionalized campaigns to be comprehensive. That, however, is an empirical question that requires contemporary exploration of campaign decision making, a project beyond the scope of the present work.

33. Actually, Nimmo found campaign consulting in the late 1960s to have "assumed the trappings, but not the substance, of a profession" (1970, 65).

34. The argument that parties have declined, especially as electoral organizations, has been a debatable one. Much of the work proffering the "party decline thesis" was written in the 1970s and early 1980s (see Broder 1972; Ranney 1975; Burnham 1982; Crotty 1984; Ranney 1975; and Sabato 1981, 284–90 and 1983). With the exception of Pomper (1981), those who rejected the thesis did so from the perspective of the mid- to late 1980s and 1990s (see Price 1984; Schlesinger 1985; Kayden and Mahe 1985; Sabato 1988; Herrnson 1986, 1988, 1989, 1994; Herrnson, Patterson, and Pitney 1996). It was, in fact, clear by the late 1980s that the parties had rejuvenated themselves. Much of the challenge in doing so resulted from the ascendancy of political consultants. Parties reacted to this development, in part, by employing consultants to do party work (Herrnson 1988, 1994).

There are two ways parties might utilize consultants; they can either hire them as professional staff, or they can contract out to them on behalf of specific candidates. This new element in the parties' electoral arsenal, along with a few other types of assistance, have led some scholars to characterize today's renovated parties as "service" parties (Beck and Sorauf 1992, 467–69), "service vendors" (Arterton 1982), or brokers (Herrnson 1986).

35. In fact, *Campaigns and Elections* regularly runs "software buying guides" to inform consultants about costs and functions of new programs. Such programs handle direct mail lists, volunteer coordination, scheduling, financial filing, voter targeting, PAC solicitation, comprehensive campaign management, and, for the candidate who makes it into office, constituency service.

36. This, of course, greatly understates the extent to which interpersonal communication affects voters' perceptions (see Lenart 1994; Kinsey and Chaffee 1996).

37. That pleasure may be derived from the ability to talk about current events with others or from the competition of the election itself. Recall Schattschneider's (1960) argument that the "contagiousness of conflict" was *"the basic pattern of all politics"* (2, emphasis in original) because "[n]othing attracts a crowd as quickly as a fight" (1). Clem Whitaker's comments along these lines are worth quoting at length—

> [T]here are two ways you can interest [the average American] in a campaign, and only two that we have ever found successful.
>
> Most every American loves *contest*. He likes a good hot battle, with no punches pulled. He likes the clash of arms! *So you can interest him if you put on a fight!*
>
> No matter what you fight for, *fight for something*, in our business, and very soon the voters will be turning out to hear you, providing you make the fight interesting.
>
> Then, too, most every American likes to be entertained. He likes the movies; he likes mysteries; he likes fireworks and parades. He likes Jack Benney and Bob Hope and Joe E. Brown!
>
> So if you can't fight, PUT ON A SHOW! And if you put on a good show, Mr. and Mrs. America will turn out to see it. (Quoted in Kelley 1956, 50)

38. To illustrate the high-speed world of consulting, the American Association of Political Consultants held a roundtable discussion in January 1995 entitled "Real-Time Campaigning: The Accelerated World of Rapid Response." Broadcast on C-SPAN, the panel had two parts: the first issued a challenge to a number of consultants, the second revealed their responses (see C-SPAN 1995a and 1995b). The challenge was to respond to a hypothetical press release from the Republicans lauding the first 100 days of the 104th Congress and the success of the "Contract with America." Direct mail, radio, print, and television consultants from both parties were given the challenge at 10:00 A.M. and returned at 3:00 P.M. with completed products. Most had taken lunch breaks, and one, Ray Strother, was finished by noon (C-SPAN 1995b). As this simulation reveals, consultants can respond to any event (e.g., a press conference or an attack ad) so quickly that operatives now say they work "in real-time."

Another example of the high-speed capabilities of technology and the consultants who use it is a new system designed to track political advertising called POLARIS, which was developed and is being offered by National Media, Inc., and Competitive Media Reporting. The service "allows real-time tracking of advertising for political and issue efforts in 75 markets" by giving clients "complete television ad information including electronic story boards, reports on when and where the spot ran, as well as the demographic make-up of the target audience" ("Inside Politics" 1996a, 8).

Chapter 3

1. Iyengar and Kinder (1987) found that the agenda-setting effect from television news is stronger for those who have less education, are less partisan, and are not involved or interested in politics (59).

2. Despite what some of its more paranoid critics may believe, there is not a press conspiracy that dictates what will become news. Consequently, the media do not attempt to set the public's agenda for the benefit of one candidate over another. Instead, news selection is largely source-driven; in other words, the media's sources generate the news (Sigal 1973; Gans 1979; Hallin 1986; Bennett 1990; Soley 1992). In addition, to the extent that they are commercial entities and therefore in pursuit of profits, the media's selection of the news is a business decision. This commercialism may have more of an impact on the way in which the news is reported than on what gets considered news. Nevertheless, we often end up with sensationalism, politics-as-a-game (Patterson 1993), and/or "attack journalism" (Sabato 1991). What does not exist, however, is a plot to help some candidates and hurt others.

3. On the other hand, at least in terms of voters' perceptions of candidates, Conover and Feldman (1986) have argued that "cognitive consistency theory remains the most prominent approach" (129).

4. Hastie (1986) notes the problems in usage of the concept "schema." Indeed, he argues that, as of 1986, there was "no unitary theoretical entity that deserves the label *schema theory* extant in current information-processing psychology" (21; emphasis in original). I think by now the terms *schema* and *schema theory* are well enough established in political science to be used here meaningfully.

5. To the extent that voters infer information based on existing knowledge rather than gathering and verifying the missing pieces, they can be considered "cognitive misers." See Conover and Feldman (1986) for a detailed treatment of the role of inference in candidate evaluation.

6. In the 1994 midterm elections, some Republicans did use ADA scores to compare their opponents to Ted Kennedy, the symbolic archetype of an ultra-liberal. One reason that such a tactic is not used more often could be that members of Congress generally "fit" the ideology of their districts quite well (see Glazer and Robbins 1985). Interest group ratings would, presumably, make that clear. Thus, challengers are more likely to use a few roll call votes against a sitting member of Congress than they are to attack the representative's overall ideology.

7. Many of the examples in this chapter are taken from presidential elections. Although this book is about congressional campaigns, the presidential examples were chosen because they are well known and thus more illustrative of the concepts discussed herein.

8. Mendelberg (1997) argues the "Horton appeal was . . . about race rather than crime; it mobilized whites' racial prejudice, not their worries about crime" (151).

9. At this point, I should acknowledge that nonprofessionally run campaigns may also engage in the process of what I will call "deliberate priming." To the extent that they do, what follows is a theory of campaign behavior rather than consultant behavior. Of course, further empirical work (e.g., field research) is needed to determine whether or not amateur campaigners deliberately prime voters. For now, I maintain that the vast majority do not, while virtually all professional campaigners (i.e., political consultants) employ the deliberate priming strategy.

10. Salmore and Salmore (1989) claim, "The information that strategists need to determine appropriate campaign themes now comes from polls" (114). It is probably true that most information used in theme creation comes from polls, but one could argue that the focus groups now provide more essential information. Of course, Salmore and Salmore include focus groups as part of an overall "polling package" (115).

11. "Actants" are "referent [or central] nodes" around which various senses or propositions in a text (e.g., a television program) are organized (Biocca 1991a, 52). Well-known politicians, for example, are often the actants in a news story. Actants can play

many roles, of course (thus, "actant role"), and they often play more than one in any given situation, e.g., mother, businesswoman, candidate for Congress (54). Obviously, consultants must determine which actant role or roles are most advantageous to their clients, something with which focus groups can also help.

12. In terms of candidate positioning, Salmore and Salmore (1989) also note that a candidate's choice of themes must be credible, must fit his/her constituency, and must be more convincing than the opponent's (114). Thus, candidate status (i.e., incumbency status), the office sought, and national trends each affect the selection of a theme (126–35).

13. Of course, a candidate's image can also refer to the composite perception that exists among the entire electorate. This meaning of "image" is something like the sum total of all individually held candidate images.

14. It is likely that the visuals in Gantt's ad contributed greatly to signifying his support for education. Nevertheless, the text of the spot would be sufficient to prime voters on that issue.

15. To be fair, one participant noted that Gantt had "built schools," a reference, apparently, to a fact mentioned in the ad (Kern and Just 1994, 9).

16. Indeed, Helms attempted to prime some voters on just this issue with the use of a now infamous "quota" ad (a.k.a. "White Hands"). In the spot, "The camera comes up on a white worker's callused hands opening an official-looking letter. The announcer says: 'You needed that job, and you were the best qualified. But they had to give it to a racial minority. Is that really fair?'" (Diamond and Bates 1992, 329). Many credit the ad with giving Helms his victory (376).

17. I cannot emphasize enough that deliberate priming based on polling does not mean candidates adopt positions based on polls; it simply means that the issues candidates emphasize are likely to be determined from polling information (see Jacobs and Shapiro 1994, 529, for a concurring opinion).

18. A quick look at the American National Election Study from 1960 suggests that priming may not have had much of a measurable effect on the voters. Jacobs and Shapiro (1994) say that "the following types of issues" appeared in Kennedy's public statements as a result of polling data: "increasing Social Security, passing Medicare legislation, reforming education, fighting unemployment, combating the high cost of living, and such foreign policy issues as bolstering America's military spending and general prestige" (532). Yet when asked why they were going to vote for Kennedy, over 40 percent of the respondents to the NES survey did not give an answer. Of those who did, the leading response (at 7.8 percent) was that he was educated or intelligent. Only 3.8 percent of the respondents gave issue-specific answers to the question. Of these, the two leading answers were that Kennedy would protect or create social welfare programs (i.e., Social Security and Medicare; 1.1 percent of the sample) and that he would lower the cost of living (.6 percent). This does not seem like much support for the success of deliberate priming.

Of course, voters may not always recall why they intend to vote for a particular candidate. Indeed, on-line models of information processing would suggest that voters typically do not remember the bits of information that helped them assess candidates. Nevertheless, much more work in this area needs to be done before we can draw conclusions about the effectiveness of deliberate priming (see the discussion of Darrell West's work in the chapter).

19. Although West (1993) claims that Gantt was also successful in priming voters on the abortion issue, his data appear to indicate the opposite (see West's table on page 137).

20. Ads may also be aired for the benefit of the media. Consultants, especially in

larger races, know that the media will report on the campaign's ads either as a regular news story or as an Ad Watch feature (on the media's coverage of ads, see West 1993, chapter 4; and Jamieson 1992, chapters 5 and 6; on Ad Watches specifically, see West 1993, 67–73; Pfau and Louden 1994; Cappella and Jamieson 1994; McKinnon et al. 1996; Tedesco, McKinnon, and Kaid 1996; Ansolabehere and Iyengar 1996; and Jamieson and Cappella 1997). This is often how the intended meaning of a spot will be disseminated.

21. Kern (1989) also discusses the use of "the wheel of emotions" as a way to advertise with affect (see 30–32).

22. Fund-raising consultants are also important to a campaign's success, but their effect is indirect. They may use signs to raise money—it is said, for instance, that Ted Kennedy and Jesse Helms are the most effective bogeymen available to conservative and liberal fund-raisers, respectively—but they do not communicate in order to garner votes. Nevertheless, the fruits of their labor enable other consultants to do their work. As a result, I will hypothesize that fund-raising consultants (whether direct mail or event fund-raisers) will not have a significant, direct effect on candidates' shares of the vote but should influence the amount of money that a candidate raises.

Likewise, voter contact consultants, who often deal solely with get-out-the-vote efforts, would only have indirect influence on voters' decisions. If they combine their GOTV work with persuasive appeals (e.g., through phone banks), their influence would then be hypothesized as direct.

23. Kaid, Downs, and Ragan (1990) offer an experimental study of the Bush-Rather encounter and the audience expectations of and reactions to it.

Chapter 4

1. In actuality, the Corrupt Practices Act of 1925 first required candidates to disclose their campaign finances, but the legislation was sufficiently ambiguous to enable candidates to avoid even the most minimal filing (Magleby and Nelson 1990, 13–14). It would be four years after the passage of the 1974 FECA amendments before the Federal Election Commission was able to fully report the financial activities of candidates for Congress (Sorauf 1992, 248n. 10).

2. In a number of specific cases it was unclear whether professional services should be considered rendered. See appendix A for the coding decisions in these cases.

3. See appendix B for a variable list, coding information, and data sources.

4. Interest group and party spending on behalf of candidates were, however, included as campaign spending variables in the data set. See text for a discussion of the relevant variables.

5. In 1975, Louisiana adopted a nonpartisan primary that allowed candidates of all parties to run for office against one another. If one candidate received more than 50 percent of the vote, that candidate would be unopposed in the general election. If, on the other hand, no candidate received the obligatory 50 percent, the top two contenders would "run-off" against each other in the general election. This system was applied to congressional candidates (both House and Senate) in 1978 (*Congressional Quarterly's Guide to U.S. Elections* 1985, 1068–69).

6. Presidential campaigns, however, were using professional consultants to a much greater extent. Between 1952 and 1957, Heard (1960) notes that partial services were performed by twenty-two firms for twenty-seven presidential nomination campaigns and by twenty-eight firms for forty-three general election efforts, including various state efforts for a single candidate. Total campaign management was rendered by five firms for nine campaigns (417). Given the fact that only two presidential contests

were held between 1952 and 1957, these figures represent extensive activity by consultants in presidential politics.

7. Huckshorn and Spencer (1971) found little difference between the parties with regard to the number of professional campaign managers hired (99).

8. When 1990 and 1992 data are combined, there is no significant difference between the level of consultant use by incumbents and open seat candidates (χ^2 = 2.413, df = 1, p = .120). The same holds for 1990 separately (χ^2 = 2.133, df = 1, p = .144). In 1992, however, the difference was significant (χ^2 = 22.128, df = 1, p = .000). In other words, significantly fewer open seat candidates hired consultants in 1992 than did incumbents, a pattern that was not found in 1990.

9. Fenno (1978, 35–36) argues, however, that the number of trips an incumbent makes back to his/her district does not increase with vulnerability.

10. For another view of the generally paradoxical nature of congressional campaigns, see Fishel (1973, 6–8).

11. Challengers may also face the bias that many consultants have of working solely for incumbents (Sabato 1981, 18; Luntz 1988, 53). This is largely because consultants are concerned about won-lost records, but it is also based on the fact that "[f]or the most part, incumbents have a clearer idea than challengers of the message they wish to convey, better general knowledge of the important issues in the campaign, far greater fund-raising ability, and an understanding of what it takes to win an election" (Luntz 1988, 53).

12. Tables summarizing the data discussed in the following paragraphs can be obtained from the author.

13. I should note that, at least at this point, I am not making causal claims about the impact of hiring a consultant on winning and losing. I am simply reporting the level of association between the two variables.

14. Some have argued, for example, that physical appearance plays a role in a candidate's ability to compete effectively for office (see Rosenberg et al. 1986). Of course, measuring physical attractiveness for more than eight hundred House candidates per election cycle would prove impossible. More commonly cited characteristics of a quality candidate include general campaign skills (Squire 1992), celebrity status (Krasno and Green 1988; Green and Krasno 1988; Abramowitz 1988), ambition (Canon 1990, 1993), and personal wealth (Wilcox 1988). See Squire (1995, 893–97) for a complete discussion of this issue.

15. The information used to determine whether or not a candidate had held elected office was found in *Congressional Quarterly*'s list of candidates for 1990 and 1992 ("1990 Candidates for Senate and House" 1990, 3359–71; "Candidates for Governor, Senate, House" 1992, 3415–30).

16. The assumption that politicians believe consultants are essential for a credible campaign is a safe one (see Sabato 1981, 4; Blumenthal 1982, 19; Luntz 1988, 42–50).

17. Even with such an advantage for quality nonincumbents, Herrnson (1995) argues, "The organizational advantages that incumbents possess over challengers are usually greater than those advantages that experienced nonincumbents have over political amateurs" (64). That should put the value of the incumbency advantage into proper perspective.

18. Witt, Paget, and Matthews (1994) show that, in actuality, "Year of the Woman" had been used in numerous elections before 1992, including 1990 (2, 6–7), and was first applied to the 1974 election cycle (285n. 2).

19. It should be noted that the "practical" literature (i.e., articles written for the consulting trade magazines by the industry's practitioners) on women's campaigns assumes differences in the obstacles women face and the issues they advocate and it ad-

vises accordingly (see Lake 1995, 23–24, 69; Fitzpatrick 1995, 25–26, 59; Lauth 1996, 55).

20. EMILY's List, a fund-raising organization supporting pro-choice Democratic women candidates, and WISH List, the Republican counterpart (also supporting only pro-choice women), are two such networks. While these groups are essentially PACs, they have also "taken on several other roles traditionally performed by political parties" (Carroll 1994, 172). For one thing, extensive fund-raising efforts mobilize donors on behalf of the candidates in terms of volunteering and voting. Fund-raising lists can easily be converted to other types of voter contact lists. This will be especially helpful when women become more active as presidential candidates because PAC lists are usually national in scope. Other roles that these networks are undertaking include identifying viable women candidates and urging them to run and conducting campaign training seminars for women candidates and campaign managers. In this last area, the National Women's Political Caucus has taken a notable lead (172).

21. None of these overall differences by incumbency status were significant. Only the differences among challengers approached statistical significance (χ^2 = 2.6088, df = 1, p = .106). The chi-square result for incumbents is χ^2 = 1.316, df = 1, p = .251; for open seat candidates it is χ^2 = .496, df = 1, p = .481.

22. "Competitive" is defined here as having received between 40 and 60 percent of the vote. Since the unit of analysis is the candidate and not the race by district, not all of the candidates who finished with vote percentages within this range were in competitive races. For example, an incumbent who received 55 percent of the vote may have been opposed by a weak opponent from the other major party and a third party candidate who garnered 30 and 15 percent of the vote, respectively. The incumbent was safe, but his/her vote total does not reflect that. Such cases were uncommon, but did occur. Thus, the number of competitive incumbents may not equal the number of competitive challengers in table 4.6.

23. I should note that in addition to examining the level of consultant use according to the previous factors, I also looked for regional differences. Breaking the nation into four regions (Northeast, Midwest, South, and West) revealed that only one differed from the rest of the nation in anything approaching a significant level. Half of all candidates in the South in 1990 hired at least one consultant; this is relatively higher than the rest of the nation, which combined to hire consultants in 43.6 percent of the cases (χ^2 = 2.777, df = 1, p = .096).

Chapter 5

1. Incumbents defeated in the primaries totaled one in 1990 and nineteen in 1992. The total number of incumbents who were not reelected in those two years, therefore, was sixteen and forty-three (Jacobson 1993a, 167).

2. While I am not analyzing 1994 data in this study, readers may be interested to note that the first congressional election since 1954 to produce a new majority in the House saw the success rate of incumbents seeking reelection climb back to 92 percent.

3. C-SPAN should not be overestimated as an influence on constituencies. Cook (1989) suggests that "the value of broadcast floor proceedings is not C-SPAN's audiences around the country but the networks' feeds or the reporters who tune in" (99). Furthermore, Maltzman and Sigelman (1996) find that members of Congress using one-minute and five-minute speeches and special orders—devices that seem to be ripe for use for electoral purposes—engage in those activities to influence policy rather than to further their electoral goals (824). Still, with potential viewers numbering in the tens of millions, any exposure incumbents get will certainly have indirect electoral consequences.

4. There has been a great deal of debate about whether or not the "marginals vanished." Among those who have argued that congressional elections became less competitive in the 1960s are Tufte (1974), Erikson (1971), Cover (1977), Bauer and Hibbing (1989), Ansolabehere, Brady, and Fiorina (1992), Garand and Gross (1984), Gross and Garand (1984), and Garand, Wink, and Vincent (1993a, 1993b). On the other hand, some political scientists denied any decrease in the number of marginal seats. They include Jacobson (1987a, 1990b, 1993b) and Alford and Brady (1993). The latter find evidence for a "sophomore surge" and a "retirement slump," both of which emerged in the 1960s, but they do not find a corresponding increase in incumbent safety (see Ragsdale 1994, 550).

5. The impact of constituency service on the electoral success of incumbents is also debatable. Serra and Cover (1992) join Fiorina (1989) in arguing for the positive benefits of such service. Cain, Ferejohn, and Fiorina (1984, 1987), however, found only a modest effect for casework, and McAdams and Johannes (1988) found no electoral effect at all.

6. Building and spending an early "war chest" does not, however, help incumbents scare off quality challengers (Krasno and Green 1988) despite attempts by incumbents to do so (Drew 1983; Jackson 1988; Sorauf 1992). On the other hand, Epstein and Zemsky (1995) offer a theoretical "signaling model" in which early fund-raising by incumbents can deter strong challengers.

7. A very good examination of early, or "seed," money and its importance to challengers was conducted by Biersack, Herrnson, and Wilcox (1993). They find that early money helps challengers, especially inexperienced ones, raise more money later in the campaign (545). For challengers who have held past elected office, only money raised from individuals (as opposed to PACs and other candidates) significantly increases the chances of raising later money (545–46). Given the overwhelming agreement that challenger money matters, their finding is very enlightening for challengers' assessments of what they need to do to be competitive. Actually doing it—that is, raising early money—is another story.

8. Some of these advantages would also be enjoyed by candidates who had been legislative staffers and/or political consultants. Indeed, a potential flaw in my operationalization is that I neglect to count such candidates as "quality." The addition of candidates with these backgrounds, however, would have added only twenty-five quality candidates to my data set (specifically, five Republicans and four Democrats in 1990 and twelve Republicans and four Democrats in 1992). Of these, only twelve would have had professionally run campaigns (one Republican and three Democrats in 1990 and five Republicans and two Democrats in 1992). More important, their inclusion in the data set did not change a single substantive finding below.

9. "Voter contact" was not a category in the original data. It is a combination of two other types of consultants: persuasion mail and direct mail handlers.

10. A complete list of variables and their data sources can be found in appendix B.

11. This is an admittedly simplistic way to measure a district's "normal" vote. However, a district's vote for president taps long-standing partisanship better than the previous vote for a particular party's congressional candidate. The latter includes short-term, candidate-specific influences like incumbency. Furthermore, Dukakis was widely considered to have run a weak to fair campaign (for an academic perspective, see Quirk 1989; for popular accounts, see Germond and Witcover 1989 and Goldman and Mathews 1989). As a result, his share of a district's vote is likely to be close to a true baseline of Democratic support. For more detailed estimations of the normal vote, see Goldenberg and Traugott (1981) and Miller (1979); for a critique of using the presidential vote to tap constituency characteristics, see LeoGrande and Jeydel (1997).

12. Taking the logged transformation of campaign expenditures is a common practice in the campaign spending literature and is used to account for the diminishing marginal return of each dollar spent. I have followed Ansolabehere and Gerber (1994) and have operationalized campaign spending narrowly. While they find "communication expenditures" (by which they mean spending on only advertising and "other activities" meant to communicate to the voters) to be the best specification for spending, I use their "general campaign expenditures" measure, which includes advertising, "other activities," campaign overhead, and polling. Either measure is an improvement over "total expenditures," which includes the aforementioned spending categories as well as fund-raising, gifts and donations, and expenses not itemized (1110).

13. Although I am not interested in estimating presidential coattail effects, they have been shown to influence the congressional vote (Burnham 1975; Calvert and Ferejohn 1983; Ferejohn and Calvert 1984; Born 1984; Campbell 1986; Chubb 1988; Jacobson 1992; Gaddie 1995a; see the following chapter of this study for a more detailed discussion of coattail effects).

14. While the ANOVA found no party effect, meaning that Democrats and Republicans did not differ in terms of variance in the percentage of the vote they received, I chose to run separate analyses for Democrats and Republicans because specific variables might still function differently for candidates of the two parties. In other words, consultants may be relatively more important (in terms of how much of the vote they add to their clients) for candidates of one party than the other even if they have a significant influence for both.

15. For all of the regression models in this chapter, only major party candidates were included. The one exception was Bernie Sanders (I-VT), who was coded as a Democrat. Furthermore, races were excluded where an incumbent was pitted against another incumbent. There were five such races in 1992—districts 5 and 6 in Louisiana, district 2 in Iowa, district 1 in Maryland, and district 1 in Montana.

16. Because spending is measured as a base-10 logged transformation, the interpretation of these coefficients is slightly different than it is for the other variables. As Gierzynski and Breaux (1996) explain in an article on campaign spending in state legislative elections, "substantive interpretations of the [spending] coefficients must be in terms of percentage changes" (347).

17. The log transformations of the spending variables explain the large estimate for the constant.

18. Of note here is work by Paul Frymer (1994), who offers an explanation of divided government wherein voters are ideologically consistent. Specifically, voters may be voting for conservative Republicans for president and conservative Democrats for Congress. While Republican congressional candidates are, presumably, also conservative, Frymer notes that he is not claiming "that ideologically identical choices are occurring, just similar choices" (302). Thus, even if the Republican House candidate is more in line with the Republican presidential nominee, a conservative Democrat is probably also fairly well aligned with the latter ideologically. In addition, it is conceivable that in conservative districts, where voters choose "Blue Dog" Democrats for Congress and Republicans for president, Republican House candidates are too far to the right and, in effect, are less ideologically aligned with their party's presidential nominees than are Democratic congressional candidates. At any rate, Fiorina (1996b, 154–55) provides a strong critique of this argument.

19. Jacobson's (1990b) argument appears not to have been borne out given the 1994 results. He argues, however, that "[a]lthough the parties have traded institutions, the same logic holds" (Jacobson 1996a, 81). In other words, people still have the same policy preferences they have always had and they continue to attribute traditional

positions to the parties. What has changed is the institutional role for the two parties. If that is the case, voters are more strategic than many political scientists were previously willing to admit.

20. Petrocik and Doherty (1996), following Petrocik (1991), offer a third theory of the origins of divided government (as opposed to Fiorina's balancing theory and Jacobson's role expectations theory). They posit an issue ownership theory which suggests that "ticket-splitting occurs when the issues dominating the presidential election differ from those attracting attention in the congressional contest" (89). Thus, when an issue at the national level is a "Republican" issue and the major issue at the district level is a "Democratic" one, most voters will cast split ballots. This theory differs from Jacobson's in that he expects presidential issues to be "collective" and House issues to be "distributive." As a result, Jacobson expected divided government to favor Republicans at the national level and Democrats at the congressional level. But 1992 set the stage for a reversal of that pattern in 1994. Petrocik and Doherty can easily explain that reversal with their theory: the congressional elections were simply dominated by GOP-owned issues in 1994 while the national issue agenda was owned by Democrats, specifically Clinton (89).

21. This finding suggests that the "year" variable in table 5.2 measures something other than coattails, as we might have suspected.

22. One objection that each of the models in this chapter is likely to face concerns potential correlation between some of the variables, or multicollinearity. That problem, along with autocorrelation, is dealt with in appendix D, a methodological note on this chapter.

Chapter 6

1. Banks and Kiewiet (1989) argue that, for political amateurs (e.g., those who have not held elected office), incumbent-held seats may be more enticing than open ones. "This is because," the logic goes,

> the current incumbent is not the only opponent potential [*sic*] that challengers must take into account. To get to Congress, they must first defeat any and all other candidates of their own party. The likelihood of defeating an incumbent representative is low, but a candidate who chooses to challenge an incumbent is more likely to avoid serious opposition in the primary. A candidate who instead waits for a seat to open up faces the additional hurdle of winning a primary against one or more strong candidates of his own party. (1013–14)

Thus, nonquality candidates may have (or at least may perceive) a better chance of being elected to Congress against an incumbent than against strong primary *and* general election opponents.

2. As throughout this study, "quality" here means that a candidate has held an elected office.

3. The number of quality Democratic open seat candidates rose from 56.7 percent to 64.4 percent between 1990 and 1992, but that increase was not significant (χ^2 = 0.58, df = 1, p = .446).

4. To test the hypothesis, Jacobson and Kernell (1983) used presidential popularity and real income levels for various time periods preceding the general election as predictors of the electoral success of the president's party. They found that, as expected, spring real income had a positive effect, yet September, not spring, presidential approval figures proved to be the most influential political consideration affecting

party success in congressional elections (68–70). That latter piece of counterevidence is weakened by eliminating 1974 from the data set because the extremely low popularity of Nixon in the spring of that year "grossly overpredicts the decline of the Republican vote that year," meaning that "the spring popularity variable tends to underpredict the vote for the remaining eight elections" (121n. 12). At any rate, because factors affecting voters' decisions and those that impress strategic politicians are likely to be different, Jacobson and Kernell's strategic politician theory holds that voters' choices in November are structured by politicians' decisions made much earlier in the year (70–71).

5. Bush's rating was the lowest election year approval average of any sitting president since Truman (Gallup 1993, 142). The fall in Bush's approval rating was all the more glaring given his record high of 89 percent in late February and early March 1991 (42).

6. An indication of how hard fought open seat races are is that roughly 60 percent of such elections are considered marginal, meaning the winner received less than 60 percent of the vote (Jacobson 1990b, 33).

7. These Democratic Party advantages disappeared in 1994 open seat races (Gaddie 1995b).

8. I am assuming, of course, that quality candidates did better than those without prior elected experience. All the ANOVA result tells us is that candidates' shares of the vote differed significantly based on quality status; it does not indicate which group received more of the vote. However, a simple comparison of means (which are not included in table 6.1) indicates that, in fact, quality open seat candidates had a higher mean share of the vote than did nonquality ones.

Chapter 7

1. Predicted probabilities will always fall between 0 and 1, but the closer a probability is to either extreme, the less effect it will have in the logistic regression equation (Lottes, Adler, and DeMaris 1996). The predicted probability in the above example was calculated using the following two steps:

A. z = Constant + b_1(variable's value) + b_2(variable's value) . . .
OR
$z = -37.211 + -1.039(0) + .079(39.06) + .007(1) + 3.628(4.6818) + -3.54(5.4714) + 8.112(1) + 7.261(0) = -10.957565$

B. predicted probability [denoted as Prob(WIN)] = $e^z/1 + e^z$, where e^z can be arrived at by entering z on a calculator and pressing the INV and LN (or ln$x$) buttons.
OR
Prob(WIN) = $e^{-10.957565}$ / $1 + e^{-10.957565}$ = 0.0000174 / 1.0000174 = 0.0000174.

2. Recall that Democratic incumbents also significantly garnered more of the vote by hiring professional campaign handlers, as did Republican challengers. Of course, the increase that Republican challengers received was obviously not enough to significantly increase their chances of winning.

3. The probabilities were figured using 46.61 as the mean vote for Dukakis in the districts under analysis, 5.5484 and 5.3596 as the mean logged expenditures for Democrats and Republicans, 0 for the year (1990), and assuming both candidates had held past elected office (i.e., were quality candidates). Incidentally, when neither candidate hired a consultant, the probability of a Republican win was .2377111, and when both did, it was .1879677.

4. Even ideological interest groups, which presumably are more concerned with

policy positions than with competitiveness, are more likely to give to candidates in close races than to sure losers (Welch 1976 and 1980).

5. This is true, but only to a certain extent. As I have noted repeatedly throughout this study, challengers find it particularly hard to both raise money and hire consultants. A candidate can hardly do one without the other and, consequently, most find it next to impossible to do either. Herrnson, however, simply means that, unlike a district's partisan distribution, the popularity of a president, or the strength of the incumbent, campaign organization is not completely out of a candidate's control.

6. Initial t-tests revealed that candidates raised significantly more money when they hired a political consultant. Challengers who employed at least one campaign operative raised $289,195.16 more than those who ran amateur efforts (t = -10.24, df = 753, p = .000). Incumbents raised an additional $241,357.90 ($t$ = -20.97, df = 630, p = .000) and the average open seat candidate garnered $392,056.99 more when they hired a professional than when he or she did not (t = -6.68, df = 234, p = .000). Of course, consultants cost money to begin with, so it is not immediately clear that it was the presence of consultants that helped candidates boost campaign coffers.

7. Herrnson (1992) makes a similar claim about using an index versus using a measure of whether or not a candidate hired a fund-raising consultant (861). There are, however, two potential factors to explore here, both of which I am trying to examine, although Herrnson studied only one. The first is whether or not general professionalism enhances fund-raising (which is what Herrnson explored). Herrnson is correct that the level of professionalization is more important than a simple dichotomous measure of professionalism because the former is more likely to be recognized by contributors (especially parties and PACs) than the latter.

The second phenomenon, however, is whether fund-raising consultants deliver what they claim to deliver. Here, the perceptions of potential donors is irrelevant. Fund-raising experts are hired to coordinate successful events or put together highly persuasive direct mail appeals. Employing fund-raising event and/or mail specialists should, *ceteris paribus,* mean more money for the candidate-client but for a different reason than having a highly professional campaign. In other words, fund-raising consultants should be effective at raising money simply because of what they do, while the level of professionalization should matter because of what it represents to potential donors (namely, a serious candidate). Thus, I will use an index (following Herrnson) to examine the effect of the level of professionalism, and I will use a dichotomous measure for fund-raising consultant use to measure those consultants' specific impact on campaign receipts.

8. Herrnson (1992) used a scale from 0 to 50 to measure candidate competitiveness (863n. 8). If a candidate received 50 percent or less of the vote, he/she got that number as his/her competitiveness score; those with more than 50 percent of the vote got a score "equal to 100 minus their percentage of the vote."

9. No Democratic challenger hired fund-raising mail consultants in 1990 or 1992. If they conducted fund-raising through the mail, it was more than likely done by general direct mail consultants. In such instances, both persuasion and fund-raising mail is handled by the same firm. To the extent that this happened, then, I am missing some of the fund-raising activity of House candidates by not including the "direct mail" variable in this model. Given my inability to determine how much of the direct mail specialists' work was persuasion and how much fund-raising, I have decided to err on the side of overlooking some fund-raising activity rather than including some consulting as fund-raising when it was, in fact, persuasive.

10. Neither parties' open seat candidates hired fund-raising mail consultants.

11. Some may object that this is an unsatisfactory definition of *efficiency.* I would

argue, however, that the operationalization I have proposed is similar to the general understanding of that term in economics. With regard to *economic efficiency*, Alan Gilpin (1970) suggests in his *Dictionary of Economic Terms* that "the lower the cost per unit of output, without sacrifice of quality, in relation to the value or price of the finished article, the greater the economic efficiency of the productive organisation" (75). While this definition is not completely applicable because campaigns are not manufacturers, the essential part of the definition—the cost per unit of output—is analogous.

12. The voting age population of districts varies to a considerable degree. The smallest district in my data set is Montana's second district, with a voting age population of 272,290 (in 1990); the largest is California's thirty-seventh district, which had 705,576 people of voting age (also in 1990).

13. With just 50 percent of the vote in 1992 (the final vote was 50 to 41), Dornan won by little more than 10,000 votes. In 1990, Dornan's cost per vote ratio had been 23.87, and in 1994 it would skyrocket to 45.12.

14. "General spending," as I explained earlier, is the total spending on advertising, overhead, polling, and other campaign-related expenditures (see Ansolabehere and Gerber 1994).

15. This is particularly true if by "potential voters" we mean the voting age population. It might make more practical sense, however, to conceive of potential voters as all those who are registered to vote. While the number of registered voters varies between election cycles, the number stays relatively constant barring any major change in registration procedures (e.g., Motor Voter legislation). Nevertheless, the number of actual voters can vary considerably from election to election.

16. Of course, one could argue that candidates hope to increase turnout by using sophisticated targeting methods. If turnout did increase as spending in a campaign went up, the cost per vote would, indeed, remain stable. Unfortunately, there is no evidence that such methods raise turnout levels (see the following section of this chapter).

17. This result was confirmed in other work by Jackson (1996a) that found campaign-related factors influencing turnout for those who had registered to vote. Registration, on the other hand, was influenced by sociodemographics.

18. Of course, consultants may actually contribute to nonvoting in two senses. The first is that the expansion of the consulting industry, when combined with other elements of the contemporary political landscape (e.g., the decline of parties, the increasing use of television, etc.), ushered in a "new politics" that, in turn, led to a decrease in turnout *over time*. Second, consultants may influence turnout levels *in the individual elections* of which they are a part. I am only examining the latter. Nevertheless, it is quite possible that I will not find a significant increase in nonvoting in those races where consultants are present, and yet consultants may have had a negative, cumulative effect on turnout.

19. For districts in states where no gubernatorial and/or senatorial races were run, the variables in question were coded as one point higher than the largest vote margin in a gubernatorial/senatorial race that year. These variables could not take zero as their value because the hypothesized effect is negative. In other words, the lower the margin in these races, the higher the turnout. If those cases where there was not a Senate or governor's race were coded as zero, they would operate as extremely close races (or, essentially, ties) instead of no race at all.

Thus, for the gubernatorial margin variable, "no race" was coded as 53 for House races with an incumbent present and 49 for open seat House races. For the senatorial margin variable, "no race" was coded as 68 for both types of House races.

20. My analysis will differ in this regard from virtually all other turnout studies, which separate midterm and presidential election years (see Jackson 1996b, who runs different models for 1988 and 1990, and Cox and Munger 1989, who look only at 1982).

21. This measure is adapted from Cox and Munger (1989) and Gilliam (1985). See appendix C for a detailed discussion of various closeness measures and turnout.

22. Out of curiosity, I ran OLS models for both incumbent/challenger and open seat races in which I replaced the dichotomous consultant variable with a measure of the total number of consultants hired by the Democrat and Republican. This alternative consultant measure was insignificant in both models.

23. Of course, consultants may influence elections in many ways that I did not investigate. Unexamined, for example, is the direct impact of consultants on voting behavior.

24. Other scholars are less sure. Ladd (1993, 1995), for example, argues that a political realignment has been taking place slowly, over the course of decades. Jacobson's (1996b and 1996c) analysis of the 1994 elections is based on the traditional explanations of congressional election outcomes, while Brady et al. (1996) find "that Democratic losses in the House followed from voters having rejected President Clinton's legislative agenda by turning against those Representatives who advanced it" (346). Finally, Jacobson and Kim (1996) directly address, and question, Abramowitz's conclusions about the electorate.

Chapter 8

1. In fact, the finding was that when Democratic incumbents hired consultants, the chances that a Republican challenger would win were significantly decreased.

2. I am well aware of the fact that columnists like Barnicle are supposed to be controversial and therefore often overstate the case they make on any topic. Yet sentiments like the ones described above are relatively commonplace.

3. Opinion on the balanced budget amendment is actually rather complex. Whether a majority of citizens favor the amendment or not is largely dependent on a survey's question wording (Rosenbaum 1997). Still, most members of Congress probably thought that a large majority of voters favored the amendment, since that was the prevailing wisdom in the media at the time of the vote.

4. These two assumptions parallel Claudia Mills's (1995, 97) two general strategies for persuasion, namely, the altering of a person's external (or objective) choice situation and altering his/her internal (or subjective) choice situation. Some actions that fall in the second category Mills calls "manipulative." Questionable practices that fall under the first strategy would be deemed "coercive."

5. Kelley recognizes that perfect rationality in the electorate is impossible. He hopes, however, to reform the system in ways that we are all willing to accept and that bring us closer to the ideal.

6. This section states, "If any licensee shall permit any person who is a legally qualified candidate for any public office to use a broadcasting station, he shall afford equal opportunities to all other such candidates for that office in the use of such broadcasting station" (U.S. Code Annotated Title 47, sec. 315; cited in Polsby and Wildavsky 1996, 110n. 64). Kelley's concern with the equal access provision is that it dissuades broadcasters from giving candidates free time. As he notes, "Any grant of free time to major party candidates during an election campaign makes all legally qualified candidates of minor parties eligible to receive comparable time without cost. . . . Thus, Section 315 really gives candidates a quite fictitious equality of access to the airwaves because it reduces the willingness of broadcasters to give free time and therefore makes

the candidate's ability to pay the principal factor that determines the extent of his time on the air" (Kelley 1960, 38, 39).

7. Kelley's wish has been granted in the form of Ad Watch features.

8. The importance of aesthetics for political behavior has not been recognized by most political scientists. Lane (1969) acknowledged the role of aesthetics in a composite set of "cognitive needs" but did little with it in terms of political thinking (32). One study, by Rosenberg et al. (1986), examined the impact of nonverbal appearance on vote preferences. To my knowledge, this is the only empirical research that taps voters' sense of aesthetics.

9. Jamieson (1996) judges the Horton ad as follows: "Although it did show the Horton mug shot, I do not consider the Horton ad racist. The racism that existed in these ads [Horton and two other crime spots] was placed there through complicity with frightened audiences. Those who interpreted the messages of the crime ads out of their fears . . . saw in William Horton's color what they supposed was a typical criminal" (477). Mendelberg (1997), on the other hand, maintains that the Horton ad "mobilized whites' racial prejudice" (151).

10. We can imagine this taking place with regard to values relating not only to race, gender, religion, sexual orientation, and age but also to honesty and civility. In fact, it is candidates' lack of compliance with those latter values that leads most people to complain about negative campaigning. Of course, the degree to which voters are willing to punish candidates for unacceptable behavior seems minimal. Instead, they heap scorn on the entire system, since all candidates appear to engage in the same activity. The media, however, are quite willing to hold candidates accountable. Thus, avoiding negative coverage serves as a relatively strong check on campaign behavior. The extent to which political consultants, specifically, are held accountable will be addressed below.

11. Mayer (1996) takes the view that negative campaigning is misunderstood and/or overstated. If one agrees with him, this particular charge against consultants would be baseless on its face.

12. Those interested in the use of the Internet in politics will want to see a Web site created by consultant Phil Noble and devoted to practical politics on the Internet, <www.politicsonline.com>. On the Internet and the political process generally, see Glass (1996).

13. The West Virginia regulation is found in the West Virginia Code § 3-8-5. The San Francisco Campaign Consultant Ordinance (S.F. Admin. Code § 16.540–16.547) was approved by voters in 1997. For more on the San Francisco ordinance, see the "campaign consultants" page on the Ethics Commission Web site at <www.ci.sf. ca.us/ethics>.

14. The "nationalization of elections" has been of some interest to election scholars. By "nationalization," we mean a "uniformity of response by geographical units to election occurrences and convergence in the level of partisan support across geographical units of the electorate" (Ragsdale 1994, 539, reporting on the work of Claggett, Flanigan, and Zingale 1984). While earlier work found some nationalization effects (Stokes 1976), recent studies have found no trends of that sort (Claggett, Flanigan, and Zingale 1984; Kawato 1987).

15. This may be due to the fact that in neither of the two most publicized cases (Ed Rollins's "street money" incident of 1993 and Dick Morris's "sex scandal" of 1996) was the public interest harmed. In the former, the claim by Rollins that Christine Todd Whitman's campaign for governor in New Jersey paid to suppress turnout among African Americans was never proved and it was later retracted by Rollins (*Congressional Quarterly Weekly Report* "New Jersey Vote Probe Finds No Suppression" 1994,

83; see also Rollins 1996). Of course, to the extent that Rollins's comments were construed to be racist, the common good was affected. But in the Morris case, the leaking of campaign strategy could only have affected the Clinton reelection effort, not the public at large. Both situations are, to be sure, examples of unethical consultant conduct (for other examples of questionable consultant practices, see Sabato 1981, 303–10; Sabato and Simpson 1996). Rollins's comments come dangerously close to being racist in that he jeopardized the reputation of black preachers. And Morris betrayed a fiduciary relationship with a client. Voters, however, are unlikely to hold candidates responsible for acts they did not commit and, in some ways, are the victims of themselves. Perhaps voters would be more likely to punish candidates for consultants' actions if they directly endangered the public interest.

Appendix C

1. While there is some empirical support for minimax regret voting (Ferejohn and Fiorina 1975 and Kenney and Rice 1989), there has been much criticism of the theory from a variety of perspectives (see Strom 1975; Stephens 1975; Mayer and Good 1975; Beck 1975; Tullock 1975; Aldrich 1993, 259–61; Blais et al. 1995). In one of the more humorous responses to the theory, Stephen Stephens (1975) calculated the odds of being in a car wreck on the way to the polls as one in ten million while the chances that one's single vote will be decisive in a presidential election are one in a million. He concluded, "If a minimax-regretter is going to dip down six factors of ten in probability to pick up the possibility that his sole vote may decide a presidential election, it is difficult for me to see that he will not dip down another factor of ten and pick up the possibility that he will be run over; I am sure there are many professors of political science who would gladly give their legs to elect a Democratic president, but I do not believe such intensity of sentiment is widely distributed in the population" (914).

2. This argument has often been called the "competitive threat theory" (e.g., Gray 1976, 154).

3. Cox (1988) also argues that one should use the raw vote margin of victory, denoted as m, along with m^2. Squaring m deals with the "mathematical necessity . . . [that] T > or = (m/e) x 100," where T is turnout and e is the number of eligible voters in a district (773). In addition, because districts are of different sizes, m can be standardized by dividing it by e (771). This accounts for the possibility that while voters are motivated by raw vote margins, party and campaign organizations may focus on vote percentage differences (770). The reason for the difference is that organizational size is proportioned to the size of the electorates. "Thus, to the extent that each candidate can command pre-existing organizations whose size is proportional to the task facing them, the relevant variable is the percentage rather than raw vote margin" (770).

4. The squared margin variable should make the unsquared variable significant, or close to it, and negative while the squared variable would be positive to account for the aforementioned increase in turnout as the margin of victory enlarges.

Appendix D

1. Kennedy (1992) claims that the "major undesirable consequence of multicollinearity is that the variances of the OLS estimates of the parameters of the collinear variables are quite large" (177). This, in turn, means that the coefficient estimates cannot be trusted (178). In other words, we cannot be confident in the results of a regression analysis that includes two collinear independent variables.

2. Democratic use of consultants and spending produced tolerance levels of .447 and .404 and VIFs of 2.235 and 2.473. While these results vary somewhat from those of the other variables, the differences are negligible and are nowhere near the levels required for finding collinearity.

3. Incidentally, diagnostics for challenger use of consultants and quality also indicate no collinearity (R^2s of .13 and .05 for Democrats and Republicans, respectively, and normal tolerance levels and VIFs).

4. The dependent variable for the 1990 and 1992 models was the incumbent's share of the vote, without regard to party. A party control was included among the independent variables.

5. If including the same incumbent twice in the same data set caused the autocorrelation problem, then the open seat models should be free of autocorrelation. However, the DW result for the most basic open seat OLS model was 1.49. This is an additional reason for thinking that the cause of autocorrelation in my models is the result of less than perfect model specification.

Bibliography

"1990 Candidates for Senate and House." 1990. *Congressional Quarterly Weekly Report*, 13 October, 3359–71.

Abramowitz, Alan I. 1980. "A Comparison of Voting for U.S. Senator and Representative." *American Political Science Review* 74:633–40.

———. 1988. "Explaining Senate Election Outcomes." *American Political Science Review* 82:385–403.

———. 1991. "Incumbency, Campaign Spending, and the Decline of Competition in U.S. House Elections." *Journal of Politics* 43:34–56.

———. 1995. "The End of the Democratic Era? 1994 and the Future of Congressional Election Research." *Political Research Quarterly* 48:873–89.

Achenbach, Joel. 1996. "Making It Look Natural." *Washington Post*, 19 September, C1–2.

Adams, William C., and Dennis J. Smith. 1980. "Effects of Telephone Canvassing on Turnout and Preferences: A Field Experiment." *Public Opinion Quarterly* 44:389–95.

Agranoff, Robert, ed. 1972a. *The New Style in Election Campaigns*. Boston: Holbrook Press.

———. 1972b. "Introduction/The New Style of Campaigning: The Decline of Party and the Rise of Candidate-Centered Technology." In *The New Style in Election Campaigns*, ed. Robert Agranoff. Boston: Holbrook Press.

———. 1976. *The Management of Election Campaigns*. Boston: Holbrook Press.

Aldrich, John H. 1980. *Before the Convention: Strategies and Choices in Presidential Nomination Campaigns*. Chicago: University of Chicago Press.

———. 1993. "Rational Choice and Turnout." *American Journal of Political Science* 37:246–78.

———. 1996. "Issue Ownership in Presidential Elections, with a 1980 Case Study." *American Journal of Political Science* 40:825–50.

Alford, John, and David Brady. 1993. "Personal and Partisan Advantage in U.S. Congressional Elections." In *Congress Reconsidered*, 5th ed., ed. Lawrence Dodd and Bruce Oppenheimer. Washington, D.C.: Congressional Quarterly Press.

Alford, John, Holly Teeters, Daniel S. Ward, and Rick K. Wilson. 1994. "Overdraft: The Political Cost of Congressional Malfeasance." *Journal of Politics* 56:788–801.

Anderson, John R. 1980. *Cognitive Psychology and Its Implications*. San Francisco: Freeman.

———. 1983. *The Architecture of Cognition*. Cambridge: Harvard University Press.

Ansolabehere, Stephen, and Alan Gerber. 1994. "The Mismeasure of Campaign Spending: Evidence from the 1990 U.S. House Elections." *Journal of Politics* 56:1106–18.

Ansolabehere, Stephen, and Shanto Iyengar. 1995. *Going Negative: How Attack Ads Shrink and Polarize the Electorate*. New York: Free Press.

———. 1996. "Can the Press Monitor Campaign Advertising? An Experimental Study." *Press/Politics* 1:72–86.

Ansolabehere, Stephen, David Brady, and Morris Fiorina. 1992. "The Vanishing Marginals and Electoral Responsiveness." *British Journal of Political Science* 22:21–38.

Ansolabehere, Stephen, Shanto Iyengar, and Adam Simon. 1995. "Evolving Perspectives on the Effects of Campaign Communication." In *Research in Political Sociology*, ed. Philo C. Wasburn. Greenwich, Conn.: JAI Press.

Ansolabehere, Stephen, Shanto Iyengar, Adam Simon, and Nicholas Valentino. 1994. "Does Attack Advertising Demobilize the Electorate?" *American Political Science Review* 88:829–38.

Armstrong, Richard. 1988. *The Next Hurrah: The Communications Revolution in American Politics*. New York: Beech Tree Books.

Arterton, F. Christopher. 1982. "Political Money and Party Strength." In *The Future of American Political Parties*, ed. Joel Fleishman. Englewood Cliffs, N.J.: Prentice-Hall.

――――. 1997. "Can Politics Be Taught?" *Campaigns and Elections*, December/January, 53–54.

Baer, Denise. 1995. "Contemporary Strategy and Agenda Setting." In *Campaigns and Elections American Style*, ed. James A. Thurber and Candice J. Nelson. Boulder, Colo.: Westview Press.

Banducci, Susan A., and Jeffrey A. Karp. 1994. "Electoral Consequences of Scandal and Reapportionment in the 1992 House Elections." *American Politics Quarterly* 22:3–26.

Banks, Jeffrey S., and D. Roderick Kiewiet. 1989. "Explaining Patterns of Candidate Competition in Congressional Elections." *American Journal of Political Science* 33:997–1015.

Barnicle, Mike. 1994. "Get Consultants Out of the Way." *Boston Globe*, 25 October.

Barthes, Roland. 1974. *S/Z*. Trans. Richard Miller. New York: Noonday Press.

Bartlett, Frederick C. 1932. *Remembering: A Study in Experimental and Social Psychology*. London: Cambridge University Press.

Barzel, Yoram, and Eugene Silberberg. 1973. "Is the Act of Voting Rational?" *Public Choice* 16:51–58.

Bauer, Monica, and John Hibbing. 1989. "Which Incumbents Lose in House Elections: A Response to Jacobson's 'The Marginals Never Vanished.'" *American Journal of Political Science* 33:262–71.

Baus, Herbert M., and William B. Ross. 1968. *Politics Battle Plan*. New York: Macmillan.

Beaudry, Ann, and Bob Schaeffer. 1986. *Winning Local and State Elections: The Guide to Organizing Your Campaign*. New York: Free Press.

Beck, Nathaniel. 1975. "The Paradox of Minimax Regret." *American Political Science Review* 69:918.

Beck, Paul Allen, and Frank J. Sorauf. 1992. *Party Politics in America*. 7th ed. New York: HarperCollins.

Behind the Scenes in Politics. 1924. New York: E. P. Dutton.

Beiler, David. 1991. "The 1990 Campaign Scorecard." *Campaigns and Elections*, December/January.

Bennett, W. Lance. 1990. "Toward a Theory of Press-State Relations in the United States." *Journal of Communication* 40:103–25.

――――. 1992. "White Noise: The Perils of Mass-Mediated Democracy." *Communication Monographs* 59:401–6.

Berelson, Bernard R., Paul F. Lazarsfeld, and William N. McPhee. 1954. *Voting: A Study of Opinion Formation in a Presidential Campaign.* Chicago: University of Chicago Press.

Berke, Richard L. 1993a. "In Trenton, Echoes of Ali-Frazier as Two Campaign Titans Clash." *New York Times,* 4 October, A1, A13 (national edition).

———. 1993b. "Whitman Campaign Paid to Curtail Black Voting." *New York Times,* 10 November, A13 (national edition).

Bianco, William T. 1984. "Strategic Decisions on Candidacy in U.S. Congressional Districts." *Legislative Studies Quarterly* 9:351–64.

Bibby, John F. 1984. "Party Renewal in the National Republican Party." In *Party Renewal in America,* ed. Gerald Pomper. New York: Praeger.

Biersack, Robert, Paul S. Herrnson, and Clyde Wilcox. 1993. "Seeds for Success: Early Money in Congressional Elections." *Legislative Studies Quarterly* 18:535–51.

Biocca, Frank. 1991a. "Viewers' Mental Models of Political Messages: Toward a Theory of the Semantic Processing of Television." In *Television and Political Advertising,* vol. 1: *Psychological Processes.* ed. Frank Biocca. Hillsdale, N.J.: Lawrence Erlbaum.

———. 1991b. "The Orchestration of Codes and Discourses: Analysis of Semantic Framing." In *Television and Political Advertising,* vol. 2: *Signs, Codes, and Images,* ed. Frank Biocca. Hillsdale, N.J.: Lawrence Erlbaum.

———. 1991c. "What Is the Language of Political Advertising?" In *Television and Political Advertising,* vol. 2: *Signs, Codes, and Images,* ed. Frank Biocca. Hillsdale, N.J.: Lawrence Erlbaum.

Blais, André, Robert Young, Christopher Fleury, and Miriam Lapp. 1995. "Do People Vote on the Basis of Minimax Regret?" *Political Research Quarterly* 48:827–36.

Bloom, Melvyn H. 1973. *Public Relations and Presidential Campaigns: A Crisis in Democracy.* New York: Thomas Y. Crowell.

Blumenthal, Sidney. 1982. *The Permanent Campaign.* Rev. ed. New York: Simon and Schuster.

Boiney, John, and David L. Paletz. 1991. "In Search of the Model Model: Political Science versus Political Advertising Perspectives on Voter Decision Making." In *Television and Political Advertising,* vol. 1: *Psychological Processes,* ed. Frank Biocca. Hillsdale, N.J.: Lawrence Erlbaum.

Bolger, Glen, and Bill McInturff. 1996. "'Push Polling' Stinks." *Campaigns and Elections,* August.

Boller, Paul F., Jr. 1984. *Presidential Campaigns.* New York: Oxford University Press.

Bond, Jon R., Cary Covington, and Richard Fleisher. 1985. "Explaining Challenger Quality in Congressional Elections." *Journal of Politics* 47:510–29.

Born, Richard. 1984. "Reassessing the Decline of Presidential Coattails: U.S. House Elections from 1952 to 1980." *Journal of Politics* 46:60–79.

———. 1986. "Strategic Politicians and Unresponsive Voters." *American Political Science Review* 80:599–612.

———. 1994a. "Split-Ticket Voters, Divided Government, and Fiorina's Policy-Balancing Model." *Legislative Studies Quarterly* 19:95–115.

———. 1994b. "Rejoinder." *Legislative Studies Quarterly* 19:126–29.

Bowman, James. 1994. "Fame Is the Spin." *Times Literary Supplement,* 21 October, 14.

Bradshaw, Joel. 1995. "Who Will Vote for You and Why: Designing Strategy and Theme." In *Campaigns and Elections American Style,* ed. James A. Thurber and Candice J. Nelson. Boulder, Colo.: Westview Press.

Brady, David W., John F. Cogan, Brian J. Gaines, and Douglas Rivers. 1996. "The Perils of Presidential Support: How the Republicans Took the House in the 1994 Midterm Elections." *Political Behavior* 18:345–67.

Brady, John. 1997. *Bad Boy: The Life and Politics of Lee Atwater.* Reading, Mass.: Addison Wesley.

Broder, David. 1972. *The Party's Over: The Failure of Politics in America.* New York: Harper and Row.

Brody, Richard A. 1986. "Candidate Evaluations and the Vote: Some Considerations Affecting the Application of Cognitive Psychology to Voting Behavior." In *Political Cognition,* ed. Richard R. Lau and David O. Sears. Hillsdale, N.J.: Lawrence Erlbaum.

Brown, Robin, and Nancy Kruse. 1993. "Consultant Scorecard." *Campaigns and Elections,* January.

Bryant, Jay. 1995. "Paid Media Advertising." In *Campaigns and Elections American Style,* ed. James A. Thurber and Candice J. Nelson. Boulder, Colo.: Westview Press.

Buchanan, Bruce. 1991. *Electing a President: The Markle Commission Research on Campaign '88.* Austin: University of Texas Press.

Budge, Ian, and Dennis J. Farlie. 1983. *Explaining and Predicting Elections: Issue Effects and Party Strategies in Twenty-three Democracies.* London: Allen and Unwin.

Burnham, Walter Dean. 1975. "Insulation and Responsiveness in Congressional Elections." *Political Science Quarterly* 90:411–35.

———. 1982. *The Current Crisis in American Politics.* New York: Oxford University Press.

———. 1987. "Elections as Democratic Institutions." In *Elections in America,* ed. Kay Lehman Schlozman. Boston: Allen and Unwin.

Burrell, Barbara C. 1994. *A Woman's Place Is in the House: Campaigning for Congress in the Feminist Era.* Ann Arbor: University of Michigan Press.

"Buyer's Guide: Political Schools and Programs." 1997. *Campaigns and Elections,* December/January.

C-SPAN. 1995a. "Political Campaign Strategy, Part 1." Tape #62683, January 13. Public Affairs Video Archives, Purdue University.

———. 1995b. "Political Campaign Strategy, Part 2." Tape #62683, January 13. Public Affairs Video Archives, Purdue University.

Cain, Bruce, John Ferejohn, and Morris Fiorina. 1984. "The Constituency Service Basis of the Personal Vote for U.S. Representatives and British Members of Parliament." *American Political Science Review* 78:110–25.

———. 1987. *The Personal Vote.* Cambridge: Harvard University Press.

Caldeira, Gregory A., and Samuel C. Patterson. 1982. "Contextual Influences on Participation in U.S. State Legislative Elections." *Legislative Studies Quarterly* 7:359–81.

Caldeira, Gregory A., Samuel C. Patterson, and Gregory A. Markko. 1985. "The Mobilization of Voters in Congressional Elections." *Journal of Politics* 47:490–509.

Calvert, Randall L., and John A. Ferejohn. 1983. "Coattail Voting in Recent Presidential Elections." *American Political Science Review* 77:407–19.

Campbell, Angus. 1960. "Surge and Decline: A Study of Electoral Change." *Public Opinion Quarterly* 24:397–418.

Campbell, Angus, Philip E. Converse, Warren E. Miller, and Donald E. Stokes. 1960. *The American Voter.* Chicago: University of Chicago Press.

Campbell, James E. 1986. "Predicting Seat Gains from Presidential Coattails." *American Journal of Political Science* 30:165–83.

———. 1991. "The Presidential Surge and Its Midterm Decline in Congressional Elections, 1868–1988." *Journal of Politics* 53:477–87.

———. 1993. *The Presidential Pulse of Congressional Elections*. Lexington: University Press of Kentucky.

———. 1996. *Cheap Seats: The Democratic Party's Advantage in U.S. House Elections*. Columbus: Ohio State University Press.

"Candidates for Governor, Senate, House." 1992. *Congressional Quarterly Weekly Report*, 24 October, 3415–30.

Canon, David T. 1990. *Actors, Athletes, and Astronauts: Political Amateurs in the United States Congress*. Chicago: University of Chicago Press.

———. 1993. "Sacrificial Lambs or Strategic Politicians? Political Amateurs in U.S. House Elections." *American Journal of Political Science* 37:1119–41.

Cappella, Joseph N., and Kathleen Hall Jamieson. 1994. "Broadcast Adwatch Effects: A Field Experiment." *Communication Research* 21:342–65.

Carmines, Edward G., and James A. Stimson. 1980. "The Two Faces of Issue Voting." *American Political Science Review* 74:78–91.

———. 1989. *Issue Evolution: Race and the Transformation of American Politics*. Princeton: Princeton University Press.

Carroll, Susan J. 1994. *Women As Candidates in American Politics*. 2d ed. Bloomington: Indiana University Press.

Chagall, David. 1981. *The New Kingmakers*. New York: Harcourt Brace Jovanovich.

Chubb, John. 1988. "Institutions, the Economy, and the Dynamics of State Elections." *American Political Science Review* 82:133–53.

Claggett, William, William Flanigan, and Nancy Zingale. 1984. "Nationalization of the American Electorate." *American Political Science Review* 78:77–91.

Clark, Charles S. 1996. "Political Consultants." *CQ Researcher* 6:865–88.

Clarke, Peter, and Susan Evans. 1983. *Covering Campaigns: Journalism in Congressional Elections*. Stanford: Stanford University Press.

Committee on Political Parties of the American Political Science Association. 1950. "Toward a More Responsible Two-Party System." *American Political Science Review* 44: supplement.

Congressional Quarterly's Guide to U.S. Elections. 1985. 2d ed. Washington, D.C.: Congressional Quarterly, Inc.

Connelly, William F., Jr., and John J. Pitney Jr. 1994. *Congress' Permanent Minority: Republicans in the U.S. House*. Lanham, Md.: Littlefield Adams.

Connolly, Ceci, Kitty Cunningham, Beth Donovan, Dave Kaplan, and Elizabeth A. Palmer. 1993. "'Street Money' under Scrutiny after Claims of Influence." *Congressional Quarterly Weekly Report*, 13 November, 3141–43.

Conover, Pamela Johnston. 1988. "Feminists and the Gender Gap." *Journal of Politics* 50:985–1010.

Conover, Pamela Johnston, and Stanley Feldman. 1986. "The Role of Inference in the Perception of Political Candidates." In *Political Cognition*, ed. Richard R. Lau and David O. Sears. Hillsdale, N.J.: Lawrence Erlbaum.

Converse, Philip E. 1962. "Information Flow and the Stability of Partisan Attitudes." *Public Opinion Quarterly* 26:578–99.

Cook, Rhodes. 1992. "Democratic Clout Is Growing as the Gender Gap Widens." *Congressional Quarterly Weekly Report*, 17 October, 3265–68.

Cook, Timothy E. 1989. *Making Laws and Making News: Media Strategies in the U.S. House of Representatives*. Washington, D.C.: Brookings Institution.

Corlett, Wilfred. 1990. "Multicollinearity." In *The New Palgrave: Econometrics*, ed. John Eatwell, Murray Milgate, and Peter Newman. New York: W. W. Norton.

Corsino, Louis. 1985. "A Case Study of Campaign Organization: Social Technology,

Conflict, and Games." In *Research in Political Sociology*, vol. 1, ed. Richard G. Braungart. Greenwich, Conn.: JAI Press.

Cover, Albert D. 1977. "One Good Term Deserves Another: The Advantage of Incumbency in Congressional Elections." *American Journal of Political Science* 21:523–41.

Covington, Cary R., Kent Kroeger, Glenn Richardson, and J. David Woodard. 1993. "Shaping a Candidate's Image in the Press: Ronald Reagan and the 1980 Presidential Election." *Political Research Quarterly* 46:783–98.

Cox, Gary W. 1988. "Closeness and Turnout: A Methodological Note." *Journal of Politics* 50:768–75.

Cox, Gary W., and Michael C. Munger. 1989. "Closeness, Expenditures, and Turnout in the 1982 U.S. House Elections." *American Political Science Review* 83:217–31.

Crain, Mark, Donald R. Leavens, and Lynn Abbot. 1987. "Voting and Not Voting at the Same Time." *Public Choice* 32:131–35.

Crick, Bernard. 1972. *In Defense of Politics*. 2d ed. Chicago: University of Chicago Press.

Crotty, William J. 1971. "Party Effort and Its Impact on the Vote." *American Political Science Review* 65:439–50.

———. 1984. *American Parties in Decline*. 2d ed. Boston: Little, Brown.

Cunningham, Noble E., Jr. 1956. "John Beckley: An Early American Party Manager." *The William and Mary Quarterly* 13:40–52.

Cutright, Phillips. 1963. "Measuring the Impact of Local Party Activity on the General Election Vote." *Public Opinion Quarterly* 27:372–86.

Dabelko, Kristen la Cour, and Paul S. Herrnson. 1997. "Women's and Men's Campaigns for the U.S. House of Representatives." *Political Research Quarterly* 50:121–35.

Dahl, Robert A. 1990. "Myth of the Presidential Mandate." *Political Science Quarterly* 105:355–66.

Danesi, Marcel. 1994. "Introduction: Thomas A. Sebeok and the Science of Signs." In *Signs: An Introduction to Semiotics*. Thomas A. Sebeok. Toronto: University of Toronto Press.

Darcy, Robert, and Sarah Slavin Schramm. 1977. "When Women Run against Men." *Public Opinion Quarterly* 41:1–12.

Darcy, Robert, Susan Welch, and Janet Clark. 1987. *Women, Elections, and Representation*. New York: Longman.

Dawson, Paul A., and James E. Zinser. 1976. "Political Finance and Participation in Congressional Elections." *Annals of the American Academy of Political and Social Science* 425:59–73.

Delli Carpini, Michael X. 1996. "Voters, Candidates, and Campaigns in the New Information Age: An Overview and Assessment." *Press/Politics* 1:36–56.

Denton, Robert E., Jr., and Gary C. Woodward. 1985. *Political Communication in America*. New York: Praeger.

DeVries, Walter, and Lance Tarrance Jr. 1972. *The Ticket-Splitter: A New Force in American Politics*. Grand Rapids, Mich.: William B. Eerdmans.

Diamond, Edwin, and Stephen Bates. 1992. *The Spot: The Rise of Political Advertising on Television*. 3d ed. Cambridge: MIT Press.

DiLeonardi, Joan W., and Patrick Almond Curtis. 1992. *What to Do When the Numbers Are In*. Chicago: Nelson-Hall.

Dimock, Michael A., and Gary C. Jacobson. 1995. "Checks and Choices: The House Bank Scandal's Impact on Voters in 1992." *Journal of Politics* 57:1143–59.

Downs, Anthony. 1957. *An Economic Theory of Democracy*. New York: Harper and Row.

Drew, Elizabeth. 1983. *Politics and Money: The New Road to Corruption*. New York: Macmillan.

Eco, Umberto. 1976. *A Theory of Semiotics*. Bloomington: Indiana University Press.

_____. 1979. *The Role of the Reader: Explorations in the Semiotics of Texts*. Bloomington: Indiana University Press.

_____. 1980. "Towards a Semiotic Inquiry into the TV Message." In *Communication Studies*, ed. J. Corner and J. Hawthorn. London: Arnold.

_____. 1984. *Semiotics and the Philosophy of Language*. Bloomington: Indiana University Press.

_____. 1989. *The Open Work*. Trans. Anna Cancogni. Cambridge: Harvard University Press.

Edelman, Murray. 1985. *The Symbolic Uses of Politics*. Urbana: University of Illinois Press.

_____. 1988. *Constructing the Political Spectacle*. Chicago: University of Chicago Press.

Edwards, George C., III. 1979. "The Impact of Presidential Coattails on Outcomes of Congressional Elections." *American Politics Quarterly* 7:94–108.

_____. 1980. *Presidential Influence in Congress*. San Francisco: Freeman.

Eldersveld, Samuel J. 1956. "Experimental Propaganda Techniques and Voting Behavior." *American Political Science Review* 50:154–65.

Eldersveld, Samuel J., and Richard W. Dodge. 1954. "Personal Contact or Mail Propaganda? An Experiment in Voting Turnout and Attitude Change." In *Public Opinion and Propaganda*, ed. Daniel Katz, Dorwin Cartwright, Samuel J. Eldersveld, and Alfred M. Lee. New York: Dryden Press.

Epstein, David, and Peter Zemsky. 1995. "Money Talks: Deterring Quality Challengers in Congressional Elections." *American Political Science Review* 89:295–308.

Erikson, Robert. 1971. "The Advantage of Incumbency in Congressional Elections." *Polity* 3:395–405.

Ezra, Marni, and Candice J. Nelson. 1995. "Do Campaigns Matter?" In *Campaigns and Elections American Style*, ed. James A. Thurber and Candice J. Nelson. Boulder, Colo.: Westview Press.

Faucheux, Ron. 1994. "The Message." *Campaigns and Elections*, May.

_____. 1996. "Unfair Ads, Push Polls." *Campaigns and Elections*, April.

Feldman, Stanley, and Pamela Johnston Conover. 1983. "Candidates, Issues, and Voters: The Role of Inference in Political Perception." *Journal of Politics* 45:810–39.

Fenno, Richard F., Jr. 1978. *Home Style: House Members in Their Districts*. Glenview, Ill.: Scott, Foresman.

Ferejohn, John A., and Randall L. Calvert. 1984. "Presidential Coattails in Historical Perspective." *American Journal of Political Science* 28:127–46.

Ferejohn, John A., and Morris P. Fiorina. 1974. "The Paradox of Not Voting: A Decision Theoretic Analysis." *American Political Science Review* 68:525–36.

_____. 1975. "Closeness Counts Only in Horseshoes and Dancing." *American Political Science Review* 69:920–25.

_____. 1985. "Incumbency and Realignment in Congressional Elections." In *The New Direction in American Politics*, ed. John E. Chubb and Paul E. Peterson. Washington, D.C.: Brookings Institution.

Ferejohn, John A., and Roger G. Noll. 1978. "Uncertainty and the Formal Theory of Political Campaigns." *American Political Science Review* 72:492–505.

Fineman, Howard. 1993. "A Round of 'Idiotic Game Playing.'" *Newsweek*, 29 November, 42.

Finkel, Steven E. 1993. "Reexamining the 'Minimal Effects' Model in Recent Presidential Campaigns." *Journal of Politics* 55:1–21.

Fiorina, Morris P. 1977a. "The Case of the Vanishing Marginals: The Bureaucracy Did It." *American Political Science Review* 71:177–81.

———. 1977b. *Congress: Keystone of the Washington Establishment.* New Haven: Yale University Press.

———. 1988. "The Reagan Years: Turning to the Right or Groping toward the Middle? In *The Resurgence of Conservatism in Anglo-American Democracies,* ed. Barry Cooper, Allan Kornberg, and William Mishler. Durham, N.C.: Duke University Press.

———. 1989. *Congress: Keystone of the Washington Establishment.* 2d ed. New Haven: Yale University Press.

———. 1990. "An Era of Divided Government." In *Developments in American Politics,* ed. Bruce Cain and Gillian Peele. London: Macmillan.

———. 1992. *Divided Government.* New York: Macmillan.

———. 1994. "Response to Born." *Legislative Studies Quarterly* 19:117–25.

———. 1996a. "The Causes and Consequences of Divided Government: Lessons of 1992–1994." In *Divided Government: Change, Uncertainty, and the Constitutional Order,* ed. Peter F. Galderisi with Roberta Q. Herzberg and Peter McNamara. Lanham, Md.: Rowman and Littlefield.

———. 1996b. *Divided Government.* 2d ed. Boston: Allyn and Bacon.

Fishel, Jeff. 1973. *Party and Opposition: Congressional Challengers in American Politics.* New York: David McKay.

Fiske, John. 1986. "Television: Polysemy and Popularity." *Critical Studies in Mass Communication* 3:391–407.

———. 1987. *Television Culture.* London: Methuen.

———. 1990. *Introduction to Communication Studies.* 2d ed. London: Routledge.

Fiske, Susan T. 1986. "Schema-Based Versus Piecemeal Politics: A Patchwork Quilt, but Not a Blanket, of Evidence." In *Political Cognition,* ed. Richard R. Lau and David O. Sears. Hillsdale, N.J.: Lawrence Erlbaum.

Fiske, Susan T., and Donald R. Kinder. 1981. "Involvement, Expertise, and Schema Use: Evidence from Political Cognition." In *Personality, Cognition, and Social Interaction,* ed. N. Cantor and J. F. Kihlstrom. Hillsdale, N.J.: Lawrence Erlbaum.

Fiske, Susan T., Donald R. Kinder, and W. M. Larter. 1983. "The Novice and the Expert: Knowledge-based Strategies in Political Cognition." *Journal of Experimental Social Psychology* 19:381–400.

Fiske, Susan T., and Shelley E. Taylor. 1984. *Social Cognition.* Reading, Mass.: Addison-Wesley.

Fitzpatrick, Kellyanne. 1995. "The Republican Warning." *Campaigns and Elections,* October/November.

Flanigan, William H., and Nancy H. Zingale. 1991. *Political Behavior of the American Electorate.* 7th ed. Washington, D.C.: Congressional Quarterly Press.

Flemming, Gregory N. 1995. "Presidential Coattails in Open-Seat Elections." *Legislative Studies Quarterly* 20:197–211.

Fritz, Sara, and Dwight Morris. 1992. *Handbook of Campaign Spending: Money in the 1990 Congressional Races.* Washington, D.C.: Congressional Quarterly Press.

Frymer, Paul. 1994. "Ideological Consensus within Divided Party Government." *Political Science Quarterly* 109:287–311.

Gaddie, Ronald Keith. 1995a. "Is There an Inherent Democratic Party Advantage in

U.S. House Elections? Evidence from the Open Seats." *Social Science Quarterly* 76:203–12.

———. 1995b. "Negating the Democratic Party Advantage in Open Seat Elections: A Research Update." *Social Science Quarterly* 76:673–80.

Gallup, George, Jr. 1993. *The Gallup Poll: Public Opinion 1992.* Wilmington, Del.: Scholarly Resources.

Gans, Herbert J. 1979. *Deciding What's News: A Study of* CBS Evening News, NBC Nightly News, Newsweek, *and* Time. New York: Pantheon Books.

Garand, James, and Donald Gross. 1984. "Changes in Vote Margins for Congressional Candidates: A Specification of Historical Trends." *American Political Science Review* 78:17–30.

Garand, James, Kenneth Wink, and Bryan Vincent. 1993a. "Changing Meanings of Electoral Marginality in U.S. House Elections, 1824–1978." *Political Research Quarterly* 46:27–48.

———. 1993b. "Similar Details, Different Interpretations: A Response to Professor Jacobson." *Political Research Quarterly* 46:55–66.

Garramone, Gina M., Charles K. Atkin, Bruce E. Pinkleton, and Richard T. Cole. 1990. "Effects of Negative Political Advertising on the Political Process." *Journal of Broadcasting and Electronic Media* 34:299–311.

Gelman, Andrew, and Gary King. 1990. "Estimating Incumbency Advantage without Bias." *American Journal of Political Science* 34:1142–64.

Germond, Jack W., and Jules Witcover. 1989. *Whose Broad Stripes and Bright Stars? The Trivial Pursuit of the Presidency 1988.* New York: Warner Books.

Gierzynski, Anthony, and David Breaux. 1996. "Legislative Elections and the Importance of Money." *Legislative Studies Quarterly* 21:337–57.

Gilliam, Franklin D., Jr. 1985. "Influences on Voter Turnout for U.S. House Elections in Non-Presidential Years." *Legislative Studies Quarterly* 10:339–51.

Gilpin, Alan. 1970. *Dictionary of Economic Terms.* London: Butterworths.

Glantz, Stanton A., Alan I. Abramowitz, and Michael P. Burkart. 1976. "Election Outcomes: Whose Money Matters?" *Journal of Politics* 38:1033–41.

Glass, Andrew J. 1996. "On-line Elections: The Internet's Impact on the Political Process." *Press/Politics* 1:140–46.

Glazer, Amihai, and Marc Robbins. 1985. "Congressional Responsiveness to Constituency Change." *American Journal of Political Science* 29:259–73.

Goffman, Erving. 1959. *The Presentation of Self in Everyday Life.* Garden City, N.Y.: Doubleday Anchor Books.

Goidel, Robert K., and Donald A. Gross. 1994. "A Systems Approach to Campaign Finance in U.S. House Elections." *American Politics Quarterly* 22:125–53.

Gold, Vic. 1977. *PR as in President.* Garden City, N.Y.: Doubleday.

Goldenberg, Edie N., and Michael W. Traugott. 1981. "Normal Vote Analysis of U.S. Congressional Elections." *Legislative Studies Quarterly* 6:247–57.

———. 1984. *Campaigning for Congress.* Washington, D.C.: Congressional Quarterly Press.

Goldman, Peter, and Tom Mathews. 1989. *The Quest for the Presidency: The 1988 Campaign.* New York: Simon and Schuster.

Gore, William J., and Robert L. Peabody. 1958. "The Functions of the Political Campaign: A Case Study." *Western Political Quarterly* 11:55–70.

Gosnell, Harold F. 1927. *Getting Out the Vote: An Experiment in the Stimulation of Voting.* Chicago: University of Chicago Press.

Gray, Jerry. 1993. "New Jersey Governor-Elect Denies Aide's Claim of Campaign Payoffs." *New York Times,* 11 November, A1, A18 (national edition).

Gray, Virginia. 1976. "A Note on Competition and Turnout in the American States." *Journal of Politics* 38:153–58.

Green, Don Philip, and Jonathan S. Krasno. 1988. "Salvation for the Spendthrift Incumbent: Reestimating the Effects of Campaign Spending in House Elections." *American Journal of Political Science* 32:884–907.

———. 1990. "Rebuttal to Jacobson's 'New Evidence for Old Arguments.'" *American Journal of Political Science* 34:363–72.

Greenfield, Jeff. 1980. *Playing to Win: An Insider's Guide to Politics.* New York: Simon and Schuster.

Gronbeck, Bruce E. 1978. "The Functions of Presidential Campaigning." *Communication Monographs* 45:268–80.

Groseclose, Timothy, and Keith Krehbiel. 1994. "Golden Parachutes, Rubber Checks, and Strategic Retirements from the 102d House." *American Journal of Political Science* 38:75–99.

Gross, Donald, and James Garand. 1984. "The Vanishing Marginals, 1824–1980." *Journal of Politics* 46:224–37.

Gurevitch, Michael, and Anandam P. Kavoori. 1992. "Television Spectacles as Politics." *Communication Monographs* 59:415–20.

Hagle, Timothy M., and Glenn E. Mitchell. 1992. "Goodness-of-Fit Measures for Probit and Logit." *American Journal of Political Science* 36:762–84.

Hagstrom, Jerry. 1984. "Hired Guns—Like It or Not, Campaign Consultants Are Clearly Here to Stay." *National Journal*, 20 October, 1976–83.

Hagstrom, Jerry, and Robert Guskind. 1986. "Advice for Hire." *National Journal*, 11 October, 2432–33.

Hallin, Daniel C. 1986. *The "Uncensored War": The Media and Vietnam.* New York: Oxford University Press.

Hamill, Ruth, Milton Lodge, and Frederick Blake. 1985. "The Breadth, Depth, and Utility of Class, Partisan, and Ideological Schemata." *American Journal of Political Science* 29:850–70.

Hamilton, Bill. 1997. "Studying Politics." *Campaigns and Elections*, December/January, 52.

Hamilton, Richard F. 1972. *Class and Politics in the United States.* New York: John Wiley.

Harris, Louis. 1963. "Polls and Politics in the United States." *Public Opinion Quarterly* 27:3–8.

Hart, Roderick P. 1994. *Seducing America: How Television Charms the Modern Voter.* Oxford: Oxford University Press.

———. 1996. "Easy Citizenship: Television's Curious Legacy." *Annals of the American Academy of Political and Social Science* 546:109–19.

Hastie, Reid. 1986. "A Primer of Information-Processing Theory for the Political Scientist." In *Political Cognition,* ed. Richard R. Lau and David O. Sears. Hillsdale, N.J.: Lawrence Erlbaum.

Hastie, Reid, and Nancy Pennington. 1989. "Notes on the Distinction between Memory-based versus On-line Judgments." In *On-line Cognition in Person Perception,* ed. John N. Bassili. Hillsdale, N.J.: Lawrence Erlbaum.

Heard, Alexander. 1960. *The Costs of Democracy.* Chapel Hill: University of North Carolina Press.

Held, David. 1987. *Models of Democracy.* Stanford: Stanford University Press.

Hellinger, Daniel, and Dennis R. Judd. 1994. *The Democratic Facade.* 2d ed. Belmont, Calif.: Wadsworth.

Herbert, Christopher J. 1994. "Stop/Look/Listen: A Guide for the Focus Group Observer." The Insight Group. Typescript.

Herrnson, Paul S. 1986. "Do Parties Make a Difference? The Role of Party Organizations in Congressional Elections." *Journal of Politics* 48:589–615.

———. 1988. *Party Campaigning in the 1980s.* Cambridge: Harvard University Press.

———. 1989. "National Party Decision Making, Strategies, and Resource Distribution in Congressional Elections." *Western Political Quarterly* 42:301–23.

———. 1992. "Campaign Professionalism and Fund-raising in Congressional Elections." *Journal of Politics* 54:859–69.

———. 1994. "The Revitalization of National Party Organizations." In *The Parties Respond: Changes in American Parties and Campaigns,* 2d ed., ed. L. Sandy Maisel. Boulder, Colo.: Westview Press.

———. 1995. *Congressional Elections: Campaigning at Home and in Washington.* Washington, D.C.: Congressional Quarterly Press.

———. 2000. "Hired Guns and House Races: Campaign Professionals in House Elections." In *Campaign Warriors,* ed. James A. Thurber and Candice J. Nelson. Washington, D.C.: Brookings Institution Press.

Herrnson, Paul S., and Kirsten Andersen. 1995. "The Battle of the Sexes? A Comparison of Women's and Men's Campaigns for the U.S. House of Representatives." Paper presented at the Midwest Political Science Association Annual Meeting, Chicago, IL.

Herrnson, Paul S., Kelly D. Patterson, and John J. Pitney Jr. 1996. "From Ward Heelers to Public Relations Experts: The Parties' Response to Mass Politics." In *Broken Contract? Changing Relationships between Americans and Their Government,* ed. Stephen C. Craig. Boulder, Colo.: Westview Press.

Hershey, Marjorie Randon. 1974. *The Making of Campaign Strategy.* Lexington, Mass.: D. C. Heath.

———. 1984. *Running for Office: The Political Education of Campaigners.* Chatham, N.J.: Chatham House.

———. 1994. "The Meaning of a Mandate: Interpretations of 'Mandate' in 1984 Presidential Election Coverage." *Polity* 27:225–54.

Hess, Carol, ed. 1989. *Political Resource Directory: National Edition 1990.* Rye, N.Y.: Political Resources.

———. 1992. *Political Resource Directory: National Edition 1993.* Rye, N.Y.: Political Resources.

———. 1999. *Political Resource Directory: National Edition 1999.* Burlington, Vt.: Political Resources.

Hiebert, Ray, Robert Jones, Ernest Lotito, and John Lorenz, eds. 1971. *The Political Image Merchants: Strategies in the New Politics.* Washington, D.C.: Acropolis Books.

Higgins, E. T., W. S. Rholes, and C. R. Jones. 1977. "Category Accessibility and Impression Formation." *Journal of Experimental Social Psychology* 13:141–54.

Hinckley, Barbara. 1980. "House Re-elections and Senate Defeats: The Role of the Challengers." *British Journal of Political Science* 10:441–60.

———. 1981. *Congressional Elections.* Washington, D.C.: Congressional Quarterly Press.

Holbrook, Thomas M. 1994. "Campaigns, National Conditions, and U.S. Presidential Elections." *American Journal of Political Science* 38:973–98.

———. 1996. *Do Campaigns Matter?* Thousand Oaks, Calif.: Sage.

Huckfeldt, Robert, and John Sprague. 1992. "Political Parties and Electoral Mobilization: Political Structure, Social Structure, and the Party Canvass." *American Political Science Review* 86:70–86.

Huckshorn, Robert Jack, and Robert C. Spencer. 1971. *The Politics of Defeat: Campaigning for Congress.* Amherst: University of Massachusetts Press.

"Inside Politics: Faster than a Speeding Bullet." 1996. *Campaigns and Elections,* August.

Isaak, Alan C. 1985. *Scope and Methods of Political Science: An Introduction to the Methodology of Political Inquiry.* 4th ed. Pacific Grove, Calif.: Brooks/Cole.

Iyengar, Shanto, and Donald R. Kinder. 1987. *News That Matters: Television and American Opinion.* Chicago: University of Chicago Press.

Jackson, Brooks. 1988. *Honest Graft: Big Money and the American Political Process.* New York: Alfred A. Knopf.

Jackson, Robert A. 1996a. "A Reassessment of Voter Mobilization." *Political Research Quarterly* 49:331–49.

———. 1996b. "The Mobilization of Congressional Electorates." *Legislative Studies Quarterly* 21:425–45.

Jacobs, Lawrence R., and Robert Y. Shapiro. 1994. "Issues, Candidate Image, and Priming: The Use of Private Polls in Kennedy's 1960 Presidential Campaign." *American Political Science Review* 88:527–40.

Jacobson, Gary C. 1976. "Presidential Coattails in 1972." *Public Opinion Quarterly* 40:194–200.

———. 1978. "The Effects of Campaign Spending in Congressional Elections." *American Political Science Review* 72:769–83.

———. 1980. *Money in Congressional Elections.* New Haven: Yale University Press.

———. 1985. "Money and Voters Reconsidered: Congressional Elections, 1972–1982." *Public Choice* 47:7–62.

———. 1987a. "The Marginals Never Vanished: Incumbency and Competition in Elections to the U.S. House of Representatives, 1952–1982." *American Journal of Political Science* 31:126–41.

———. 1987b. "Running Scared: Elections and Congressional Politics in the 1980s." In *Congress: Structure and Policy,* ed. Mathew McCubbins and Terry Sullivan. Cambridge: Cambridge University Press.

———. 1989. "Strategic Politicians and the Dynamics of House Elections, 1946–1986." *American Political Science Review* 83:773–93.

———. 1990a. "The Effect of Campaign Spending in House Elections: New Evidence for Old Arguments." *American Journal of Political Science* 34:334–62.

———. 1990b. *The Electoral Origins of Divided Government: Competition in U.S. House Elections, 1946–1988.* Boulder, Colo.: Westview Press.

———. 1992. *The Politics of Congressional Elections.* 3d ed. New York: HarperCollins.

———. 1993a. "Congress: Unusual Year, Unusual Election." In *The Elections of 1992,* ed. Michael Nelson. Washington, D.C.: Congressional Quarterly Press.

———. 1993b. "Getting the Details Right: A Comment on 'Changing Meanings of Electoral Marginality in U.S. House Elections, 1824–1978.'" *Political Research Quarterly* 46:49–54.

———. 1996a. "Divided Government and the 1994 Elections." In *Divided Government: Change, Uncertainty, and the Constitutional Order,* ed. Peter F. Galderisi with Roberta Q. Herzberg and Peter McNamara. Lanham, Md.: Rowman and Littlefield.

———. 1996b. "The 1994 House Elections in Perspective." In *Midterm: The Elections of 1994 in Context,* ed. Philip A. Klinkner. Boulder, Colo.: Westview Press.

———. 1996c. "The 1994 House Elections in Perspective." *Political Science Quarterly* 111:203–23.

Jacobson, Gary C., and Michael Dimock. 1994. "Checking Out: The Effects of Bank Overdrafts on the 1992 House Elections." *American Journal of Political Science* 38:601–24.

Jacobson, Gary C., and Samuel Kernell. 1983. *Strategy and Choice in Congressional Elections*. 2d ed. New Haven: Yale University Press.

Jacobson, Gary C., and Thomas P. Kim. 1996. "After 1994: The New Politics of Congressional Elections." Presented at the annual meeting of the Midwest Political Science Association, Chicago.

Jamieson, Kathleen Hall. 1984. *Packaging the Presidency: A History and Criticism of Presidential Campaign Advertising*. New York: Oxford University Press.

———. 1992. *Dirty Politics: Deception, Distraction, and Democracy*. New York: Oxford University Press.

———. 1996. *Packaging the Presidency: A History and Criticism of Presidential Campaign Advertising*. 3d ed. New York: Oxford University Press.

Jamieson, Kathleen Hall, and Joseph N. Cappella. 1997. "Setting the Record Straight: Do Ad Watches Help or Hurt?" *Press/Politics* 2:19–28.

Javits, J. K. 1947. "How I Used a Poll in Campaigning for Congress." *Public Opinion Quarterly* 11:222–26.

Jensen, Klaus Bruhn. 1995. *The Social Semiotics of Mass Communication*. Thousand Oaks, Calif.: Sage.

Jervis, Robert. 1986. "Cognition and Political Behavior." In *Political Cognition*, ed. Richard R. Lau and David O. Sears. Hillsdale, N.J.: Lawrence Erlbaum.

Johnson, Dennis W. 2000. "The Business of Political Consulting." In *Campaign Warriors*, ed. James A. Thurber and Candice J. Nelson. Washington, D.C.: Brookings Institution Press.

Johnson-Laird, Philip N. 1983. *Mental Models: Towards a Cognitive Science of Language, Inference, and Consciousness*. Cambridge: Harvard University Press.

Johnson-Parker, Karen, and Tony Parker. 1994. "Politics Is a Contact Sport: Use the Telephone!" *Campaigns and Elections*, July.

Joyner, Conrad F. 1969. "Running a Congressional Campaign." In *Practical Politics in the United States*, ed. Cornelius P. Cotter. Boston: Allyn and Bacon.

Kaid, Lynda Lee, Valerie Cryer Downs, and Sandra Ragan. 1990. "Political Argumentation and Violations of Audience Expectations: An Analysis of the Bush-Rather Encounter." *Journal of Broadcasting and Electronic Media* 34:1–15.

Katz, Daniel, and Samuel J. Eldersveld. 1961. "The Impact of Local Party Activity upon the Electorate." *Public Opinion Quarterly* 25:1–24.

Katz, Elihu. 1957. "The Two-Step Flow of Communication: An Up-to-Date Report on an Hypothesis." *Public Opinion Quarterly* 21:61–78.

———. 1963. "The Diffusion of New Ideas and Practices." In *The Science of Human Communication*, ed. W. Schramm. New York: Basic Books.

Katz, Elihu, and Paul Lazarsfeld. 1955. *Personal Influence: The Part Played by People in the Flow of Mass Communications*. Glencoe, Ill.: Free Press.

Kawato, Sadafumi. 1987. "Nationalization and Partisan Realignment in Congressional Elections." *American Political Science Review* 81:1235–50.

Kayden, Xandra. 1978. *Campaign Organization*. Lexington, Mass.: D. C. Heath.

Kayden, Xandra, and Eddie Mahe Jr. 1985. *The Party Goes On: The Persistence of the Two-Party System in the United States*. New York: Basic Books.

Keith, Bruce E., David B. Magleby, Candice J. Nelson, Elizabeth Orr, Mark C. Westlye, and Raymond E. Wolfinger. 1992. *The Myth of the Independent Voter*. Berkeley: University of California Press.

Kelley, Stanley, Jr. 1956. *Professional Public Relations and Political Power.* Baltimore: Johns Hopkins University Press.

———. 1960. *Political Campaigning: Problems in Creating an Informed Electorate.* Washington, D.C.: Brookings Institution.

Kennedy, Peter. 1992. *A Guide to Econometrics.* 3d ed. Cambridge: MIT Press.

Kenney, Patrick J., and Tom W. Rice. 1989. "An Empirical Examination of the Minimax Hypothesis." *American Politics Quarterly* 17:153–62.

Kenny, Christopher, and Michael McBurnett. 1992. "A Dynamic Model of the Effect of Campaign Spending on Congressional Vote Choice." *American Journal of Political Science* 36:923–37.

Kern, Montague. 1989. *30–Second Politics: Political Advertising in the Eighties.* New York: Praeger.

Kern, Montague, and Marion Just. 1994. "How Voters Construct Images of Political Candidates: The Role of Political Advertising and Televised News." Joan Shorenstein Barone Center, Kennedy School of Government, Harvard University. Research Paper R-10.

———. 1995. "The Focus Group Method, Political Advertising, Campaign News, and the Construction of Candidate Images." *Political Communication* 12:127–45.

Kernell, Samuel. 1977. "Presidential Popularity and Negative Voting: An Alternative Explanation of the Midterm Congressional Decline of the President's Party." *American Political Science Review* 71:44–66.

Kessel, John H. 1968. *The Goldwater Coalition: Republican Strategies in 1964.* New York: Bobbs-Merrill.

Key, V. O., Jr. 1949. *Southern Politics.* New York: Vintage Books.

———. 1958. *Politics, Parties, and Pressure Groups.* New York: Thomas Y. Crowell.

Key, V. O., Jr. with Milton C. Cummings Jr. 1966. *The Responsible Electorate: Rationality in Presidential Voting, 1936–1960.* New York: Vintage Books.

Kinder, Donald R., and Susan T. Fiske. 1986. "Presidents in the Public Mind." In *Political Psychology,* ed. Margaret G. Hermann. San Francisco: Jossey-Bass.

King, Anthony. 1997. *Running Scared: Why America's Politicians Campaign Too Much and Govern Too Little.* New York: Free Press.

King, Gary, Robert O. Keohane, and Sidney Verba. 1994. *Designing Social Inquiry: Scientific Inference in Qualitative Research.* Princeton: Princeton University Press.

King, Robert, and Martin Schnitzer. 1968. "Contemporary Use of Private Political Polling." *Public Opinion Quarterly* 32:431–36.

Kingdon, John W. 1966. *Candidates for Office: Beliefs and Strategies.* New York: Random House.

Kinsey, Dennis F., and Steven H. Chaffee. 1996. "Communication Behavior and Presidential Approval: The Decline of George Bush." *Political Communication* 13:281–91.

Klapper, Joseph T. 1960. *The Effects of Mass Communication.* Glencoe, Ill.: Free Press.

Kolbert, Elizabeth. 1995. "The Vocabulary of Votes: Frank Luntz." *New York Times Magazine,* 26 March, 46–49.

Kolodny, Robin, and Angela Logan. 1998. "Political Consultants and the Extension of Party Goals." *PS: Political Science and Politics* 31:155–59.

Kramer, Gerald H. 1970–71. "The Effects of Precinct-Level Canvassing on Voter Behavior." *Public Opinion Quarterly* 34:560–72.

Krasno, Jonathan S., and Donald Philip Green. 1988. "Preempting Quality Challengers in House Elections." *Journal of Politics* 50:920–36.

Krasno, Jonathan S., Donald Philip Green, and Jonathan A. Cowden. 1994. "The Dynamics of Fund-raising in House Elections." *Journal of Politics* 56:459–74.

Kuklinski, James H., Robert C. Luskin, and John Bolland. 1991. "Where Is the Schema? Going Beyond the 'S' Word in Political Psychology." *American Political Science Review* 85:1341–56.

Ladd, Evett Carll. 1993. "The 1992 Vote for President Clinton: Another Brittle Mandate." *Political Science Quarterly* 108:1–28.

———. 1995. "The 1994 Congressional Elections: The Postindustrial Realignment Continues." *Political Science Quarterly* 110:1–23.

Lake, Celinda. 1995. "The Democratic Puzzle." *Campaigns and Elections,* October/November.

Lamb, Karl A., and Paul A. Smith. 1968. *Campaign Decision Making: The Presidential Election of 1964.* Belmont, Calif.: Wadsworth.

Lane, Robert E. 1969. *Political Thinking and Consciousness: The Private Life of the Political Mind.* Chicago: Markham.

———. 1986. "What Are People Trying to Do with Their Schemata? The Question of Purpose." In *Political Cognition,* ed. Richard R. Lau and David O. Sears. Hillsdale, N.J.: Lawrence Erlbaum.

Larson, Magali Sarfatti. 1977. *The Rise of Professionalism: A Sociological Analysis.* Los Angeles: University of California Press.

Lau, Richard R. 1986. "Political Schemata, Candidate Evaluations, and Voting Behavior." In *Political Cognition,* ed. Richard R. Lau and David O. Sears. Hillsdale, N.J.: Lawrence Erlbaum.

Lau, Richard R., and R. Erber. 1985. "An Information Processing Approach to Political Sophistication." In *Mass Media and Political Thought,* ed. S. Kraus and R. Perloff. Beverly Hills, Calif.: Sage.

Lau, Richard R., and David O. Sears. 1986. "Social Cognition and Political Cognition: The Past, the Present, and the Future." In *Political Cognition,* ed. Richard R. Lau and David O. Sears. Hillsdale, N.J.: Lawrence Erlbaum.

Lauth, Laura E. 1996. "Strategic Media Tips for Women Candidates." *Campaigns and Elections,* February.

Lazarsfeld, Paul F., Bernard Berelson, and Hazel Gaudet. [1944] 1968. *The People's Choice: How the Voter Makes Up His Mind in a Presidential Campaign.* 3d ed. New York: Columbia University Press.

"Lessons Learned." 1997. *Campaigns and Elections,* February.

Leeds-Hurwitz, Wendy. 1993. *Semiotics and Communication: Signs, Codes, Cultures.* Hillsdale, N.J.: Lawrence Erlbaum.

Lenart, Silvo. 1994. *Shaping Political Attitudes: The Impact of Interpersonal Communication and Mass Media.* Thousand Oaks, Calif.: Sage.

LeoGrande, William M., and Alana S. Jeydel. 1997. "Using Presidential Election Returns to Measure Constituency Ideology: A Research Note." *American Politics Quarterly* 25:3–18.

Leuthold, David A. 1968. *Electioneering in a Democracy: Campaigns for Congress.* New York: John Wiley.

Levin, Murray B. 1962. *The Compleat Politician: Political Strategy in Massachusetts.* New York: Bobbs-Merrill.

Levine, Peter. 1994. "Consultants and American Political Culture." *Philosophy and Public Policy* 14(3/4):1–6.

Lewis-Beck, Michael S. 1990. *Applied Regression: An Introduction.* Newbury Park, Calif.: Sage.

Liley, Betsy. 1994. "Ads Accentuate Negative." *Burlington Free Press,* 1 November, A1.

Lodge, Milton, and Ruth Hamill. 1986. "A Partisan Schema for Political Information Processing." *American Political Science Review* 80:505–19.

Lodge, Milton, and Kathleen M. McGraw. 1991. "Where Is the Schema? Critiques." *American Political Science Review* 85:1357–64.

Lodge, Milton, Kathleen M. McGraw, and Patrick Stroh. 1989. "An Impression-driven Model of Candidate Evaluation." *American Political Science Review* 87:399–419.

Lodge, Milton, Marco R. Steenbergen, and Shawn Brau. 1995. "The Responsive Voter: Campaign Information and the Dynamics of Candidate Evaluation." *American Political Science Review* 89:309–26.

Loomis, Burdett. 1988. *The New American Politician: Ambition, Entrepreneurship, and the Changing Face of Political Life.* New York: Basic Books.

Lottes, Ilsa L., Marina A. Adler, and Alfred DeMaris. 1996. "Using and Interpreting Logistic Regression: A Guide for Teachers and Students." *Teaching Sociology* 24:284–98.

Luntz, Frank I. 1988. *Candidates, Consultants, and Campaigns: The Style and Substance of American Electioneering.* New York: Basil Blackwell.

Lupfer, Michael, and David E. Price. "On the Merits of Face-to-Face Campaigning." *Social Science Quarterly* 53:534–43.

McAdams, John, and John Johannes. 1988. "Congressmen, Perquisites, and Elections." *Journal of Politics* 50:412–39.

McCubbins, Mathew D., ed. 1992. *Under the Watchful Eye: Managing Presidential Campaigns in the Television Era.* Washington, D.C.: Congressional Quarterly Press.

McGinniss, Joe. 1969. *The Selling of the President 1968.* New York: Trident Press.

McGraw, Kathleen M., Milton Lodge, and Patrick Stroh. 1990. "On-line Processing in Candidate Evaluation: The Effects of Issue Order, Issue Salience, and Sophistication." *Political Behavior* 12:41–58.

McKinnon, Lori Melton, Lynda Lee Kaid, Janet Murphy, and Cynthia K. Acree. 1996. "Policing Political Ads: An Analysis of Five Leading Newspapers' Responses to 1992 Political Advertisements." *Journalism and Mass Communication Quarterly* 73:66–76.

McLeod, Jack M., and Lee B. Becker. 1981. "The Uses and Gratifications Approach." In *Handbook of Political Communication,* ed. Dan D. Nimmo and Keith R. Sanders. Beverly Hills: Sage.

Magleby, David B., and Candice J. Nelson. 1990. *The Money Chase: Congressional Campaign Finance Reform.* Washington, D.C.: Brookings Institution.

Magleby, David B., and Kelly D. Patterson. 1998a. "Consultants and Direct Democracy." *PS: Political Science and Politics* 31:160–69.

———. 1998b. "Campaign Consultants and Direct Democracy: The Politics of Citizen Control." Paper presented at the conference Role of Political Consultants in Elections, Washington, D.C.

Maisel, L. Sandy. 1993. *Parties and Elections in America: The Electoral Process.* 2d ed. New York: Random House.

———. 1992. "Quality Candidates in House and Senate Elections, from 1982 to 1990." In *The Atomistic Congress: An Interpretation of Congressional Change,* ed. Allen D. Hertzke and Ronald M. Peters Jr. Armonk, N.Y.: M. E. Sharpe.

Maltzman, Forrest, and Lee Sigelman. 1996. "The Politics of Talk: Unconstrained Floor Time in the U.S. House of Representatives." *Journal of Politics* 58:819–30.

Mancini, Paolo, and David L. Swanson. 1996. "Politics, Media, and Modern Democracy: Introduction." In *Politics, Media, and Modern Democracy: An International Study of Innovations in Electoral Campaigning and Their Consequences,* ed. David L. Swanson and Paolo Mancini. Westport, Conn.: Praeger.

Manheim, Jarol B. 1975. *The Politics Within: A Primer in Political Attitudes and Behavior.* Englewood Cliffs, N.J.: Prentice-Hall.

Mann, Thomas. 1977. *Unsafe at Any Margin.* Washington, D.C.: American Enterprise.

Mann, Thomas, and Raymond E. Wolfinger. 1980. "Candidates and Parties in Congressional Elections." *American Political Science Review* 74:617–32.

Marquette, Jesse. 1996. "How to Become a Wise Consumer of Campaign Polling." In *Campaign Craft: The Strategies, Tactics, and Art of Political Campaign Management,* ed. Daniel M. Shea. Westport, Conn.: Praeger.

Matalin, Mary, and James Carville. 1994. *All's Fair: Love, War, and Running for President.* New York: Random House and Simon and Schuster.

Mauser, Gary A. 1983. *Political Marketing: An Approach to Campaign Strategy.* New York: Praeger.

Mayer, Lawrence S., and I. J. Good. 1975. "Is Minimax Regret Applicable to Voting Decisions?" *American Political Science Review* 69:916–17.

Mayer, William G. 1996. "In Defense of Negative Campaigning." *Political Science Quarterly* 111:437–55.

Mayhew, David R. 1974a. *Congress: The Electoral Connection.* New Haven: Yale University Press.

———. 1974b. "Congressional Elections: The Case of the Vanishing Marginals." *Polity* 6:295–317.

Meadow, Robert G., ed. 1984. *New Communication Technologies in Politics.* Washington, D.C.: Washington Program of the Annenberg School of Communications.

———. 1985. "Political Campaigns, New Technology, and Political Communications Research." In *Political Communication Yearbook, 1984,* ed. Keith R. Sanders, Lynda Lee Kaid, and Dan Nimmo. Carbondale: Southern Illinois University Press.

———. 1989. "Political Campaigns." In *Public Communication Campaigns,* 2d ed., ed. Ronald E. Rice and Charles K. Atkin. Newbury Park, Calif.: Sage.

Medvic, Stephen K. 1997. "Party Support and Consultant Use in Congressional Elections." Presented at the annual meeting of the American Political Science Association, Washington, D.C.

———. 1998. "The Effectiveness of the Political Consultant as a Campaign Resource." *PS: Political Science and Politics* 31:150–54.

———. 2000. "Professionalization in Congressional Campaigns." In *Campaign Warriors,* ed. James A. Thurber and Candice J. Nelson. Washington, D.C.: Brookings Institution Press.

Medvic, Stephen K., and Silvo Lenart. 1997. "The Influence of Political Consultants in the 1992 Congressional Elections." *Legislative Studies Quarterly* 22:61–77.

Mendelberg, Tali. 1997. "Executing Hortons: Racial Crime in the 1988 Presidential Campaign." *Public Opinion Quarterly* 61:134–57.

Milburn, Michael A. 1987. "Ideological Self-Schemata and Schematically Induced Attitude Consistency." *Journal of Experimental Social Psychology* 23:383–98.

———. 1991. *Persuasion and Politics: The Social Psychology of Public Opinion.* Pacific Grove, Calif.: Brooks/Cole.

Miller, Arthur H. 1979. "Normal Vote Analysis: Sensitivity to Change over Time." *American Journal of Political Science* 23:406–25.

———. 1986. "Partisan Cognitions in Transition." In *Political Cognition,* ed. Richard R. Lau and David O. Sears. Hillsdale, N.J.: Lawrence Erlbaum.

———. 1991. "Where Is the Schema? Critiques." *American Political Science Review* 85:1369–77.

Miller, Arthur H., Martin P. Wattenberg, and Oksana Malanchuk. 1986. "Schematic

Assessments of Presidential Candidates." *American Political Science Review* 80:521–40.

Mills, Claudia. 1995. "Politics and Manipulation." *Social Theory and Practice* 21:97–112.

Minogue, Kenneth. 1996. "Machiavelli and the Duck/Rabbit Problem of Political Perception." *Government and Opposition* 31:216–26.

Mitchell, Greg. 1992. *The Campaign of the Century: Upton Sinclair's Race for Governor of California and the Birth of Media Politics.* New York: Random House.

Mondak, Jeffrey J. 1990. "Determinants of Coattail Voting." *Political Behavior* 12:265–88.

———. 1993. "Presidential Coattails and Open Seats: The District-Level Impact of Heuristic Processing." *American Politics Quarterly* 21:307–19.

Mondak, Jeffrey J., and Carl McCurley. 1994. "Cognitive Efficiency and the Congressional Vote: The Psychology of Coattail Voting." *Political Research Quarterly* 47:151–75.

Moore, David W. 1992. *The Superpollsters: How They Measure and Manipulate Public Opinion in America.* New York: Four Walls Eight Windows.

Moore, Jonathan, ed. 1981. *The Campaign for President: 1980 in Retrospect.* Cambridge: Ballinger.

———. 1986. *Campaign for President: The Managers Look at '84.* Dover, Mass.: Auburn House.

Moore, Jonathan, and Janet Fraser, eds. 1977. *Campaign for President: The Managers Look at '76.* Cambridge: Ballinger.

Morris, Dick. 1997. *Behind the Oval Office: Winning the Presidency in the Nineties.* New York: Random House.

———. 1999. *The New Prince: Machiavelli Updated for the Twenty-first Century.* Los Angeles: Renaissance Books.

Morris, Dwight, and Murielle E. Gamache. 1994. *Handbook of Campaign Spending: Money in the 1992 Congressional Races.* Washington, D.C.: Congressional Quarterly Press.

Mundy, Alicia. 1993. "Victory Has a Thousand Fathers." *Campaigns and Elections,* January.

Napolitan, Joseph. 1972. *The Election Game and How to Win It.* New York: Doubleday.

Neuman, W. Russell, Marion R. Just, and Ann N. Crigler. 1992. *Common Knowledge: News and the Construction of Political Meaning.* Chicago: University of Chicago Press.

"New Jersey Vote Probe Finds No Suppression." 1994. *Congressional Quarterly Weekly Report,* 15 January, 83.

Newman, Bruce I. 1994. *The Marketing of the President: Political Marketing as Campaign Strategy.* Thousand Oaks, Calif.: Sage.

Nie, Norman H., Sidney Verba, and John R. Petrocik. 1976. *The Changing American Voter.* Cambridge: Harvard University Press.

Niemi, Richard G., and Herbert F. Weisberg, eds. 1993. *Controversies in Voting Behavior.* 3d ed. Washington, D.C.: Congressional Quarterly Press.

Nimmo, Dan. 1970. *The Political Persuaders: The Techniques of Modern Election Campaigns.* Englewood Cliffs, N.J.: Prentice-Hall.

———. 1978. *Political Communication and Public Opinion in America.* Santa Monica, Calif.: Goodyear.

———. 1996. "Politics, Media and Modern Democracy: The United States." In *Politics, Media, and Modern Democracy: An International Study of Innovations in Elec-*

toral Campaigning and Their Consequences. ed. David L. Swanson and Paolo Mancini. Westport, Conn.: Praeger.

Nimmo, Dan, and James E. Combs. 1980. *Subliminal Politics: Myths and Mythmakers in America.* Englewood Cliffs, N.J.: Prentice-Hall.

———. 1983. *Mediated Political Realities.* New York: Longman.

———. 1992. *The Political Pundits.* Westport, Conn.: Praeger.

Nimmo, Dan, and Robert L. Savage. 1976. *Candidates and Their Images: Concepts, Methods, and Findings.* Pacific Palisades, CA: Goodyear Publishing.

Norquist, Grover, Dick Woodward, and Rick Arnold. 1994. "Citizen Initiatives." *Campaigns and Elections,* May.

Norusis, Marija J. 1994. *SPSS 6.1 Base System User's Guide, Part 2.* Chicago: SPSS.

Nuessel, Frank. 1996. "Introducing Semiotics." *Semiotica* 110:145–55.

O'Donnell, Karen Fling. 1986. "Consultant Scorecard." *Campaigns and Elections,* November/December.

Ornstein, Norman J., Thomas E. Mann, and Michael J. Malbin. 1994. *Vital Statistics on Congress, 1993–1994.* Washington, D.C.: Congressional Quarterly Press.

O'Shaughnessy, N. J. 1990a. "High Priesthood, Low Priestcraft: The Role of Political Consultants." *European Journal of Marketing* 24(2):7–23.

———. 1990b. *The Phenomenon of Political Marketing.* New York: St. Martin's Press.

Page, Benjamin I. 1976. "The Theory of Political Ambiguity." *American Political Science Review* 70:742–52.

———. 1978. *Choices and Echoes in Presidential Elections.* Chicago: University of Chicago Press.

Page, Benjamin I., and Richard A. Brody. 1972. "Policy Voting and the Electoral Process: The Vietnam War Issue." *American Political Science Review* 66:979–95.

Parenti, Michael. 1995. *Democracy for the Few.* 6th ed. New York: St. Martin's Press.

Patterson, Samuel C., and Gregory A. Caldeira. 1983. "Getting Out the Vote: Participation in Gubernatorial Elections." *American Political Science Review* 77:675–89.

Patterson, Thomas E. 1993. *Out of Order.* New York: Alfred A. Knopf.

Peele, Gillian. 1982. "Campaign Consultants." *Electoral Studies* 1:355–62.

Perry, James M. 1968. *The New Politics: The Expanding Technology of Political Manipulation.* New York: Clarkson N. Potter.

Petracca, Mark P. 1989. "Political Consultants and Democratic Governance." *PS: Political Science and Politics* 22:11–14.

Petracca, Mark P., and Courtney Wiercioch. 1988. "Consultant Democracy: The Activities and Attitudes of American Political Consultants." Presented at the annual meeting of the Midwest Political Science Association, Chicago.

Petrocik, John R. 1991. "Divided Government: Is It All in the Campaigns?" In *The Politics of Divided Government,* ed. Gary W. Cox and Samuel Kernell. Boulder, Colo.: Westview Press.

Petrocik, John R., and Joseph Doherty. 1996. "The Road to Divided Government: Paved without Intention." In *Divided Government: Change, Uncertainty, and the Constitutional Order,* ed. Peter F. Galderisi with Roberta Q. Herzberg and Peter McNamara. Lanham, Md.: Rowman and Littlefield.

Pfau, Michael, and Allen Louden. 1994. "Effectiveness of Adwatch Formats in Deflecting Political Attack Ads." *Communication Research* 21:325–41.

Pitchell, Robert J. 1958. "The Influence of Professional Campaign Management Firms in Partisan Elections in California." *Western Political Quarterly* 11:278–300.

Pitney, John F., Jr., and William F. Connelly Jr. 1996. "'Permanent Minority' No More: House Republicans in 1994." In *Midterm: The Elections of 1994 in Context,* ed. Philip A. Klinkner. Boulder, Colo.: Westview Press.

Political pages, 1996–97. 1996. *Campaigns and Elections*, March.

Polsby, Nelson W., and Aaron Wildavsky. 1996. *Presidential Elections: Strategies and Structures in American Politics.* 9th ed. Chatham, N.J.: Chatham House.

Pomper, Gerald M. 1968. *Elections in America: Control and Influence in Democratic Politics.* New York: Dodd, Mead.

——. 1972. "From Confusion to Clarity: Issues and American Voters, 1956–1968." *American Political Science Review* 66:415–28.

——, ed. 1981. *Party Renewal in America.* New York: Praeger.

Popkin, Samuel L. 1994. *The Reasoning Voter: Communication and Persuasion in Presidential Campaigns.* 2d ed. Chicago: University of Chicago Press.

Pressman, Steven. 1984. "From Television to Potholders, Consultants Leave Their Mark on 1984 Congressional Races." *Congressional Quarterly Weekly Report*, 22 December, 3151–54.

Price, David E. 1984. *Bringing Back the Parties.* Washington, D.C.: Congressional Quarterly Press.

Price, David E., and Michael Lupfer. 1973. "Volunteers for Gore: The Impact of a Precinct-Level Canvass in Three Tennessee Cities." *Journal of Politics* 35:410–38.

Purcell, Edward A., Jr. 1973. *The Crisis of Democratic Theory: Scientific Naturalism and the Problem of Value.* Lexington: University Press of Kentucky.

Putnam, Robert D. 2000. *Bowling Alone: The Collapse and Revival of American Community.* New York: Simon and Schuster.

Quirk, Paul J. 1989. "The Election." In *The Elections of 1988*, ed. Michael Nelson. Washington, D.C.: Congressional Quarterly Press.

Ragsdale, Lyn. 1981. "Incumbent Popularity, Challenger Invisibility, and Congressional Voters." *Legislative Studies Quarterly* 6:201–18.

——. 1985. "Legislative Elections and Electoral Responsiveness." In *Handbook of Legislative Research*, ed. Gerhard Loewenberg, Samuel C. Patterson, and Malcolm E. Jewell. Cambridge: Harvard University Press.

——. 1989. "Do Voters Matter? Democracy in Congressional Elections." In *Congressional Politics*, ed. Christopher Deering. Chicago: Dorsey Press.

——. 1994. "Old Approaches and New Challenges in Legislative Election Research." *Legislative Studies Quarterly* 19:537–82.

Ragsdale, Lyn, and Timothy E. Cook. 1987. "Representatives' Actions and Challengers' Reactions: Limits to Candidate Connections in the House." *American Journal of Political Science* 31:45–81.

Rahn, Wendy M., John H. Aldrich, Eugene Borgida, and John L. Sullivan. 1990. "A Social-Cognitive Model of Candidate Appraisal." In *Information and Democratic Processes*, ed. John A. Ferejohn and James H. Kuklinski. Urbana: University of Illinois Press.

Ranney, Austin. 1962. *The Doctrine of Responsible Party Government: Its Origin and Present State.* Urbana: University of Illinois Press.

——. 1975. *Curing the Mischiefs of Faction.* Berkeley: University of California Press.

RePass, David E. 1971. "Issue Salience and Party Choice." *American Political Science Review* 65:389–400.

Riker, William H., and Peter C. Ordeshook. 1968. "A Theory of the Calculus of Voting." *American Political Science Review* 62:25–42.

Robeck, Bruce W. 1982. "State Legislator Candidates for the U.S. House: Prospects for Success." *Legislative Studies Quarterly* 7:507–14.

Rollins, Ed. 1996. *Bare Knuckles and Back Rooms: My Life in American Politics.* New York: Broadway Books.

Roper, William L. 1978. *Winning Politics: A Handbook for Candidates and Campaign Workers*. Radnor, Penn.: Chilton.

Rosenbaum, David E. 1997. "Deficit: Public Enemy No. 1, It's Not." *New York Times*, 15 February.

Rosenberg, Shawn W., Lisa Bohan, Patrick McCafferty, and Kevin Harris. 1986. "The Image and the Vote: The Effect of Candidate Presentation on Voter Preference." *American Journal of Political Science* 30:108–27.

Rosenbloom, David Lee. 1973. *The Election Men: Professional Campaign Managers and American Democracy*. New York: Quadrangle Books.

Rosenstone, Steven J., and John Mark Hansen. 1993. *Mobilization, Participation, and Democracy in America*. New York: Macmillan.

Rumelhart, Donald E. 1980. "Schemata: The Building Blocks of Cognition." In *Theoretical Issues in Reading Comprehension: Perspectives from Cognitive Psychology, Linguistics, Artificial Intelligence, and Education*, ed. R. J. Spiro, B. C. Bruce, and William F. Brewer. Hillsdale, N.J.: Lawrence Erlbaum.

———. 1983. "Schemata and the Cognitive System." In *Handbook of Social Cognition*, ed. Robert S. Wyer and Thomas K. Srull. Hillsdale, N.J.: Lawrence Erlbaum.

Runkel, David R., ed. 1989. *Campaign for President: The Managers Look at '88*. Dover, Mass.: Auburn House.

Sabato, Larry J. 1981. *The Rise of Political Consultants: New Ways of Winning Elections*. New York: Basic Books.

———. 1983. "Political Consultants and the New Campaign Technology." In *Interest Group Politics*, ed. Allan J. Cigler and Burdett A. Loomis. Washington, D.C.: Congressional Quarterly Press.

———. 1984. *PAC Power: Inside the World of Political Action Committees*. New York: W. W. Norton.

———. 1988. *The Party's Just Begun*. Glenview, Ill.: Scott Foresman/Little, Brown.

———. 1989. "Political Influence, the News Media, and Campaign Consultants." *PS: Political Science and Politics* 22:15–17.

———. 1991. *Feeding Frenzy: How Attack Journalism Has Transformed American Politics*. New York: Free Press.

Sabato, Larry J., and Glenn R. Simpson. 1996. *Dirty Little Secrets: The Persistence of Corruption in American Politics*. New York: Times Books.

Salmore, Barbara G., and Stephen A. Salmore. 1989. *Candidates, Parties, and Campaigns: Electoral Politics in America*. 2d ed. Washington, D.C.: Congressional Quarterly Press.

Saussure, Ferdinand de. 1959. *Course in General Linguistics*. Ed. Charles Bally and Albert Sechehaye. New York: Philosophical Library.

Schantz, Harvey. 1980. "Contested and Uncontested Primaries for the U.S. House." *Legislative Studies Quarterly* 5:545–62.

Schattschneider, E. E. 1942. *Party Government*. New York: Farrar and Rinehart.

———. 1960. *The Semi-Sovereign People: A Realist's View of Democracy in America*. New York: Holt, Rinehart and Winston.

Schlesinger, Joseph A. 1985. "The New American Political Party." *American Political Science Review* 79:1152–69.

Schlozman, Kay Lehman, and Sidney Verba. 1987. "Sending Them a Message—Getting a Reply: Presidential Elections and Democratic Accountability." In *Elections in America*, ed. Kay Lehman Schlozman. Boston: Allen and Unwin.

Schneier, Edward V., Jr. 1987. "Is Politics a Profession? A New School Says Yes." *PS: Political Science and Politics* 20:889–95.

Schumpeter, Joseph A. [1942] 1975. *Capitalism, Socialism, and Democracy.* New York: Harper Torchbooks.

Schunn, Christian D., and Kevin Dunbar. 1996. "Priming, Analogy, and Awareness in Complex Reasoning." *Memory and Cognition* 24:271–84.

Schwartz, Tony. 1973. *The Responsive Chord.* New York: Anchor/Doubleday.

Schwartzman, Edward. 1989. *Political Campaign Craftsmanship: A Professional's Guide to Campaigning for Public Office.* 3d ed. New Brunswick, N.J.: Transaction.

Sebeok, Thomas A. 1994. *Signs: An Introduction to Semiotics.* Toronto: University of Toronto Press.

Selnow, Gary W. 1994. *High-Tech Campaigns: Computer Technology in Political Communication.* Westport, Conn.: Praeger.

Serra, George, and Albert D. Cover. 1992. "The Electoral Consequences of Perquisite Use: The Casework Case." *Legislative Studies Quarterly* 17:233–46.

Shadegg, Stephen C. 1972. *The New How to Win an Election.* New York: Taplinger.

Shafer, Byron E., and William J. M. Claggett. 1995. *The Two Majorities: The Issue Context of Modern American Politics.* Baltimore: Johns Hopkins University Press.

Sharp, C., and Milton Lodge. 1985. "Partisan and Ideological Belief Systems: Do They Differ?" *Political Behavior* 7:147–62.

Shea, Daniel M., ed. 1996. *Campaign Craft: The Strategies, Tactics, and Art of Political Campaign Management.* Westport, Conn.: Praeger.

Shepsle, Kenneth A. 1972. "The Strategy of Ambiguity: Uncertainty and Electoral Competition." *American Political Science Review* 66:555–68.

Sigal, Leon V. 1973. *Reporters and Officials: The Organization and Politics of Newsmaking.* Lexington, Mass.: D.C. Heath.

Silberman, Jonathan, and Garey Durden. 1975. "The Rational Choice Theory of Voter Participation." *Public Choice* 23:101–8.

Silverman, Kaja. 1983. *The Subject of Semiotics.* New York: Oxford University Press.

Skocpol, Theda, and Morris P. Fiorina, eds. 1999. *Civic Engagement in American Democracy.* Washington, D.C.: Brookings Institution Press.

Smith, Paul A. 1982. *Electing a President: Information and Control.* New York: Praeger.

Soley, Lawrence. 1992. *The News Shapers: The Sources Who Explain the News.* New York: Praeger.

Sorauf, Frank J. 1992. *Inside Campaign Finance: Myths and Realities.* New Haven: Yale University Press.

Squire, Peverill. 1989. "Challengers in U.S. Senate Elections." *Legislative Studies Quarterly* 14:531–48.

———. 1992. "Challenger Quality and Voting Behavior in Senate Elections." *Legislative Studies Quarterly* 17:247–63.

———. 1995. "Candidates, Money, and Voters: Assessing the State of Congressional Elections Research." *Political Research Quarterly* 48:891–917.

Stanley, Harold W. 1991. "The Reagan Legacy and Party Politics in the South." In *The 1988 Presidential Election in the South,* ed. Laurence W. Moreland, Robert P. Steed, and Tod A. Baker. New York: Praeger.

Steinberg, Arnold. 1976. *Political Campaign Management: A Systems Approach.* Lexington, Mass.: D. C. Heath.

Stephens, Stephen V. 1975. "The Paradox of Not Voting: Comment." *American Political Science Review* 69:914–15.

Stephenson, William. 1967. *The Play Theory of Mass Communication.* Chicago: University of Chicago Press.

Stewart, Charles. 1994. "Let's Go Fly a Kite: Causes and Consequences of the House Bank Scandal." *Legislative Studies Quarterly* 19:521–35.

Stokes, Donald E. 1966. "Some Dynamic Elements in Contests for the Presidency." *American Political Science Review* 60:19–28.

———. 1976. "Parties and the Nationalization of Election Forces." In *Controversies in American Voting Behavior*, ed. Richard Niemi and Herbert Weisberg. San Francisco: Freeman.

Strahinich, John. 1995. "The Spinmeisters." *Boston Globe Magazine*, 1 January, 14–15, 19, 24–28.

Strom, Gerald S. 1975. "On the Apparent Paradox of Participation: A New Proposal." *American Political Science Review* 69:908–13.

Sullivan, John L., John H. Aldrich, Eugene Borgida, and Wendy M. Rahn. 1990. "Candidate Appraisal and Human Nature: Man and Superman in the 1984 Election." *Political Psychology* 11:459–84.

Swanson, David L. 1992. "The Political-Media Complex." *Communication Monographs* 59:397–400.

Swanson, David L., and Paolo Mancini, eds. 1996a. *Politics, Media, and Modern Democracy: An International Study of Innovations in Electoral Campaigning and Their Consequences*. Westport, Conn.: Praeger.

———. 1996b. "Patterns of Modern Electoral Campaigning and Their Consequences." In *Politics, Media, and Modern Democracy: An International Study of Innovations in Electoral Campaigning and Their Consequences*. ed. David L. Swanson and Paolo Mancini. Westport, Conn.: Praeger.

Sweeney, William R. 1995. "The Principles of Planning." In *Campaigns and Elections American Style*, ed. James A. Thurber and Candice J. Nelson. Boulder, Colo.: Westview Press.

Switzer, Jo Young, Virginia H. Fry, and Larry D. Miller. 1990. "Semiotic and Communication: A Dialogue with Thomas A. Sebeok." *Southern Communication Journal* 55:388–401.

Taylor, Paul. 1990. *See How They Run: Electing the President in an Age of Mediaocracy*. New York: Alfred A. Knopf.

Taylor, Shelley E. 1981. "The Interface of Cognitive and Social Psychology." In *Cognition, Social Behavior, and the Environment*, ed. J. Harvey. Hillsdale, N.J.: Lawrence Erlbaum.

Tedesco, John C., Lori Melton McKinnon, and Lynda Lee Kaid. 1996. "Advertising Watchdogs: A Content Analysis of Print and Broadcast Ad Watches." *Press/Politics* 1:76–93.

Thomas, Evan. 1996. "Victory March." *Newsweek*, November 18.

Thomas, Martin. 1985. "Electoral Proximity and Senatorial Roll Call Voting." *American Journal of Political Science* 29:96–111.

Thomas, Scott J. 1989. "Do Incumbent Campaign Expenditures Matter?" *Journal of Politics* 51:965–76.

Thorson, Esther, William G. Christ, and Clarke Caywood. 1991. "Selling Candidates like Tubes of Toothpaste: Is the Comparison Apt?" In *Television and Political Advertising*, vol. 1: *Psychological Processes*, ed. Frank Biocca. Hillsdale, N.J.: Lawrence Erlbaum.

Thurber, James A. 1998. "The Study of Campaign Consultants: A Subfield in Search of Theory." *PS: Political Science and Politics* 31:145–49.

Thurber, James A., and Candice J. Nelson, eds. 2000. *Campaign Warriors: Political Consultants in Elections*. Washington, D.C.: Brookings Institution Press.

Thurber, James A., Candice J. Nelson, and David A. Dulio, eds. 2000. *Crowded Air-*

waves: Campaign Advertising in Elections. Washington, D.C.: Brookings Institution Press.

Trent, Judith S. 1978. "Presidential Surfacing: The Ritualistic and Crucial First Act." *Communication Monographs* 45:281–92.

Trent, Judith S., and Robert V. Friedenberg. 1995. *Political Campaign Communication: Principles and Practices.* 3d ed. Westport, Conn.: Praeger.

Troy, Gil. 1996. *See How They Ran: The Changing Role of the Presidential Candidate.* Rev. ed. Cambridge: Harvard University Press.

Tufte, Edward R. 1974. "Communication." *American Political Science Review* 68:211–13.

———. 1975. "Determinants of the Outcomes of Midterm Congressional Elections." *American Political Science Review* 69:812–26.

Tullock, Gordon. 1975. "The Paradox of Not Voting for Oneself." *American Political Science Review* 69:919.

Van Riper, Paul P. 1967. *Handbook of Practical Politics.* New York: Harper.

Vermeer, Jan Pons, ed. 1987. *Campaigns in the News: Mass Media and Congressional Elections.* Westport, Conn.: Greenwood Press.

Welch, William P. 1976. "The Economics of Campaign Funds." *Public Choice* 25:84.

———. 1980. "The Allocation of Political Monies: Economic Interest Groups." *Public Choice* 29:97–120.

West, Darrell M. 1993. *Air Wars: Television Advertising in Election Campaigns, 1952–1992.* Washington, D.C.: Congressional Quarterly Press.

Wilcox, Clyde. 1988. "I Owe It All to Me: Candidates' Investments in Their Own Campaigns." *American Politics Quarterly* 16:266–79.

Witt, Linda, Karen M. Paget, and Glenna Matthews. 1994. *Running as a Woman: Gender and Power in American Politics.* New York: Free Press.

Wolfinger, Raymond E. 1963. "The Influence of Precinct Work on Voting Behavior." *Public Opinion Quarterly* 27:387–98.

Zaller, John R. 1992. *The Nature and Origins of Mass Opinion.* Cambridge: Cambridge University Press.

Zarefsky, David. 1992. "Spectator Politics and the Revival of Public Argument." *Communication Monographs* 59:411–14.

Index